GATE OF LODORE.

DEPARTMENT OF THE INTERIOR.

U. S. GEOLOGICAL AND GEOGRAPHICAL SURVEY OF THE TERRITORIES.

SECOND DIVISION.—J. W. POWELL, GEOLOGIST IN CHARGE.

REPORT

ON THE

GEOLOGY

OF THE

EASTERN PORTION OF THE UINTA MOUNTAINS

AND

A REGION OF COUNTRY ADJACENT THERETO.

WITH ATLAS.

BY J. W. POWELL.

WASHINGTON:
GOVERNMENT PRINTING OFFICE.
1876.

DEPARTMENT OF THE INTERIOR.
U. S. GEOLOGICAL AND GEOGRAPHICAL SURVEY OF THE TERRITORIES.
SECOND DIVISION.—J. W. POWELL, GEOLOGIST IN CHARGE.

REPORT

ON THE

GEOLOGY

OF THE

EASTERN PORTION OF THE UINTA MOUNTAINS

AND

A REGION OF COUNTRY ADJACENT THERETO.

WITH ATLAS.

BY J. W. POWELL.

WASHINGTON:
GOVERNMENT PRINTING OFFICE.
1876.

PREFACE.

The region of country embraced in the map which accompanies this report is one of great geological interest. Three great categories of facts are here represented on a grand scale, viz: facts relating to displacement, facts relating to degradation, and facts relating to sedimentation. The displacements are of great magnitude, and because the beds involved are sedimentary strata but rarely altered, the characteristics of these displacements are plainly revealed, so that in our studies of them we have been able to arrive at conclusions, both quantitative and qualitative, with some degree of certainty.

While displacement has been great, degradation has also been great, yet the country has not been planed down to a general base-level, but stands in mountain cliffs and escarped hills, where the strata are plainly revealed.

The formations which we are able to study here have an aggregate thickness of 50,000 feet, and embrace groups of Paleozoic, Mesozoic, and Cenozoic Ages. Throughout nearly the entire region there is a condition of surface which renders the study of the geology comparatively easy. By reason of great altitude and extreme aridity the rocks are rarely masked by subaerial gravels, soil, or vegetation, and the book of geology lies open. We have thus been able to collect a large body of facts, which, in the following volume, have been arranged in such order as it seemed would best present to the reader the general geology of the country. Many details have been omitted which would have been given had the facts been presented as they were collected in the form of an itinerary, but it was though that such a method would result in encumbering geological literature with a mass of undigested facts of little value.

It may be well to indicate here the general routes of travel by which the country has been explored. In the fall of 1868 with a small party of men I crossed from the White River to the Yampa, and camped at the foot of Junction Mountain; thence I passed northward across the Snake River to the Pine Bluffs, and thence westward across Aspen Mountain to the Green River, and up the bank of that stream to Green River Station; thence I crossed to Bryan, on Black's Fork, and down that stream to its mouth, then went south to the Cameo Mountains; thence eastward to Quien Hornet Mountain; thence to Flaming Gorge, and from this latter point to Ashley Park, and from Ashley Park to Brown's Park. From Brown's Park I went through the Escalante Peaks, near the junction of the Yampa with the Green; thence eastward past Junction Mountain to the White River.

The course thus laid down is the general one of the pack train, but I myself branched from it in many ways.

On this journey I first discovered the succession of Cenozoic and Mesozoic groups, but did not divide the Upper from the Lower Green River, nor did I draw the plane of separation between the Upper Green River and Bridger Groups where I do now.

Early in the spring of 1869 I again crossed from the White River to the Yampa, camped at the foot of Junction Mountain, and spent a few days in the study of the adjacent region. I proceeded thence to Brown's Park, in which I camped for a few days, reviewing the geological studies of the previous fall. I then passed out of the park through Red Creek Cañon, from its head, crossed the divide, and proceeded westward to the Green River, and camped again at Flaming Gorge for a few days. Thence I went up Henry's Fork, studying the region on my way, and crossed the divide to Fort Bridger.

A few weeks subsequent I started on a boat trip to explore the lower Green and the Colorado River of the West. On my way I passed through the Uinta Mountains, stopping from time to time to make sections and to make geological studies of the country along the walls of the cañons.

Again, in 1871, I had a boat ride down the river. On this trip Mr. John F. Steward, of Plano, Illinois, was my assistant. We extended our studies on either side of the river for a distance of from ten to twenty miles.

In 1874, I started with a pack train from Green River Station, went up Little Bitter Creek, across Quien Hornet Mountain, through Red Creek Cañon into Brown's Park; thence southeastward to the junction of the Snake River with the Yampa, where it was crossed; thence across the Yampa Plateau to the foot of Split Mountain Cañon, and thence to the Uinta Valley. Returning from the Uinta Valley I visited the region drained by Ashley's Fork and Brush Creek, crossed the Uinta Mountains to the head of Sheep Creek, and returned to Green River Station.

The course thus marked down was that followed by the pack train, which moved but slowly, usually resting two days out of three, while my own line of travel was in diverse directions from this general route.

In 1875, I again started with a pack train from Green River Station, went east to Rock Springs and Salt Wells, thence south to the mouth of the Vermilion, thence to the eastern foot of the Dry Mountains, thence west through Brown's Park, past Flaming Gorge to the head of Sheep Creek, and thence through the Cameo Mountains to Green River Station. On this trip also the train moved slowly, and my studies were extended many miles in either direction from the general route.

A few days later I made a trip to Salt Wells and Bitter Creek Stations, and particularly examined the region about Black Butte.

The last part of the descriptive geology has been greatly condensed; this is especially the case with the description of the structure of the Yampa Plateau, Junction Mountain, Diamond Peak, the Dry Mountains, Brown's Park, and the Aspen Mountain district. It was intended to illustrate the structural characteristics of these regions with a series of diagrams and sections, but the plan was abandoned because the appropriation was exhausted. It was intended also to prepare a chapter on the physical features of the region, treating of the mountains, plateaus, monoclinal ridges, hills, parks, bad-lands, and alcove lands, and further treating of the three great kinds of drainage found in the region, viz, antecedent, consequent, and superimposed; but the necessity for immediate publication was so great that this plan has also been abandoned, and to this subject I hope to recur at a future time.

On my travels during the year 1875, Prof. C. A. White was my geological companion, and the trip was made largely for the purpose of collecting fossils at localities where they had previously been discovered, but to which sufficient time had not been given to make good collections. But many places of interest on account of geological structure were also visited, and I had the good fortune to have with me an experienced geologist on this my final review of the region; and to Professor White, whose paper on paleontology appears in this volume, I am greatly indebted. Nor must I fail to mention the valuable services of Mr. Steward; as he was with me in one of the earlier years of the work, and only in a portion of the region, his studies were but fragmentary, and the results have not been directly incorporated in my general account of the geology of the country. I feel that I have not done him full justice in this matter, but the plan of publication would not permit the incorporation of his notes bodily; nor would such a course have done him justice, from the fact that a more extended study has greatly modified opinions entertained by both Mr. Steward and myself at that time.

For the map I am indebted primarily to the labor and skill of Prof. A. H. Thompson, who has been my collaborator for many years, but in the work he has had several able assistants; and in the year 1874, Prof. H. C. De Motte, of the Illinois Wesleyan University, traveled with me for the purpose of more thoroughly studying the details of the geography more distant from the river, and he somewhat extended the area of the survey embraced on the map.

To Mr. Gilbert, I am indebted for great assistance in the preparation of the graphic representation employed in illustrating the Report.

The diagram, Plate VII of the atlas, was prepared for me by Mr. Archibald R. Marvine. In the earlier years of my travels in the Rocky Mountain region, I studied to some extent the Park Mountains. Subsequently the region was more thoroughly studied by parties under the direction of Dr. Hayden, and in his connection with that work Mr. Marvine traveled over much of the same ground that I had seen. It thus happened that we frequently discussed together the country which had been visited by both of us, and when I came to the preparation of this volume Mr. Marvine kindly proposed to construct this illustration for my use. This is perhaps the last work done by Mr. Marvine; at the time he was in very ill health, and a few days after sank into a condition from which he never recovered, and we now have to mourn the loss of a conscientious, able, and vigorous geologist, and it is with profound sorrow that I am compelled in acknowledging his courtesy to record his death.

Mr. J. C. Pilling, for the past three years, has traveled with me as stenographer and assistant geologist, and to him I am indebted for the collection of a great body of details of diverse character, but especially in the measurement of many sections.

Mr. W. Cleburn, one of the engineers of the Union Pacific Railroad, and who has been engaged in that work for many years, has at the same time interested himself in the geology and paleontology of the region, and to him I am indebted for many favors, and especially for the use of his valuable collection of fossils.

To many of the citizens of the region I am indebted for courtesy and substantial favors, but especially to Capt. Pardon Dodds, of the Uinta Valley, and Mr. S. I. Field, of Green River Station.

J. W. P.

The following note from Professor White is inserted:

Dear Sir: Since my report, comprising Chapter III of this volume, was put in type, further investigation of the fossils collected from the Cañon of Desolation has led me to doubt the correctness of the reference I have there made of them to the Point of Rocks Group. It now seems probable that they properly belong to the Bitter Creek Group, notwithstanding the close relationship of two or three of the species with some of those found in strata that are still referred without doubt to the Point of Rocks Group.

Further collections and investigations in the field will, however, be necessary before this question can be definitely settled.

Very truly yours,

C. A. WHITE.

Prof. J. W. Powell.

CONTENTS.

CHAPTER I.

THREE GEOLOGICAL PROVINCES.

CHAPTER II.

SEDIMENTARY GROUPS OF THE PLATEAU PROVINCE.

CHAPTER III.

INVERTEBRATE PALEONTOLOGY OF THE PLATEAU PROVINCE.

CHAPTER IV.

GEOGRAPHIC DISTRIBUTION OF THE GEOLOGICAL FORMATIONS IN THE UINTA MOUNTAINS.

CHAPTER V.

STRUCTURAL GEOLOGY.

CHAPTER I.

THREE GEOLOGICAL PROVINCES.

The Colorado River of the West drains a vast system of plateaus. On these plateaus are lone mountains, short ranges and groups of volcanic cones, and the principal affluents of the river have their sources in high mountains that stand on the rim of the great drainage basin. There is no considerable valley along the course of the Colorado River north of the thirty-fifth parallel nor along the course of any of its principal tributaries. The streams run chiefly in deep cañons which, with other important topographic features, serve to divide the area into plateaus. The district of country of which I thus speak is, in its important characteristics, a plateau region.

This plateau character was well recognized by Dr. Newberry. In his report to Lieutenant Ives, page 41, he says: "The Colorado rises in a thousand sources at an elevation of from ten to twelve thousand feet above the sea, on the western side of the Rocky Mountains. Descending from their fountain heads, its tributaries fall upon a high plateau of sedimentary rocks which forms the western base of these mountains and occupies all the interval between them and the great bend of the Colorado River where the river enters the volcanic district already described;" and elsewhere in that volume he makes frequent mention of these characteristics.

Mr. Blake, in the third volume of the Pacific Railroad Surveys, Part 4, page 42, also mentions this topographic character as follows:

"*Extent of the table lands west of the Sierra Madre.*—This is a convenient point from which to take a general view of the broad expanse of the great plain that lies between the Sierra Madre and the mountains which form the eastern rim of the Great Basin. From the Sierra Madre up to this place the survey followed the eroded valleys of the streams, and the vision was bounded on both sides by their high and rocky banks, composed not only of the edges of thick horizontal strata, but often capped with the harder and more unyielding solid lava. The observer as he passes westward from the mountains is thus placed below the general level of the plateau, which does not become apparent to him unless he stands upon the top of the mesas and can thus cast the eye over the whole. The point already reached in the description is about half way between the Sierra Madre and the high mountains of San Francisco, and here, as we have seen, the upper strata of the plain are denuded and washed away, so that the banks of the streams are not so high, and the country appears more level or gently rolling. From this place the vision is unbounded toward the north, except by the horizon. The plain stretches far away, without any vestige of a mountain range. Indeed, it is the continuation of this plateau which rises upon the flanks of the Park and Wasatch Mountains at the far north, and through which the waters of Grand and Green Rivers cut their deep cañoned channels. Farther south, these streams unite to form the great Colorado, which is also found traversing this grand plateau."

Our studies of this great plateau region have not progressed so far that we are able to clearly define its boundaries, but these studies have shown that the region is complex topographically as well as geologically and is in fact composed of many tables.

In this region the succession of sedimentary strata is unlike any series which has been studied elsewhere in North America; different groups and different groupings of fossils are found; a different series of unconformities is observed and the displacements by faulting and folding have characteristics not commonly observed elsewhere. All these facts seem to warrant the conclusion that this plateau region should be considered as a distinct geological province, and in this brief report and others which are to follow I shall so consider it.

A notice of its geographic connection with the surrounding country is needed. That portion of the United States west of the one hundredth meridian lies at a great altitude above the sea. The exceptions to this, as immediately along the Pacific coast and the narrow valleys of some of the principal streams, are but trivial. The rivers descend so rapidly from the upper regions that few of them are of value as highways of commerce; the valleys proper are narrow; treeless plains, cold, arid table lands, and desolate mountains are the principal topographic features. The more conspicuous of these are the mountains; lone mountains, single ranges and great groups of ranges or systems of mountains prevail. Owing to great and widely spread aridity, the mountains are scantily clothed with vegetation, and the indurated lithologic formations are rarely masked with soils, and the rocks, as they are popularly called, are everywhere exposed; hence all these mountains are popularly known as the Rocky Mountains. But there is more than one system of mountains, and later writers wishing to be more definite speak of the Cascade Mountains, the Coast ranges, the Sierra Nevada, the Wasatch Mountains, &c. But in an important sense the region is a unit; it is the generally elevated region of the United States; it is the principal region of the precious metals; it is the region without important navigable streams; it is the arid land of our country where irrigation is necessary to successful agriculture. But above all it is the rocky region; rocks are strewn along the valleys, over the plains and plateaus; the cañon walls are of naked rock; long escarpments or cliffs of rock stand athwart the country, and everywhere are mountains of rock. It is the Rocky Mountain region. There is a necessity for popular purposes for some general name and this one so appropriate will doubtless continue to be used, and it would seem best not to attempt to confine its application to any more restricted area; but as our geographic and geological knowledge increases so that we are able to reasonably and appropriately define distinct ranges and systems of mountains within this great group, other distinctive names should be given to such ranges and groups.

Influenced by this consideration, in speaking of the mountains that stand about the Plateau Province I shall use names for certain systems which seem appropriate to characterize them as distinct from other systems within the great Rocky Mountain region.

The eastern affluents of the Colorado River have their sources in the lofty mountains that stand as walls about the great parks of Southern Wyoming, Colorado, and Northern New Mexico, and these mountains constitute a system as well defined as we may hope for geographic systems to be defined by nature; and since my studies in that region in 1867–'68, I have been accustomed to speak of them as the Park Mountains. The system is composed of many ranges, some well defined, others complex, inclosing, or nearly so, the North, Middle, South, and San Luis Parks, with many minor valleys and parks; and there are short outlying spurs and ranges with other parks and valleys. The principal mountain ranges are composed of metamorphic rocks with unaltered sedimentary beds on their flanks. Some of the more western mountains are chiefly of this latter material, and many of the subsidiary mountains are of eruptive origin. Altogether they constitute a geological province characterized by a great development of metamorphic crystalline schists with patches and structural basins of marine and lacustrine sediments, and a complicated series of vulcanic formations.

Southward from the Oregon line, through Western Utah, Nevada, Southeastern California, and perhaps across the Colorado River in Western Arizona, many short and more or less distinct north and south ranges are found. The valleys and plains separating these ranges are covered with rather late subaërial gravels masking the underlying formations. The ranges are composed of metamorphic crystalline schists with Paleozoic beds on their flanks, or sometimes, even in large part of Paleozoic materials both complicated to a greater or less extent with eruptive beds; these eruptive beds themselves sometimes forming the principal component parts of the ranges.

The little streams that have their sources in these mountains empty into salt lakes, or elsewhere their waters are lost in the sands; as it is popularly said they disappear in sinks. The most important of these is the Great Salt Lake, but there are many other basins without drainage to the sea. A few of the ranges are drained into the Colorado River. To this group Mr. G. K. Gilbert has given the name Basin Range System, which seems appropriate.

It will be found convenient also to treat the area occupied by this group as a distinct geological province. It has a series of sedimentary beds differing widely from the Plateau Province; they are older, and the sediments of the latter were in large part derived from the former. The Basin Province was the dry land that fed the sea and great lakes of the Plateau Province through a long period, while many groups, each thousands of feet in thickness, were deposited.

Thus, for convenience of geological discussion, I speak of three great geological provinces—the Park Province, the Plateau Province, and the Basin Province—in order from east to west.

The area included in these three provinces lies east of the Sierra Nevada and west of the Great Plains. In a general way the northern boundary is marked by the North Platte, with its proper upper continuation the Sweetwater River whose minute upper ramifications interlock with those of the Shoshoni River, which latter is a continuation of the northern boundary until it is crossed by the forty-third parallel of north latitude. When the region along the middle course of the Shoshoni River is more thoroughly studied, the Basin Range System may be carried much farther north than we are warranted in doing with our present knowledge; but I am inclined to the opinion, from the fragments of geological description which we have from that country, that another distinctly marked group will eventually be recognized here, having for one of its characteristics a great development of eruptive rocks. The southern boundary of the three provinces I am not able to clearly define.

It may be well to state somewhat more categorically the characteristics, geographic and geological, on which I propose to divide this great area into three provinces.

GEOGRAPHIC CHARACTERISTICS OF THE THREE PROVINCES.

The Basin Ranges are short, more or less distinct north and south ridges separated by desert valleys which reveal broad stretches of subaërial gravels concealing the underlying formations. The general drainage is to interior salt lakes and sinks, but in the northeast corner there is a limited district drained by some small tributaries of the Shoshoni, and in the southeast there is a small district drained by the Rio Virgen into the Colorado River of the West.

The Plateau Province is composed of many tables bounded by cañon and cliff escarpments. On these tables stand lone mountains, irregular groups of mountains, and short ranges. It is drained by the Colorado River of the West and its tributaries.

The Park Province is characterized by broad, massive ranges, sometimes distinct, sometimes coalescing so as to include the great parks. The lofty peaks that serrate these ranges stand over snow banks that are perennial reservoirs for a multitude of streams whose waters on one hand are gathered into the Colorado River of the West, and finally discharged into the Gulf of California; and on the other hand they are gathered into the Mississippi and the Rio Grande del Norte to be discharged into the Gulf of Mexico.

Thus, in the three provinces, we have, first, desert valleys between naked ridges; second, high plateaus severed by profound gorges; and, third, massive, high mountains with shining snow fields.

GENERAL CHARACTERISTICS OF THE SEDIMENTARY GROUPS OF THREE PROVINCES.

The Basin ranges are composed of Paleozoic rocks with Eozoic schists below, and in the Humboldt Mountain district some Mesozoic and Cenozoic rocks are found. In the Plateau Province, Cenozoic and Mesozoic rocks prevail, though some of the important plateaus are of Carboniferous beds; and in a few places deep corrasion has revealed still older Paleozoic and even Eozoic formations. The Park Mountains are chiefly Eozoic. Since that age the region has been intermittently under the dominion of the waters, and Paleozoic, Mesozoic, and Cenozoic rocks are found at horizons interrupted by gaps in the general series that are represented by dry land periods, while the last orographic agencies have left but fragments of these antecedent formations.

CHARACTERISTICS OF THE OROGRAPHIC STRUCTURE OF THE THREE PROVINCES.

TYPES OF OROGRAPHIC STRUCTURE.

It seems convenient to give a general account of the types of orographic structure in the region under consideration before characterizing each province by its special type.

In this discussion I wish to use certain terms with a restricted or relative meaning; *i. e.*, in treating of anticlinal and synclinal flexures I shall speak of those portions of the sedimentary beds which are adjacent to the anticlinal axes as having been upheaved, and those portions near their synclinal axes as having subsided. Again, in blocks which are bounded by faults and tilted, I shall speak of such portions as are at a higher level as having been uplifted, and portions occupying a lower level as thrown. In such cases I do not wish to commit myself to any theory of upheaval or collapse in the change of the relation of the several parts of these beds to the center of the earth.

In treating of the structure of the mountains under consideration it is necessary to distinguish two great classes, viz, those composed of sedimentary strata, altered or unaltered, and those composed of extravasated material.

MOUNTAINS COMPOSED OF SEDIMENTARY STRATA.

I.—APPALACHIAN STRUCTURE.

The structure of the Appalachian Mountains, with closely appressed folds and axial planes tipped back from the sea, the modifications of these folds by faults, and the primary and concomitant forms of the mountains, have been clearly explained by the Messrs. Rogers and later writers, and have formed the basis of many discussions concerning geological dynamics. This Appalachian structure needs no further mention here, as it is a type of structure which so far has not been found in the region described above, and should it be found hereafter it will simply be an exceptional type to those known to prevail.

II.—SIMPLE ANTICLINAL STRUCTURE.

Mountains or short ranges carved from simple anticlinals are sometimes found, though this type of structure is not a prevailing one. Usually in such a case the great mountain mass lies in the central zone of the uplift. The fold is, of course, always found truncated by erosion, and the mountains represent but the difference between the amount of upheaval and the amount of such erosion. When not complicated by other types of structure the strata dip on all sides from the center of upheaval, gently or more abruptly, but the sides of the folds are never closely appressed. Such mountains in primary form are gently rounded in general outline, modified by the erosion of the streams running down their sides. Sometimes such

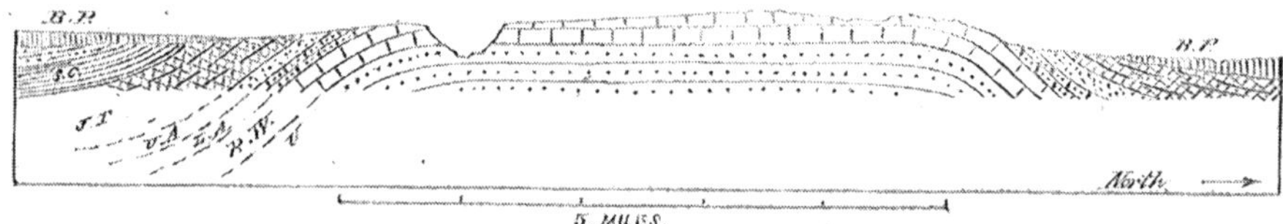

FIG. 1.—Section through Junction Mountain, north and south.

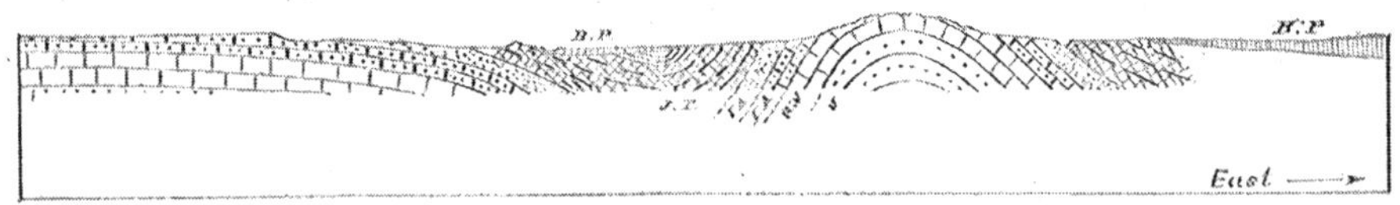

FIG. 2.—Section through Junction Mountain, east and west.

B. P., Brown's Park; S. C., Sulphur Creek; J. T., Jura Trias; U. A., Upper Aubrey; L. A., Lower Aubrey; R. W., Red Wall; U., Uinta.

mountains are severed by rivers running longitudinally, transversely or obliquely through them; the rivers themselves having their sources in regions far away and passing through the mountains in their courses to the sea. In Northeastern Colorado a short distance above the junction of the Snake River with the Yampa, stands Junction Mountain, which serves as a fine illustration of this type of structure. The mountain is divided into two unequal parts by a cañon, through which the Yampa River runs. The axis of the mountain has a north and south direction.

Figure 1 is a section through this mountain, in a north and south direction, along the axis of upheaval. Figure 2 is a section through it in a transverse direction.

CONCOMITANT FORMS.

1. *Monoclinal Ridges on the Flanks.*—Under conditions which are so well known as to need no further explanation here, monoclinal ridges or hog-backs are formed on the flanks of such upheavals, and sometimes such monoclinal ridges are of such magnitude as to be dignified with the name of mountains. Where two or more series of indurated, inclined beds are separated by extensive series of softer material, two or more monoclinal ridges may be formed.

2. *Monoclinal Ridges only.*—Sometimes we find that an anticlinal upheaval has been eroded in *intaglio*, so that there is no great central mountain mass, but the axis of upheaval is the site of a valley or low plain, but the monoclinal ridges on the flanks remain.

3. *Inclined Plateaus.*—Where the anticlinal upheaval has a great amplitude, as compared with the vertical uplift, the beds incline but slightly. Under such conditions inclined plateaus or mesas are found instead of monoclinal ridges, usually having steep escarpments facing the axis of the flexure.

III.—UINTA STRUCTURE.

In the Uinta Mountains we have a great range carved from an anticlinal upheaval, the axis of which has an easterly and westerly trend, and is more than one hundred and fifty miles in length. It terminates abruptly against the Wasatch Mountains on the west and is cut off by the short, abrupt anticlinal of Junction Mountain on the east, the latter having its axis in a north and south direction. There are several important facts observed in the study of this great flexure. Its axis has been lifted above the level of the sea about thirty thousand feet, and above the level of the adjacent country about twenty-five thousand feet. From flank to flank the flexure is about fifty miles, but varies much in width. We find on either flank, many miles from the axis, a line of maximum flexure, which line presents a subparallelism with the meandering axis. These lines have the effect of two monoclinal flexures in opposite directions, separated by the broad table, diversified by elevated valleys and peaks of which the great mass of the Uinta Mountains is composed. But the portion between these monoclinal flexures or lines of greatest flexure is itself gently flexed. In many places that which I have called the line of greatest flexure is indeed a fault, in one place on the north side of the Uinta Mountains having a throw of twenty thousand feet. On the south side the line of greatest flexure is very irregular, being complicated in some places by faults having uplifts opposed to the downthrow of the flexure. On either side the great displacement is partly by faulting, partly by flexing, and either flank is a zone of diverse displacement where the strata are faulted, flexed, twisted and contorted in many ways.

The character of these displacements in the Uinta Mountains is illustrated in Plates 1, 2, and 3 of the Atlas, and in a subsequent chapter the subject will be more fully discussed.

The simplest topographic forms produced by such displacements under conditions of erosion in general outline, are plateaus with gently rounded summits and abrupt shoulders on the flanks; but such general outline is often modified by the corrasion due to antecedent or superimposed drainage; that is, by the corrasion of streams that head in remote regions and pass through these uplifts either longitudinally, transversely or obliquely, as in the case of Simple Anticlinals.*

There are other modifications which sometimes greatly obscure the general topographic outline due to consequent drainage, *i. e.*, the local drainage which is due to the upheaval itself and which produces interesting

CONCOMITANT FORMS.

1. *Subsidiary Plateaus.*—Sometimes the streams which head near the axis of such an upheaval, as they meander to the flanks, excavate valleys

* For an explanation of what is meant by antecedent and superimposed drainage, the reader is referred to the Report on the Exploration of the Colorado River and its Tributaries, page 160, *et seq.*

and divide the great block, which is a plateau in general outline, into minor plateaus which are separated by intervening but elevated valleys. This is especially the case where the streams in their upper courses follow for some distance the strike of the beds before turning to cross the more or less abrupt lines of maximum flexure. Sometimes these streams run in deep gorges; in such cases the plateaus are bounded by cañons.

2. *Projecting Ridges.*—When these consequent streams starting near the axis of upheaval take a somewhat direct course across the strike, the general plateau is cut into a series of sharp, abrupt ridges having a trend at right angles to the strike or general axis of upheaval. Thus the points of the ridges face the plain below and are separated by deep gulches and cañons, and the observer on the plain below sees before him what appears to be a line of peaks separated by intervening gulches and valleys, and is apt to misunderstand the topographic character of the great mass which is before him.

3. *Axial Peaks.*—At some stages in the progress of erosion the channels of consequent drainage inosculate, and about their heads gorges are formed. with towering amphitheaters. In such cases an irregular line of crags and peaks will be found along the axis of upheaval. These I call axial peaks.

4. *Flanking Peaks.*—Sometimes we find a very hard bed or group of beds underlaid by more friable strata on a flank of the upheaval, which harder beds have been carried away by erosion from those portions of the upheaved mass nearer the axis. In such cases each projecting ridge is crowned with a true peak. I call these flanking peaks.

5. *Interrupted Monoclinal Ridges.*—On the flanks of these upheavals, but farther from the axis than the flanking peaks, monoclinal ridges are often found sometimes broken by gaps which are the channels of intermittent or permanent streams, and these ridges are very irregular and often interrupted. Where the downthrow is by simple flexure, a complete series is formed. Where it is partly by flexing and partly by faulting, some of the monoclinal ridges disappear. Where the faulting is on the side of the zone of maximum flexure nearest to the axis, the ridges of the

upper beds appear; but where the faulting is on the side of the zone of maximum flexure farthest from the axis, the ridges of the lower beds appear; and where the displacement is chiefly or entirely by faulting, there are no monoclinal ridges.

IV.—KAIBAB STRUCTURE.

In the region under discussion we often find the sedimentary beds broken into great blocks by faults or their homologues, monoclinal flexures, and these blocks have been gently tilted in broad masses. I have discussed this subject somewhat at length in my Report on the Exploration of the Colorado River of the West and its Tributaries, published in 1875; and in Figure 3 I reproduce a section and bird's eye view of the plateaus north of the Grand Cañon, which was used in that volume. An examination of this will fully reveal the characteristics of what I have called the Kaibab structure. The grand topographic features which result from this structure are plateaus with broken edges where they are bounded by faults, flexed edges where they are bounded by monoclinal flexures, and with escarpments where they are bounded by cañons or lines of cliffs.

CONCOMITANT FORMS.

1. *Cliffs of Displacement.*—When a plateau is bounded on one side by a fault, the edge of the plateau is an escarpment often so abrupt as to present a more or less irregular line of cliffs.

2. *Slopes of Displacement.*—When the displacement is a flexure rather than a fold, the edge of the plateau is a broken slope. I have discussed these cliffs and slopes of displacement somewhat at length in the volume already quoted several times, page 182 *et seq.*

3. *Monoclinal Ridges on the Flanks.*—On the flanks of these monoclinal flexures, under proper conditions which have already been described, monoclinal ridges are formed.

4. *Monoclinal Ridges with Plateau Carried Away.*—As in simple anticlinal upheavals the central mass may be entirely carried away leaving but monoclinal ridges, in like manner in the Kaibab structure the principal plateau mass may be carried away leaving only the monoclinal ridges. This I have also discussed in the volume already quoted.

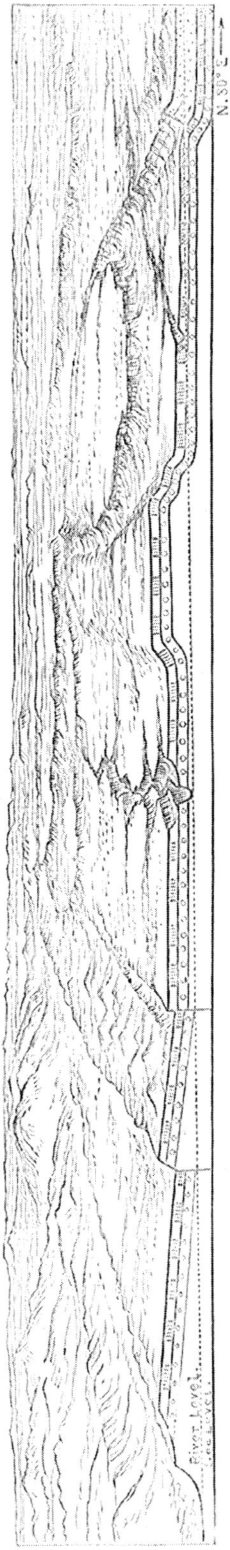

FIG. 3.—Section from west to east across the plateaus north of the Grand Cañon, with bird's-eye view of terraces and plateaus above. Horizontal scale, 16 miles to the inch; vertical scale, 4 miles to the inch.

5. *Projecting Ridges.*—It is seldom, perhaps never the case that the strata of one of these plateaus are left by the general displacement in a horizontal position; but every block is tilted more or less, and often a valley appears at the foot of the slope, and the streams which head on the opposite brink of the plateau have excavated valleys, leaving intervening ridges which project into the valley, having an effect somewhat like that described as one of the concomitant forms of the Uinta structure.

6. *Cliffs of Erosion.*—An inclined plateau may be bounded on the upheaved side by an escarpment of erosion, and such an escarpment is gradually carried back by an undermining process from the line of greatest upheaval. The drainage of such a plateau is usually from the brink of this escarpment toward the valley on the opposite side; yet a minor drainage is found which carves out deep gulches, and the cliffs of erosion have deep reëntrant and sharp salient angles.

7. *Buttes.*—Sometimes the gulches which form the deep, reëntrant angles of a line of cliffs have lateral gulches, which by continued erosion coalesce, and the salient angles are gradually cut off from the escarpment, which is ever retreating. In this manner buttes are formed as outliers of cliffs.

8. *Cameo Mountains.*—Wherever considerable areas of horizontal or nearly horizontal strata are found sufficiently elevated above the base level of erosion, and such areas are drained by two or more subparallel water courses, the lateral drainage of these water courses will gradually inosculate in their upper ramifications, and, carving out deep channels, will leave behind mountains of horizontal strata. Such mountains are often of great beauty. This is especially the case where the beds are of different texture and color, when the mountains will be terraced and buttressed in beautiful regularity, and banded with the colors which are characteristic of the several beds of which they are composed.

A few miles north of the Uinta Mountains, on the west side of the Green River, a group of such mountains are found, to which I have given the name Cameo Mountains, and I call this the Cameo structure.

V.—BASIN RANGE STRUCTURE.

When the blocks into which a district of country has been broken by faults are greatly tilted so that the strata dip at high angles, the uplifted edges of such blocks often form long mountain ridges. Such ridges have the general appearance of the monoclinal ridges already described as concomitants of other types of structure; but in this case the ridges constitute the chief mountain masses themselves, and form another general structural type. The monoclinal ridges are due to the erosion of upheaved strata; these ridges are due to displacement; they may also be eroded, but in so far as erosion has progressed the ridge like structure is obscured. Many of the ridge like mountains of the Basin Province have this structure. Such a ridge is composed of monoclinal strata, the one side presenting a bold escarped front, the other a more gently sloped back conforming to a greater or less degree with the dip. Sometimes the ridges themselves are faulted longitudinally, transversely or obliquely, and the faults may be slight or of great magnitude; but the more common structure is a simple ridge with slight transverse or oblique faults.

CONCOMITANT FORMS.

1. *Monoclinal Ridges on the Back.*—On the backs of these Basin ranges monoclinal ridges have been observed.

VI.—ZONES OF DIVERSE DISPLACEMENT.

In this region many zones or irregular areas of country are found to be divided into small blocks by faults and flexures running in diverse directions, and these may be horizontal or be tipped at high or low angles, or even be overturned. The total effect of this diverse displacement may be to uplift the area above or depress it below the adjacent country or not to change its relative altitude. These features are exhibited on a small scale within a limited area, usually so elongated as to be termed a zone.

During the past season Mr. G. K. Gilbert has studied an area where this diverse displacement is by faulting, and the faults are of no great magnitude, and the blocks into which the area has been severed are either not tilted or but slightly so. This presents the simplest illustration of this type that has

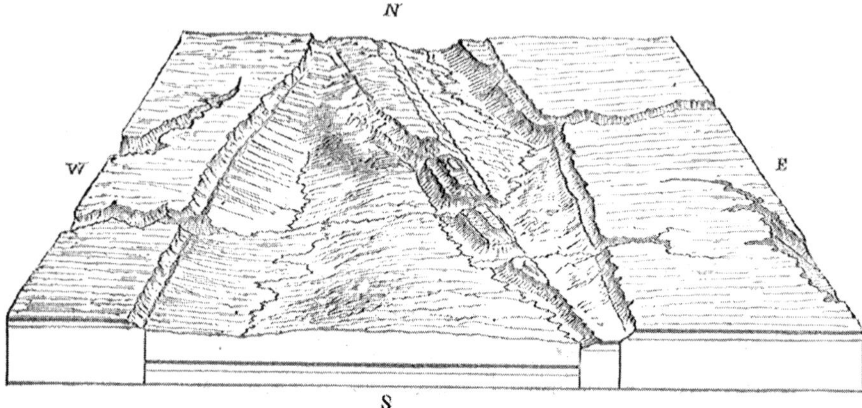

FIG. 4.—Bird's-eye view of a portion of the Musinia Zone of Diverse Displacement. The area represented is six miles square. The base line shows the sea-level. The tract is drained by Salina Creek, which unites its branches in the center and flows through the cañon on the left.

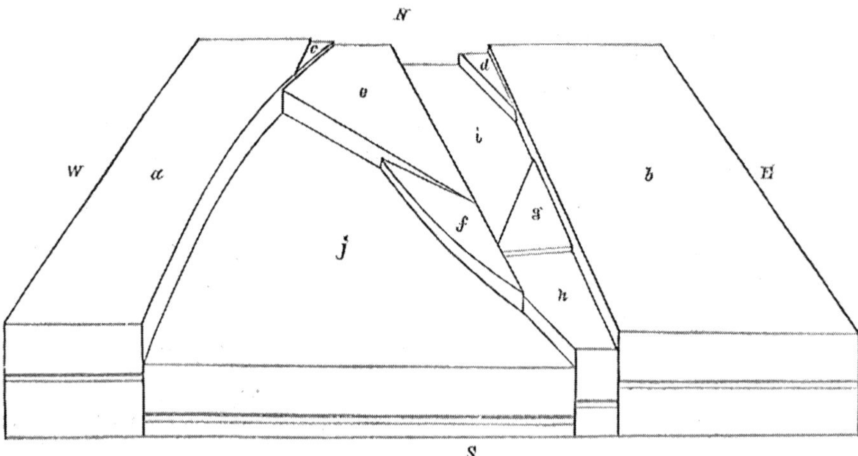

FIG. 5.—Deduced from Fig. 4. A restoration of the displaced rocks as they would appear had there been displacement but no degradation.

yet been discovered. It is simply the Kaibab structure on a very small scale. Fig. 4 is a bird's eye view of the blocks mentioned. In the section, in the foreground, the heavy line represents the summit of the highest Cretaceous group. Fig. 5 is a diagram of the same region showing the blocks into which it is severed, and the same restored to the condition they would have, had there been no denudation.

On the south side of the Uinta Mountains, and east of the Green River, another comparatively simple area has been studied by myself. This zone of diverse displacement is on the flank of the great Uinta upheaval. These displacements are chiefly by flexures rather than by faults, and the blocks are more tilted and contorted than in the last.

In Atlas, Plate No. 4, we have a stereogram representing these displacements, and in a subsequent chapter the subject will be more fully discussed.

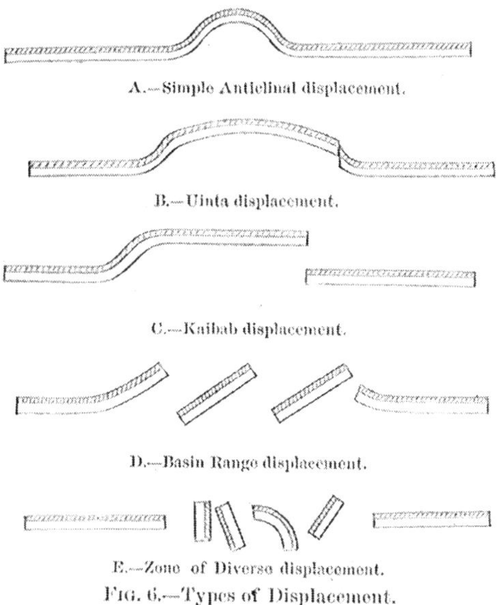

FIG. 6.—Types of Displacement.

Many other areas far more complex than these have been discovered where a zone has been broken into blocks, and these blocks tipped and contorted in diverse ways and directions like the blocks of ice crowded in an eddy of a northern river at the time of its spring flood. The topographic features found in such areas are zones of irregular hills. Figure 6 is a diagram illustrating the general types of displacement heretofore discussed. A represents a Simple Anticlinal displacement; B a Uinta displacement; C a Kaibab displacement; D a Basin Range displacement; and E a Zone of Diverse displacement.

MOUNTAINS COMPOSED IN WHOLE OR IN PART OF EXTRAVASATED MATERIAL.

We are not able in the present state of our knowledge to draw legitimate conclusions concerning the relation of the eruptive rocks so widely distributed through all three of these geological provinces, but the following types of structure have been observed.

VII.—TABLE MOUNTAIN STRUCTURE.

We often find beds of sedimentary strata preserved from erosion by a capping of lava. Such are usually called table mountains; the underlying strata may be horizontal or inclined. Earlier stages of this structure are seen in mesas or low tables, and sometimes in valleys or gulches which have been filled with extravasated material, and erosion has proceeded to a limited extent on either side of these harder masses carrying away the softer sedimentary material and leaving the harder volcanic rocks in the midst of the valley, and this may have an elevation lesser or greater than that of the adjacent country beyond the rim of the valley.

A fine example of a table mountain is found in Pilot Butte, in Wyoming Territory.

VIII.—UINKARET STRUCTURE.

Simple sheets of lava may be poured into a valley or on a plain, and serve as a protection to the sedimentary beds which are immediately underlying them and, as the erosion of the adjacent country not thus protected progresses, new vents may be formed along the edges of such sheets and at a lower level. Still erosion progresses, and still new floods of lava are poured out, and still at lower levels, until a mountain is left behind with its central mass composed of sedimentary material, but covered on the summit and flanks with irregular and overlapping patches of lava. Thus lava bed is imbricated on lava bed, but unlike the tiles of a roof, the upper edge of the lower sheet is placed on the lower edge of the upper. This structure is well represented in the Uinkaret Mountains in Northern Arizona, and has been more fully discussed by me elsewhere, *vide* The Exploration of the Colorado River, &c., page 199 *et seq.*

IX.—TU-SHAR STRUCTURE.

When a plain or valley which receives extravisated material from below remains at a base level of erosion during the period of successive eruptions, flood of lava is piled on flood of lava until a vast mass of material is accumulated from which the rains and streams carve mountains. The several beds of which such a mountain mass is composed are exceedingly irregular, from three causes: first, each bed as poured out was an irregular mass, due to its degree of fluidity and the character of the ground on which it was poured; second, each bed was more or less modified by erosion, which occurred after it was poured out, and before it was covered by a subsequent flood; and, third, the general mass has been eroded to a greater or less extent in producing the present forms.

The volcanic activity being in a region where movements of displacement are in progress, it is often the case that the structure of this class of mountains is greatly modified by such displacements. Mountains composed of such irregular beds of lava are of frequent occurrence in the region under discussion. A fine example is seen in the vicinity of the town of Beaver, Utah Territory, in what are known as the Tu-shar Mountains.

X.—VOLCANIC STRUCTURE.

When many eruptions come successively from the same vent, and each is a comparatively small amount, cones are built. Cones of such simple structure are of frequent occurrence in the region under discussion. Great complex cones such as are found in other parts of the world do not occur, but a few double and one triple cone has been observed. The great majority of the cones observed are built of cinders on broad sheets of lava, and are in fact concomitant forms of lava mesas. Such cones are comparatively ephemeral, as the scoria and ashes of which they are composed yield readily to atmospheric degradation. Where such a cone exists, still having a well defined crater, its condition testifies to the lateness of its origin, and all the facts relating to the sheet of lava on which it rests fully corroborate the conclusion. From such evidence we are able to infer the recency of much of the volcanic activity in the three provinces. If the human history of America could be carried back to as early a date as it has been in Asia, it cannot be doubted that the earlier chapters of that history would be replete with the accounts of volcanic fires.

XI.—HENRY MOUNTAIN STRUCTURE.

Sometimes we find the sedimentary strata displaced by a quaquiversal upheaval and the same fractured, and through these fractures floods of lava have poured, and these may lie in patches about the flanks of the mountains, or stand in dikes where the walls of the crevice have been swept away by denudation. In the Henry Mountains we have a fine illustration of this type of structure. These mountains have been studied by Mr. Gilbert during the past season, and in his preliminary report he says: "The eruptions of the Henry Mountains are of a character entirely novel to me, and they were studied with an interest stimulated by surprise. A description of a single one, though it will not stand for all, will serve to illustrate the type.

Mount Ellsworth is round, and its base is six or eight miles broad. The strata of the plain about it are horizontal on every side. Near the mountain the level strata become slightly inclined, rising from all sides toward the mountain. At its base the dip steadily increases until on the steep flanks it reaches a maximum of forty-five degrees. Then it begins to diminish, and the strata arch over the crest in a complete dome. But the top of the dome has cracked open, and tapering fissures have run out to the flanks, and they have been filled with molten rock, which has congealed and formed dikes. Moreover, the curving strata of sandstone and shale have in places cleaved apart and admitted sheets of lava between them. So the mountain is a dome or bubble of sedimentary rocks with an eruptive core, with a system of radial dikes, and with a system of dikes interleaved with the strata. It is a mountain of uplifted strata, distended and permeated by eruptive rock."

* * * * * *

In the foregoing characterization of certain types of structure found in these regions, I have not attempted to adopt a system of exact classification, which should be both inclusive and exclusive as the types do not admit of such classification. No "hard and fast lines" can be drawn. I have simply attempted to indicate the important types with their primary and concomitant forms.

It is manifest that the structure of a sedimentary mountain will depend primarily upon two elements—the type of the displacement and the character and extent of erosion. The erosion may be antecedent or superimposed, or it may be consequent, or these methods may be combined, and the erosion may be modified by dip, texture, and other characteristics of the beds producing concomitant forms.

For convenience, I subjoin the following:

SYNOPSIS OF THE TYPES OF MOUNTAIN STRUCTURE RECOGNIZED IN THE FOREGOING DISCUSSION.

MOUNTAINS COMPOSED OF SEDIMENTARY STRATA, ALTERED OR UNALTERED.

I.—APPALACHIAN STRUCTURE.

(Not found in the three provinces.)

II.—SIMPLE ANTICLINAL STRUCTURE.

Primary topographic form. Plateau with rounded vertical outline.

Concomitant forms: 1. Monoclinal Ridges on the Flanks.
2. Monoclinal Ridges only.
3. Inclined Plateaus.

III.—UINTA STRUCTURE.

Primary topographic form. Plateau with rounded summit and abrupt shoulders on the flank.

Concomitant forms: 1. Subsidiary Plateaus.
2. Projecting Ridges.
3. Axial Peaks.
4. Flanking Peaks.
5. Interrupted Monoclinal Ridges.

IV.—KAIBAB STRUCTURE.

Primary topographic form. Plateau with angular outlines.

Concomitant forms: 1. Cliffs of Displacement.
2. Slopes of Displacement.
3. Interrupted Monoclinal Ridges on the Flanks.
4. Monoclinal Ridges with Plateau Carried Away.
5. Projecting Ridges.
6. Cliffs of Erosion.
7. Buttes.
8. Cameo Mountains.

V.—BASIN RANGE STRUCTURE.

Primary topographic form. Monoclinal ridges of displacement.

Concomitant forms: 1. Monoclinal ridges on the back.

VI.—ZONES OF DIVERSE DISPLACEMENT.

Topographic form. Irregular hills.

MOUNTAINS COMPOSED IN WHOLE OR IN PART OF EXTRAVASATED MATERIAL.

VII.—TABLE MOUNTAIN STRUCTURE.

VIII.—UINKARET STRUCTURE.

IX.—TU-SHAR STRUCTURE.

X.—VOLCANIC STRUCTURE.

XI.—HENRY MOUNTAIN STRUCTURE.

OROGRAPHIC STRUCTURE OF THE BASIN PROVINCE.

In this province that orographic type which I have described as the Basin Range structure prevails.

In the consideration of the structure of these ridge like mountains, it is necessary to distinguish clearly the two more important elements involved, viz, that of the metamorphic and unaltered sedimentary formations, and that of the eruptive beds.

The former appear in simple monoclinal ridges of displacement, but the extravasated material may occupy any position in relation to the simple ridges; sometimes it is found appearing on the flanks, sometimes burying portions of the ranges, sometimes extending in subequal masses in transverse or oblique directions to the ridges proper, and in many ways complicating the topographic structure. It is of the structure of the monoclinal ridges only that I now speak. These ridges are not residuary fragments of anticlinal flexures eroded in *intaglio*, for wherever the structure at the foot of the escarpment is not concealed by subaërial gravels, the beds seen at the summit of the ridge, or known to belong to a still higher horizon, appear again at the foot of the escarped face, showing that they have been thrown to that position by a fault. The ridges themselves occupy the place of maximum upheaval. In the summer of 1870 I had some opportunity to examine a few of these ridges while on a trip from Salt Lake City to Fillmore, Beaver, and Saint George, in Utah. In the winter of 1871–'72, I spent a few weeks studying the mountains west of the Rio Virgen, and again in 1873 while engaged in prosecuting some ethnographic studies I visited many points in Western Utah, Nevada, and Southern California, making cursory examinations of mountain structure on my way; but Mr. G. K. Gilbert, while engaged as geologist of the Wheeler expedition, made a much more thorough study of this region. In his report of the geology of that region for 1872, and published in 1874, page 50, under the head of "Mountain Building," Mr. Gilbert presents a "diagram of generalized mountain sections discounting denudation," which I reproduce (Fig. 7), preserving his lettering.

In explanation of the diagram Mr. Gilbert remarks:

"The sections accumulated by our geological observers admit of the following classifications:

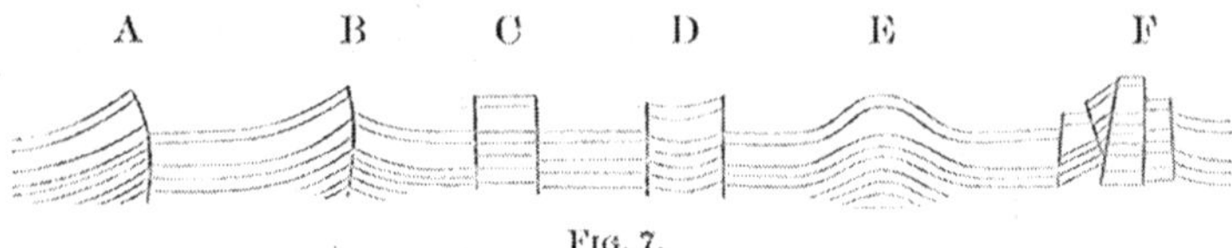

Fig. 7.

"1. Faulted monoclinals occur, in which the strata on one side of the fault have been lifted, while those on the opposite side either do not appear (A), or (less frequently) have been elevated a less amount (B). Two-thirds of the mountain ridges can be referred to this class.

"2. Other ridges are uplifts limited by parallel faults (C), and to these may be assigned a few instances of isolated synclinals (D), occurring under circumstances that preclude the idea that they are remnants omitted by denudation.

"3. True anticlinals (E) are very rare, except as local, subsidiary features, but many ranges are built of faulted and dislocated rock masses (F), with an imperfect anticlinal arrangement.

"Not only is it impossible to formulate these features, by the aid of any hypothetical denudation, in such a system of undulations and foldings as the Messrs. Rogers have so thoroughly demonstrated in Pennsylvania and Virginia, but the structure of the Basin Range system stands in strong contrast to that of the Appalachians. In the latter, corrugation has been produced commonly by folding, exceptionally by faulting; in the former, commonly by faulting, exceptionally by flexure. In the latter, few eruptive rocks occur; in the former volcanic phenomena abound, and are intimately associated with ridges of upheaval. The regular alternations of curved anticlinals and synclinals of the Appalachians demand the assumption of great horizontal diminution of the space covered by the disturbed strata, and suggest lateral pressure as the immediate force concerned; while in the Basin Ranges, the displacement of comparatively rigid bodies of strata by vertical or nearly vertical faults involves little horizontal diminution, and suggests the application of vertical pressure from below."

Thus a characteristic range of this country is the edge of a great block upheaved by the production of a fault and *pari passu* with the upheaval, eroded into irregular forms and modified by flows of eruptive matter from beneath. While this is the general structure throughout the region under consideration, there are many exceptions, as indicated by Mr. Gilbert. Of especial interest are the "uplifts limited by parallel faults (C), and to these may be assigned a few instances of isolated synclinals (D), occurring under circumstances that preclude the idea that they are remnants omitted by denudation," and the "many ranges built of faulted and dislocated rock-masses (F) with an imperfect anticlinal arrangement."

Perhaps the latter are what I have called Zones of Diverse Displacement.

In the northern portion of the province other modifications of the general structure seem to appear. Mr. King, in the third volume of the "Geological Survey of the Fortieth Parallel," page 451, says: "These low mountain chains which lie traced across the desert with a north and south trend are ordinarily the tops of folds whose deep synclinal valleys are filled with Tertiary and Quaternary detritus."

That there should be exceptions to the general type of structure in this province is not strange, for similar exceptions occur in each of the other provinces, as will appear hereafter; but I have myself seen no true anticlinal mountains in the Basin Province.

The mountains of eruptive origin in this province are chiefly accessory masses to the simple ridges of upheaval, and so far as my observations extend, are of the Tu-shar type.

OROGRAPHIC STRUCTURE OF THE PLATEAU PROVINCE.

In the Plateau Province the Kaibab structure prevails, but other types of structure are found. The Uinta Range, which furnishes the type for the Uinta structure is found within this province, and a number of simple anticlinals have been discovered; we have also found many Zones of Diverse Displacement.

The mountains of eruptive origin are of all the types above mentioned; table mountains have been observed in the region drained by the Grand, White, and Yampa Rivers. Pilot Butte has already been mentioned, and other mountains of this type are found in the Sevier district The Uinkaret Mountains, which have been taken as a type of structure, are on the north side of the Grand Cañon of the Colorado. San Francisco Mountain and other mountains in that vicinity are known to be of this structure, but this great group of mountains, of which San Francisco Mountain is the culminating peak, has not been sufficiently studied to enable us to characterize them. The Navajo Mountain, Sierra la Sal, and others in this region are known to be of the Henry Mountain type.

The principal number of important peaks and great mountain masses of the Plateau Province are divided about equally between the last two classes. Some mountains of the Tu-shar structure are found in the Sevier district. Volcanic cones are found in great numbers throughout the southern portion of the province.

OROGRAPHIC STRUCTURE OF THE PARK PROVINCE.

The great mountain masses of the Park Province, especially those to the north standing about the South, Middle, and North Parks, which I have myself seen, are composed of metamorphic crystalline schists. It would appear that these schists were metamorphosed antecedent to the deposition of the Paleozoic, Mesozoic and Cenozoic rocks, which are found in many places resting unconformably upon them; for all these later sedimentary beds contain to a greater or less extent conglomerates which are composed of fragments of metamorphic materials resembling those of the principal mountain masses; and it further appears from my brief studies that this series of rocks was profoundly plicated, perhaps on the Appalachian type, *i. e.*, with closely appressed folds, and this also prior to the deposition of the upper sediments. Through Paleozoic and Mesozoic times minor changes of level have occurred, now lifting the area above the sea, now submerging it, so that many gentle unconformities are found with an interrupted succession of sedimentary beds. But the last great orographic displacements are represented by broad upheavals which appear to have the structure of the Uinta Mountains, so far as can be made out from the fragmentary evidence left by the great erosion to which the country has been subjected in late geological times. The plateau like structure of these great ranges with sedimentaries dipping at high angles on their flanks, sometimes recurved so as to cause inversion of the succession of strata, was a feature which made a deep impression upon me in my travels through this country some years ago, and in my imagination I continued the later sedimentary beds in high curves over these plateaus, and dimly conjectured that tens of thousands of feet had been eroded from some of the ranges, and that the table or plateau like character of the ranges was due to some epoch of this later denudation of the ranges when they were planed down to a common level under conditions which I have explained in the volume several times quoted. Such a planing down occurs when the channels of the eroding streams remain for a great length of time at a general base level. But when I came to study the Uinta Mountains it seemed to me that all the facts which I had observed in the Park Province were duly explained by supposing that that province had the same structure as that observed in the Uinta Mountains. Since my study of that country Mr. Arch. R. Marvine has made a much more thorough and careful survey of it as one of the members of Dr. Hayden's corps. In the report of the United States Geological and Geographical Survey of Colorado, 1873, Hayden, on page 188, Mr. Marvine, under the head of "Blue River or Mount Powell Group", says: "The Park Range, after its abrupt rise from the broad rolling ridge at the north, entirely changes in its characters. It appears to be a rectangular shaped mountain mass cut into the most profound amphitheatral headed gorges, which are separated by the most rugged and sharp saw-like ridges of rock imaginable. The main ridge lies along the southwestern side of the mass, and from it the valleys and their sharp separating ridges trend in a general northeast direction. The northernmost spur was composed of a very distinctly and evenly bedded series of schists, gneisses, and granites which had a strike nearly with the ridge, and a dip of 40° or 50° to the southward. Looked at from the east, the general impression is received that all of the large ridges of the range have a similar structure. These rugged ridges, in their easternmost portions, present a pretty uniform general elevation, and as the northern ridge expands at its end into an even-surfaced table-like mass of rock, the impression is given that all of these sharp ridges are but the remnants left from the cutting away of a plateau like step which once followed along the mountain face. These ridges also end quite similarly along a pretty straight line, and descend to rather a uniform level. Regarding now more particularly the northern ten or fifteen miles of the high range, which includes but four or five of the ridges, it is observed that at the base of each steep end the lowered spur does not continue on as a sharp ridge but slopes off, a flat surfaced, plateau like area, descending gently eastward. Since, upon the corresponding area at the base of the northernmost ridge, great quantities of *débris* of the Lower Cretaceous sandstones were found, abundantly proving that they covered the area, it appears that all of these flattish areas either are now, or have comparatively recently been, covered with the same sandstones. Such features would seem to indicate that the Cretaceous had once extended high up, or quite over the whole range, and that the latter, in its upfolding, had received the most pronounced uplifts along certain well-defined lines, the intervening portions not being tilted up at high angles. It is by such a process that the front range, at least from the Big Thompson to the South Platte, has received much of its uplift. Major Powell and Mr. Gilbert have noticed similar folds in the Kaibab Plateau and adjacent regions on the great Colorado Plateau of Northern Arizona, though there the sedimentary beds have not (by many a thousand feet) been stripped by erosion from off the underlying rocks. It is a form of mountain building which I think is not uncommon in the West."

I am inclined to think that the purposes of orology will be better subserved by classing this structure as a type distinct from that of the Kaibab structure, rather than as a modification of it. The general arching of the strata between the lines of maximum flexure or faulting, allies it somewhat to a true anticlinal; and so far as my studies go these lines of greatest flexure have many more complexities than the faults and monoclinal flexures usually found in the Plateau Province. Hence I have classed it as a distinct type and called it the Uinta structure.

We already know that the spaces between the broad upheavals, of which the ranges themselves are composed, are complicated by many anticlinal and synclinal flexures and by many faults, but the whole structure of the parks, as these interspaces are often called, is exceedingly complex, and much study is necessary, and a great accumulation of facts must be obtained before any safe generalization can be made; but these interspaces or park areas are sometimes Zones of Diverse Displacement.

Atlas Plate No. 6 presents a section across three of the great ranges of the Park Province. This section has been prepared for me by Mr. Marvine. The scale on which it is drawn does not admit of great detail, but the general orographic characteristics are well represented. In a single section it is impossible to present all of the facts upon which this generalization is based. In the quotation from Mr. Marvine already given some of the facts on which his opinions are based appear, and I have myself seen patches of sandstone high up on the Front Range in the vicinity of Long's Peak, and also on the northern end of the Park Range in an area of country not visited by Mr. Marvine, but the shreds of evidence are too multifarious to be assembled here. The park spaces between the great ranges are seen to be complex in the section, but the full extent of this complexity could be illustrated only by the most full and graphic representation. Doubtless when the reports of the several members of the First Division of the United States Geological and Geographical Survey of the Territories are published, the general structure of this country will be more fully revealed.

I have quoted Mr. Marvine and discussed this subject with him more fully from the fact that he and I have visited many of the same points.

I have not myself studied the eruptive mountains of this province.

SUMMARY OF THE STRUCTURAL CHARACTERISTICS OF THE THREE PROVINCES.

The Basin Province is characterized by north and south ranges that are monoclinal ridges of upheaval, and these monoclinal ridges are separated by stretches of subaërial gravels that mask the structure of the areas of subsidence. But while this is the prevailing structure, other types are found.

In the Plateau Province the Kaibab structure is the characteristic. Here on a grand scale the primary and concomitant forms are found; but

Simple Anticlinals, the Uinta structure, and Zones of Diverse Displacement are found as exceptional types.

In the Park Province the Uinta structure prevails and its primary and concomitant topographic forms are grandly shown. Doubtless a more thorough study of this region will result in the discovery of exceptional types.

THESE PROVINCES NOT SEPARATED BY WELL DEFINED LINES.

No line of demarcation can be drawn between the Plateau Province and the Park Province. There is an irregular belt of country separating the better defined portions of the two provinces, which is complicated by characteristics belonging to each. The Kaibab structure of the plateaus does not change abruptly into the Uinta structure, which prevails in the latter province. In fact there are many areas lying along the border separating the two provinces which are characterized by a great development of eruptive beds, which serve to a greater or less extent to mask the orographic structure of the sedimentary beds.

In like manner on the south and west of the Plateau Province there is a belt of country separating it from the Basin Province, itself forming a subprovince of great interest. This region has already been the subject of much study, and although these studies have not been completed, many facts have been discovered from which we can with safety make some important deductions. Through late Mesozoic and earlier Tertiary times there was an old shore line here, now retreating eastward, now advancing westward. It is a region of many movements by faulting and flexing, and during these movements, in Tertiary times at least, many lavas were poured out, so that we have many unconformities both abrupt and gentle, many shore deposits, many faults and flexures and many beds of eruptive matter. But the northern portion of the Basin Province is separated geographically as well as geologically from the Plateau Province by the Wasatch Mountains which constitute a distinct geographic system; but geologically it is but a northern extension of the intervening belt which I have already described, characterized as distinct from that by the fact that the movements of displacement—

faulting and flexing—were on a grander scale and as a consequence of this greater displacement, the accumulations of sediments are greater and the unconformities more apparent and complex. Another consequence of the greater displacement is that the deep lying metamorphic rocks are brought up and exposed by denudation, so that extensive groups of crystalline schists and quartzites appear.

This geographic district, the Wasatch Subprovince, terminates on the south at Mount Nebo, and is quite distinct geographically as well as geologically from the subprovince to the southward, which may be termed the Sevier and Rio Virgen Sub-province.

Thus the Wasatch and Sevier districts separate the Basin and Plateau Provinces, not by the introduction of new types of structure, but by a combination of the types observed on either hand and being complicated by conditions consequent on their forming for a long time the shore line between the two. In the Sevier portion of the belt the Kaibab structure prevails, while in the Wasatch portion the Basin Range structure prevails.

The great Wasatch Range presents a bold front to the west due in a general way to a great fault or rather a series of faults such as I have described as occurring in the Basin Ranges; but on the east or back slope of the range the structure is complex. An irregular belt of country stretching from the crest of the mountains eastward many miles is faulted and flexed in many ways.

In the northeast angle formed by the Wasatch and Uinta Mountains there is a long but narrow and irregular zone stretching toward the northeast from the head-waters of the Bear River. Sulphur Creek drains a part of this, and the well known Bear River coal lands are found in the district. From Aspen to a point near Carter, the Union Pacific Railroad runs along the eastern border of the belt. Its extension in either direction beyond the points indicated are unknown to me. This belt also exemplifies what I have called Zones of Diverse Displacement, and the general effect is upheaval. The belt seems to have been broken into very irregular blocks by lines of faulting or flexure which so far as my observation has extended preserve no law of direction.

The blocks into which the country has been broken have been tilted, greatly sometimes, sometimes turned quite on edge, and even in some cases reversed. One of these blocks standing on edge afforded Professor Meek the opportunity to make his section on Sulphur Creek published in Dr. Hayden's Report on the Geological Survey of Montana, Idaho, Wyoming, and Utah, 1872. Professor Meek evidently recognized the difficulty of correlating the strata in that section with those outcropping elsewhere in the district. I mention these excessively complex zones without attempting to explain them. Some student of geology will eventually find here a subject rich in results.

SUMMARY OUTLINE OF THE HISTORY OF THE THREE PROVINCES DURING CENOZOIC TIME.

In the latter part of Mesozoic time the greater part of the Basin Province was dry land. The Plateau Province was an open but shallow sea. In the Park Province a chain of islands extended to the south. The Cenozoic time was inaugurated by a series of movements, which, continued to the present time, have produced the topographic features now observed. This part of the crust of the earth, and I mean by the term "crust" simply that portion of the earth which we are able to study by actual observation in truncated folds and eroded faults—this portion of the crust, then, was gradually broken and contorted. The Plateau and Park Provinces were cut off from the sea, and great bodies of fresh water accumulated in the basins, while to the east in the region of the Great Plains, in earlier Tertiary times at least, there was an open sea. Slowly through Cenozoic times the outlines of these lakes were changed, doubtless in two ways: first, by the gradual displacement of the rock beds in upheaval and subsidence here and there; and, second, by the gradual desiccation due to the filling up of the basins by sedimentation and the erosion of their barriers; and the total result of this was to steadily diminish the lacustrine area. But the movements in the displacement extended over the Basin Province, for that region was then a comparatively low plain, constituting a general base level of erosion to which that region had been denuded in Mesozoic and early Tertiary time when it was an area of dry land; for I think that from the known facts we may reasonably infer that the Basin Ranges, though composed of Paleozoic and Eozoic rocks, are, as mountains, of very late upheaval. For some purposes, and in broad generalization, erosion furnishes a valuable measure of geological times. A mountain, as a mountain, is comparatively ephemeral. The evidence of this is found on every hand as we study the Rocky Mountain region. There can be no conclusion reached from reasoning on geological data more certain than that the Uinta upheaval began at the close of Mesozoic time, and has continued intermittently near to the present, and during that time this upheaval has suffered a degradation in areas of maximum erosion of no less than 30,000 feet; and there is evidence also which leads to the conclusion that the conditions for great erosion were not persistently maintained during this time. I have already stated that the Basin Ranges occupy the area of maximum upheaval, and they are monoclinal ridges. Had these ridges been upheaved greatly beyond their present altitudes it is manifest that erosion would have carried them far back from the lines of faults, a condition not found to obtain.

In the erosion of these ridges, as an independent subject of study, the geologist is impressed with the magnitude of the work which has been performed by atmospheric agencies. It appears that each ridge is but a small residuary fragment of the great inclined block, and the interrange spaces are filled with clays, sands and gravels, the waste of these blocks, in such a manner as to bury the underlying rocks over broad areas; and whether we consider the amount which has been lost from the blocks or the amount which has been accumulated in the valleys, the loss here or the gain there, this transferred material is very great. It is worthy of remark that over much of the area, the deposit of this transferred material in the valleys was subaërial, but in the northwestern portion of the province it was lacustrine.

But when we compare the erosion which these inclined blocks have suffered with that of many of the great blocks in the Plateau Province of the Kaibab structure, or with that of the Uinta uplift, or with the great uplifts in the Park Province, the erosion of the Basin Range ridges sinks into insignificance. And when we consider, further, that the erosion in the Plateau and Park Provinces which we are able to study has all been performed during Cenozoic time, and that the conditions of maximum erosion were but intermittent during that time, we are forced to the conclusion that the conditions for great erosion now found in the Basin Ranges have existed but for a short period, *i. e.*, the blocks were certainly not upheaved antecedent to Cenozoic time; and it would seem probable that it must have been in late Tertiary.

It seems proper to add here a remark concerning certain conditions of erosion, though I have elsewhere discussed the subject more fully.

The lesser or greater rapidity of erosion depends chiefly upon three conditions: first, elevation above the base level of erosion; second, the induration of the rocks; and, third, the amount of rain fall. But erosion does not increase in ratio with the increase of the precipitation of moisture, for increasing moisture serves to increase the protection derived from vegetation.

Nor does induration greatly preserve rocks from erosion, for on most exposures the action of the elements in disintegrating the rocks is in excess of the power of the streams to carry the material away. The exceptional exposures are found on steep slopes; yet the difference in the induration of beds has an effect as seen in the minor or concomitant forms of all mountain regions. The principal factor in maximum erosion is elevation above the base level, and the power of erosion increases in geometric ratio with the elevation. The power of the streams to transport the material of erosion is increased in geometric ratio and the power of the water in corrasion is in like manner increased; and the corrasion of deep channels by rapid streams filled with sands, gravels and bowlders produces another condition of surface favorable to general degradation—that is, the walls of these deep channels are broken down by gravity, which is further increased by an undermining process where harder and softer beds alternate. With these facts in view, we need not enter into a consideration of the difference of texture or induration of the rocks of the Plateau and Park Provinces and those of the Basin Province; but we may remark that of the 30,000 feet eroded from the Uinta uplift, more than 16,000 feet were of beds of Paleozoic Age, and with a texture as firm as the rocks of the Basin Ranges.

It is manifest that the result of all these movements of displacement in the three provinces was general upheaval. But this upheaval in the three provinces was unequal; it was great in the Basin Province, greater in the

Plateau Province, and greatest in the Park Province. The Basin Province was already above the sea level, but a comparatively low plain. In such a condition, erosion would be slight; and as the ranges were lifted, the material derived from them was deposited in the valleys, and it is probable that no considerable amount was transported beyond the province into the sea, and the general uplift of the province was little or no greater than the change from that of the low plain near the sea level to its present elevation—that is, the Basin Province as a body is not the result of the difference between erosion and elevation; but the ranges themselves do thus mark the difference between erosion and elevation. That which was taken from the mountains was added to the valleys. Much of the Plateau Province was still an area of rapidly accumulating sediments long into Tertiary time; but at last the movements which began at the commencement of Tertiary time succeeded in bringing the whole area not only above the level of the sea, but above the general level of the Basin Province itself; so that while the Basin Province was drained into the Plateau Province in earlier Tertiary time, in late Tertiary time the drainage was reversed, and the streams of the Plateau Province found their way to the sea by passing through the Basin Province, and many of them, especially those in the Sevier and Wasatch regions which head along the old shore line, are now drained into the basins which characterize the province thus designated.

It is the opinion of Mr. Howell, and I believe also that of Captain Dutton, that this drainage was in some cases reversed along the very channels occupied by the ancient streams which ran from the Basin Province into the Plateau lakes. In the Park Province the general upheaval was still greater, and the Colorado River, which empties into the Gulf of California, heads in the very heart of the Park Province and drains the greater part of the Plateau Province by carrying its waters across the Basin Province. While the general surface of the last two mentioned provinces was in Mesozoic time not above the level of the sea, at the present time the general surface is from four to fourteen thousand feet above the sea level; but there are portions now marked by great ranges which have been upheaved twenty and thirty thousand feet; but these portions during the progress of upheaval suffered denudation, and a part at least of the material thus denuded was not carried away to the sea but was deposited in fresh water basins. But at last these fresh water basins themselves were drained and their beds faulted and flexed and eroded, and their sites are now found marked by broad stretches of bad-lands.

I speak of an open sea to the east of the Park Mountains, where now the Great Plains stretch in broad expanse. That there was a sea or arm of the sea here is manifest, for I have collected marine Tertiary fossils of Vicksburgh types in several places east of Denver; but from my exceedingly brief studies in that region, merely as a passing traveler, I can only say that the region, though simple in its topographic features, is indeed complex in its geological structure.

Throughout this great area, from the eastern slope of the Park Mountains on the east to the eastern slope of the Sierra Nevada on the west, and from the sources of the Green and Shoshoni Rivers on the north to the San Francisco Mountains on the south, the whole region is broken, flexed, and contorted along innumerable lines. But the great structure lines have a north and south trend; the ranges of the Basin Province run from north to south; the great faults of the Plateau Province also run north and south, and the Park Ranges have a north and south trend. But these general outlines are broken by oblique and transverse displacements, usually of a minor magnitude, though in some cases, as in the Uinta Mountains, these transverse displacements assume as great proportions as the north and south flexures and faults. While the whole region is exceedingly complex by displacement, it is also exceedingly complex by reason of the unconformity of its sedimentary beds. And all this complexity is greatly increased by reason of the floods of lava which have been poured out here and there over the entire area, and now and then through Cenozoic up to the present time. And all these floods of lava, all these thousands of eruptive mountains, thousands of mesa sheets, thousands of volcanic cones, testify to a period of great volcanic activity while the region was in fact a great continental area, thus contradicting the generalization which has obtained in some quarters that volcanic activity is adjacent to the sea. And further, very much of this volcanic activity has been exhibited since the desiccation of the lakes.

CHAPTER II.

SEDIMENTARY GROUPS OF THE PLATEAU PROVINCE.

We turn now to a consideration of the Plateau Province. Throughout its extent it is traversed by profound gorges or cañons; high cliffs are found; long ridges and lone buttes are seen, all presenting escarpments unclad with vegetation where the geological structure is plainly revealed, and it is nowhere concealed to any important extent by subaërial gravels, river deposits, deep soil, or rich vegetation. The whole region has been flexed and faulted on a vast scale; the flexures are truncated by erosion, and the faults are crossed by cañons and lines of cliffs; and thus by a combination of circumstances the whole region is an open book to the geologist, revealing a wonderfully complicated structure and a grand succession of formations. Accumulations of sediments may be studied of Cenozoic, Mesozoic, and Paleozoic Ages, each represented by formations that are measured by thousands of feet. In the hearts of the mountains and depths of the cañons Eozoic rocks are found; on the mesas and elevated valleys sheets of lava have been spread; and naked volcanic cones crown the geological series. A general section of the sedimentary beds alone sums up a total of nearly 60,000 feet, and the relations of the groups into which they can be divided can be determined with a certainty rarely attainable in the eastern portion of the United States. When we group these beds in such a manner as the structural geology demands we have a series of groups or succession of formations separated by epochs of change, producing unconformities or resulting in extensive stratigraphic peculiarities, and in constructing a general section of this country this natural series cannot be ignored without greatly distorting the facts. But a section thus arranged presents a series of limestones, shales, sandstones and conglomerates totally unlike that which has been established in the New York and Appalachian Province or in the Valley of the Mississippi. Again in several of the groups we discover the remains of rich faunas and floras, but the series of fossils belonging to any of the natural groups in the Plateau Province is unlike that of any group or formation in the earlier studied rocks of the east; either entirely new series are found or the old types are regrouped so as to present a new aspect. Hence it would be manifestly absurd to introduce into this newly studied province the nomenclature adopted in those provinces which had been previously studied, as it would involve the necessity of explaining in each case that the name was used with a new meaning, and that the adoption of the older names was intended simply to express the opinion that the group to which it was given should be referred to some period in the geological time scale about the same as that held by the group to which the name was originally applied; and this would involve the re-adjustment of the names from time to time on the collection of new suites of fossils. While it does not seem possible to consider a particular sandstone or limestone, or a particular group of strata as identical with or closely similar to one in New York or Illinois, this does not preclude the possibility of establishing a general synchronism. The Cenozoic, Mesozoic and Paleozoic Ages seem to be as well defined as elsewhere, and in each age there are formations which are earlier or later, but the details of this general synchronism can only be discovered after a far more thorough study of the paleontology of the province has been made.

The conclusions thus stated have been reached after a study of the province which has occupied the greater part of the last eight years. During the earlier years I attempted here to find the formations of the east, or at least formations corresponding to them, and thus years of study were in part fruitless for that reason. I then determined if possible to discover the natural series of the province itself independent of other regions, and the general section below is the result. Perhaps, from *a priori* reasons, I should have commenced with this plan. The supposition that at the same time sediments should have been carried into the

Colorado sea similar to those in the New York sea, is not warranted by a study of the deposits now forming in existing seas. The Hudson River carries a very different deposit into the Atlantic Ocean from that carried by the Colorado River into the Gulf of California. Nor should we expect that the faunas or floras of regions so widely separated should be the same or closely similar. In the earlier times, which we study as geologists, there seem to have been physical conditions in the two regions as widely differing as those of the present. The Cenozoic formations of the plateaus are lacustrine; the Cenozoic formations of the Atlantic slope are marine. The Mesozoic of the plateaus is of great extent and thickness, while that age is but scantily represented on the Atlantic slope. Nor do the Paleozoic formations exhibit a close similarity.

The names which I have selected for the groups are geographic, as such a system admits of easy interpolation, and the localities serve well in fitting the name to the group and refer at once to the typical strata. For obvious reasons I should have been pleased to have commenced with a clean slate, selecting such localities as would serve for the best types; but I did not feel at liberty to ignore the labors of geologists who had preceded me.

In the Cenozoic groups and the first Mesozoic I found great confusion, as these groups had been seen at many places, and some of them received several names each; and often different groups were confounded by being included under one geographic name. With these groups I have tried to select such localities as would serve to fairly represent the groups and at the same time do no injustice to other laborers.

We now append the general section.

TABLE OF THE GROUPS OF SEDIMENTARY STRATA OF THE PLATEAU PROVINCE.

	Scale in feet.	Thickness of groups in feet.	Groups.		
CENOZOIC.		300	Bishop Mt Conglomerate.	Unconformable by plication and erosion with underlying rocks.	
	2,000	1,800	Brown's Park.	Sandstones, gravels, limestones, concretionary and stratified flints. Unconformable with all underlying rocks.	
	4,000	2,000	Bridger.	Bad-land sandstones, (chiefly green-sands,) limestones, shells—marls, and concretionary and stratified flints.	
		500	Upper Green River	Plant beds	Sandstones, sometimes argillaceous, and limestones, Carbonaceous shales and lignitic coal near middle.*
				Tower Sandstone	A massive or irregularly bedded sandstone, ferruginous. Unconformable by erosion with lower group.
		800	Lower Green River	Shales, often bituminous; sandstones and limestones; carbonaceous shales and lignitic coal near the base.	
	6,000 8,000	3,000	Bitter Creek.	Bad-land sandstones, often with much gypsum; indurated sandstones; ferruginous; shell-marls; many beds of carbonaceous shales and lignitic coal. To the southward the group is composed of indurated sandstones and limestones. Unconformable by plication and erosion with the next.	
MESOZOIC. CRETACEOUS.	10,000	1,800	Point of Rocks.	Upper Hogback Sandstone. Middle Hogback Sandstone. Golden Wall Sandstone.	Sandstones, usually indurated, sometime ferruginous, with many beds of carbonaceous shales and lignitic coal.
	12,000	1,800	Salt Wells.	Sandstones or arenaceous shales; often very friable, producing bad-lands, with carbonaceous shales and lignitic coal.	
	14,000	2,000	Sulphur Creek.	Black shales; occasionally friable sandstones with carbonaceous shales and lignitic coal.	
		500	Henry's Fork.	Sandstones, bad-land rocks, conglomerates, and shales, with carbonaceous shales and lignitic coal.	

COAL HORIZON

* Unconformable by erosion with the next.

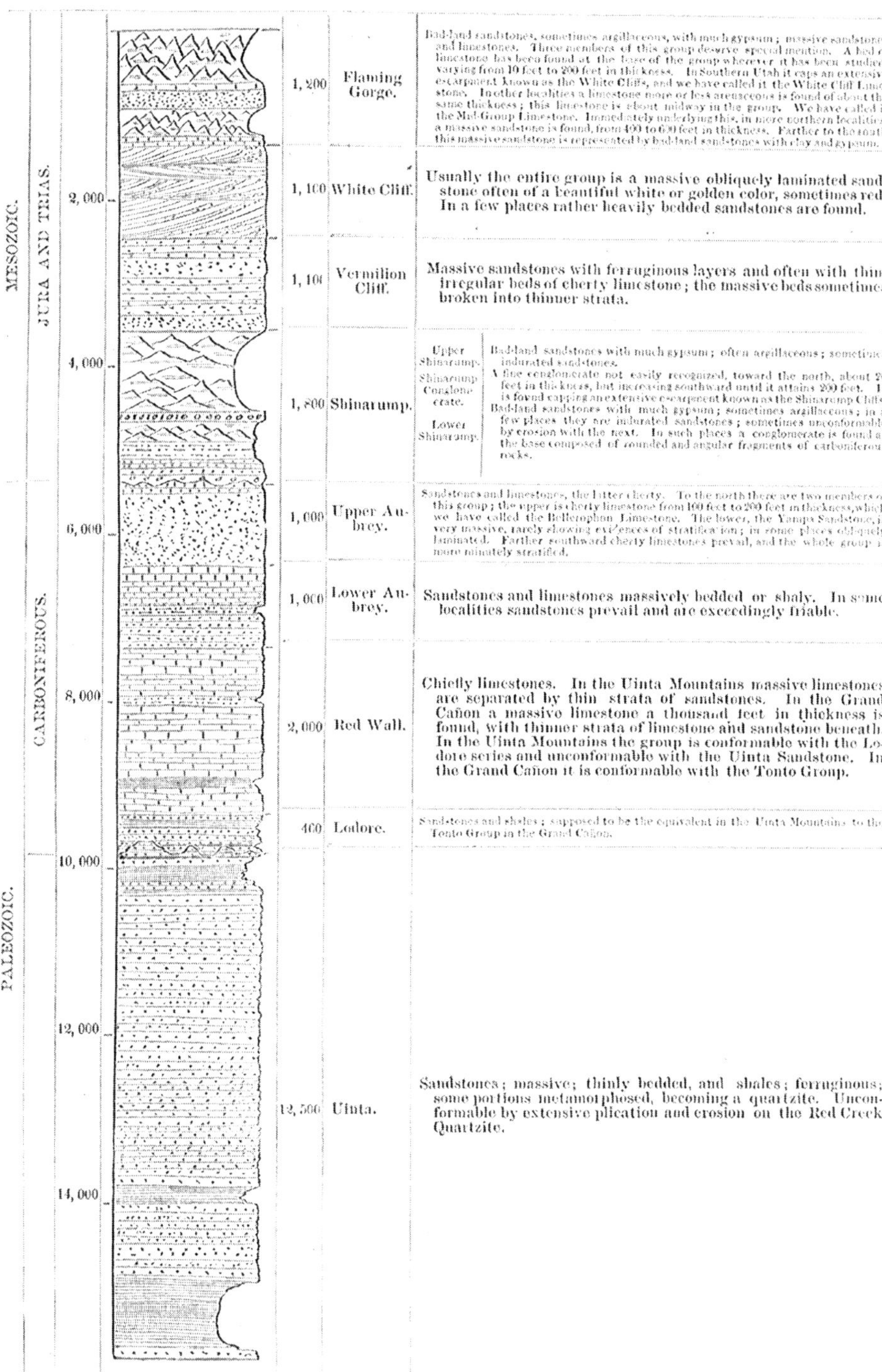

Thickness	Group	Description
1,200	Flaming Gorge.	Bad-land sandstones, sometimes argillaceous, with much gypsum; massive sandstones and limestones. Three members of this group deserve special mention. A bed of limestone has been found at the base of the group wherever it has been studied, varying from 10 feet to 200 feet in thickness. In Southern Utah it caps an extensive escarpment known as the White Cliffs, and we have called it the White Cliff Limestone. In other localities a limestone more or less arenaceous is found of about the same thickness; this limestone is about midway in the group. We have called it the Mid-Group Limestone. Immediately underlying this, in more northern localities, a massive sandstone is found, from 400 to 600 feet in thickness. Farther to the south this massive sandstone is represented by bad-land sandstones with clay and gypsum.
1,100	White Cliff.	Usually the entire group is a massive obliquely laminated sandstone often of a beautiful white or golden color, sometimes red. In a few places rather heavily bedded sandstones are found.
1,100	Vermilion Cliff.	Massive sandstones with ferruginous layers and often with thin, irregular beds of cherty limestone; the massive beds sometimes broken into thinner strata.
1,800	Shinarump.	Upper Shinarump. — Bad-land sandstones with much gypsum; often argillaceous; sometimes indurated sandstones. Shinarump Conglomerate. — A fine conglomerate not easily recognized, toward the north, about 20 feet in thickness, but increasing southward until it attains 200 feet. It is found capping an extensive escarpment known as the Shinarump Cliffs. Lower Shinarump. — Bad-land sandstones with much gypsum; sometimes argillaceous; in a few places they are indurated sandstones; sometimes unconformable by erosion with the next. In such places a conglomerate is found at the base composed of rounded and angular fragments of carboniferous rocks.
1,000	Upper Aubrey.	Sandstones and limestones, the latter cherty. To the north there are two members of this group; the upper is cherty limestone from 100 feet to 200 feet in thickness, which we have called the Bellerophon Limestone. The lower, the Yampa Sandstone, is very massive, rarely showing evidences of stratification; in some places obliquely laminated. Farther southward cherty limestones prevail, and the whole group is more minutely stratified.
1,000	Lower Aubrey.	Sandstones and limestones massively bedded or shaly. In some localities sandstones prevail and are exceedingly friable.
2,000	Red Wall.	Chiefly limestones. In the Uinta Mountains massive limestones are separated by thin strata of sandstones. In the Grand Cañon a massive limestone a thousand feet in thickness is found, with thinner strata of limestone and sandstone beneath. In the Uinta Mountains the group is conformable with the Lodore series and unconformable with the Uinta Sandstone. In the Grand Cañon it is conformable with the Tonto Group.
400	Lodore.	Sandstones and shales; supposed to be the equivalent in the Uinta Mountains to the Tonto Group in the Grand Cañon.
12,500	Uinta.	Sandstones; massive; thinly bedded, and shales; ferruginous; some portions metamorphosed, becoming a quartzite. Unconformable by extensive plication and erosion on the Red Creek Quartzite.

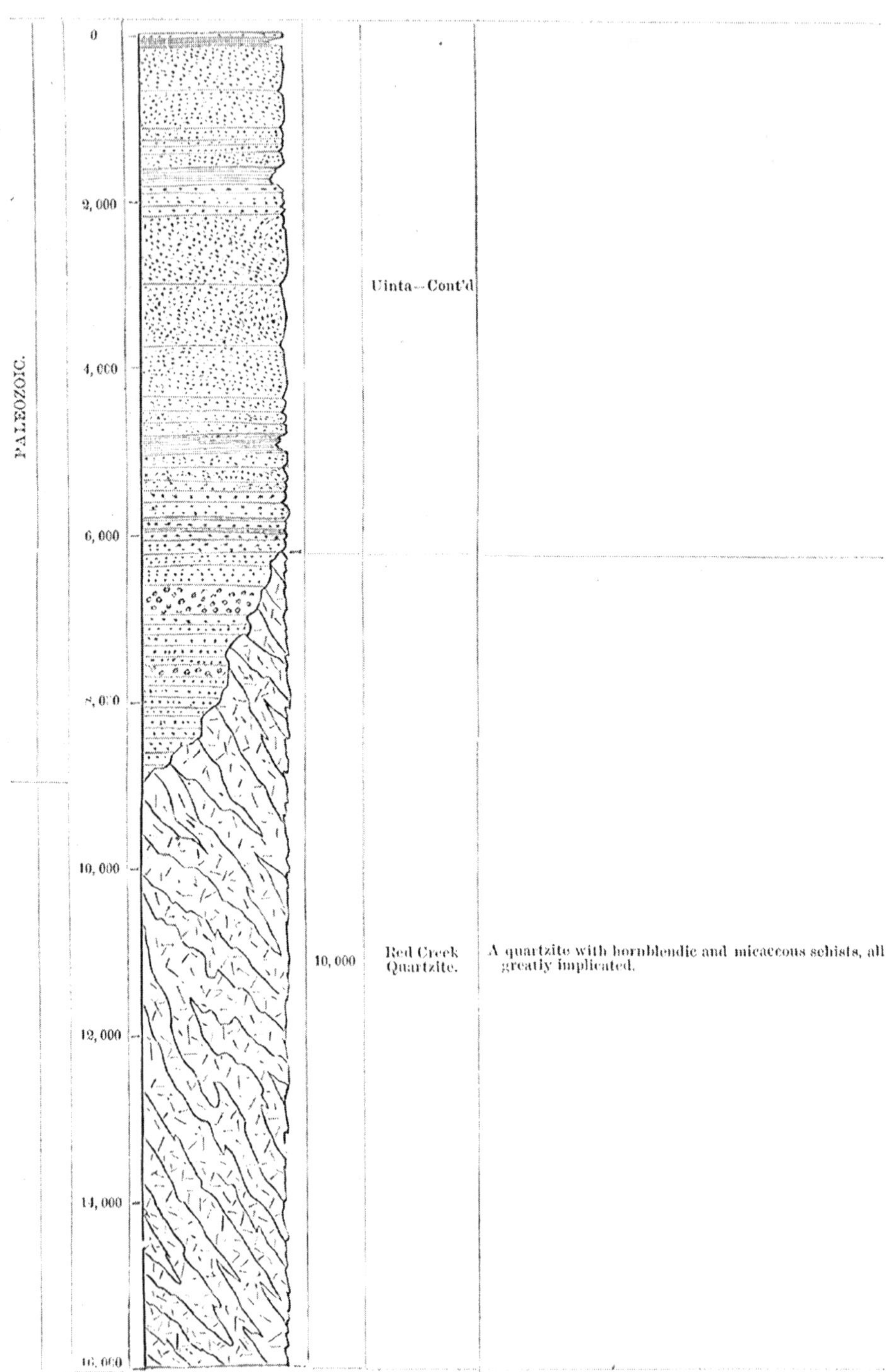
PALEOZOIC.
0
2,000
4,000
6,000
8,000
10,000
12,000
14,000
16,000
Uinta—Cont'd
10,000
Red Creek Quartzite.
A quartzite with hornblendic and micaceous schists, all greatly implicated.

BASE OF THE SECTION IN THE GRAND CAÑON OF THE COLORADO.

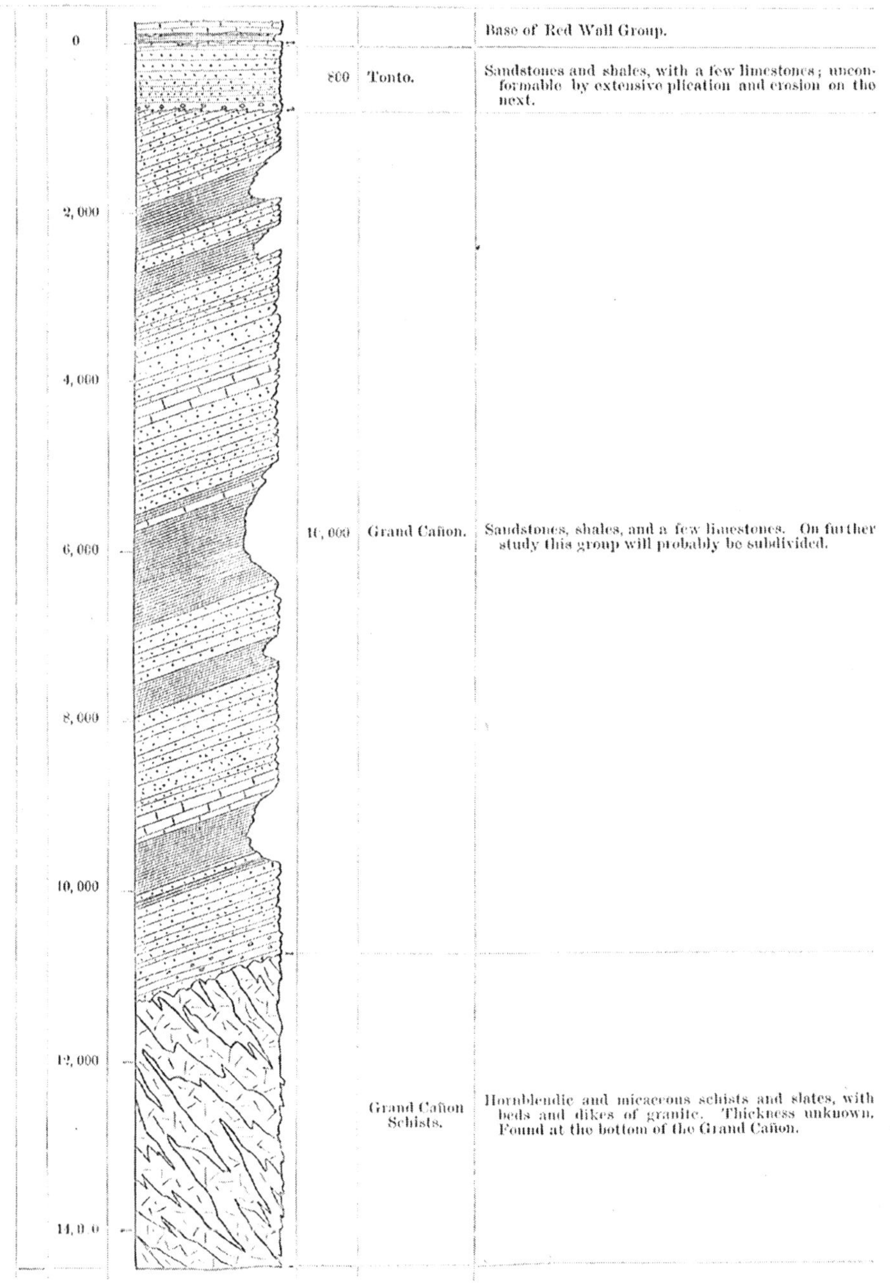

REMARKS ON THE GENERAL SECTION.

The thicknesses which I have given in the table are considered to be nearly an average. Many of the groups are much thicker in some places, and thinner in others. If the maximum thickness of each had been given, the sum would have been more than 70,000 feet; while if the minimum had been given the sum would have been reduced nearly to 50,000 feet. The Mesozoic and Paleozoic sediments in all latitudes where they have been studied, are found to attenuate as you pass from the western to the eastern border of the province.

In characterizing the rocks I have attempted to give only those features which are general throughout the province so far as it has been studied; but there are many local peculiarities which we have observed and which will appear in the detailed reports.

LOCALITIES WHERE THE SEVERAL GROUPS CAN BE STUDIED.

I now append a few localities where these several groups can be seen under favorable circumstances. They might be multiplied greatly, but perhaps no good purpose would thus be served.

BISHOP MOUNTAIN CONGLOMERATE.

The Bishop Mountain Conglomerate can be seen on the summit of Bishop Mountain, where it lies unconformably on the eroded beds of the Bitter Creek Group. A fine exposure can also be seen on the summit of the Quien Hornet Mountain.

BROWN'S PARK GROUP.

This group is well represented at Brown's Park, in Northeastern Utah and Northwestern Colorado.

A good section can be obtained in the high bluffs on the west side of the Snake River by commencing about five miles above its confluence with the Yampa where these beds are seen to rest unconformably against Carboniferous strata at the foot of the mountain. In going north two minor flexures are passed where the upper members of the group are exposed; and, on reaching a third and greater upheaval, the group is exposed from summit to base, and is seen to rest unconformably upon Bridger beds.

BRIDGER GROUP.

This group can be well studied in the vicinity of Fort Bridger, at Church Buttes, and in the Cameo Mountains. It has an extensive development in this region, *i. e.*, west of the Green River and north of the Uinta Mountains, and is usually well exposed. An outlying patch can be seen between Vermilion Creek and the Snake River, on the north side of the Dry Mountains. It can also be finely studied at Haystack Mountain.

UPPER GREEN RIVER GROUP.

The Plant Beds of this group are well exposed to the north of Green River Station, and between that point and Alkali Stage Station in many gulches and cañons. They are also well exposed in the cuts of the Union Pacific Railroad between Green River Station and Bryan. Another good exposure can be seen in the escarpments on either side of Henry's Fork, commencing about five miles above its mouth and continuing up the stream for several miles.

The Tower Sandstone is well shown in the cliffs at Green River Station and in that vicinity, especially up and down the river for several miles. This sandstone is also well exposed on the eastern side of the Green River, below the mouth of Currant Creek.

LOWER GREEN RIVER GROUP.

This group is well exposed along the Green River from Green River Station southward for ten miles where a detailed section has been made and will be given hereafter. It is also well exposed in many of the escarpments of the Quien Hornet Mountain. We again find it well exposed in the escarpments a few miles northeast from the head of Vermilion Cañon. Fine exposures are seen on the Snake River six miles above the northern foot of Junction Mountain. The elevated ledges known as Pine Bluffs, near the sources of the eastern tributaries of Vermilion Creek, are capped with the limestones and bituminous shales of this group.

BITTER CREEK GROUP.

This group is well exposed along Bitter Creek in the vicinity of Bitter

Creek and Black Buttes Stations. A fine section can be obtained by commencing at Pine Bluffs at the foot of the limestone beds and passing in a direction a little north of west until the massive gray sandstone of the next group is reached. Across this stretch of country the beds dip to the east, and their outcropping edges stand in a succession of ledges and can be well studied. It is better to follow the line which I have indicated than to make a section along Bitter Creek, as there is a fault passing between old Hallville and Black Buttes Station, and it is difficult along that line to determine the amount of the fault, and hence there is a liability of duplicating or omitting some of the lower members of this section. This fault will be explained hereafter.

The junction of the Bitter Creek Group with the Lower Green River can be very well seen in the escarpment at Pine Bluffs; one hand can be placed upon a limestone of the upper group and the other on a massive bad-land sandstone of the lower. In like manner the junction between this group and the next lower can be well seen in an escarpment east of and facing Black Butte. There is an escarpment on the northeast side of Bitter Creek, facing that stream and extending from Hallville Section House to Point of Rocks, where the upper sandstones of the Point of Rocks Group stand in an almost vertical cliff, and the lower members of the Bitter Creek series can be seen to rest upon this sandstone unconformably. These beds are exceedingly friable, ferruginous sandstones and shales, and in many places a shelf or terrace is seen between the foot of the Bitter Creek shales and the brink of the cliffs formed of the Point of Rocks sandstone.

This group can be studied along the Union Pacific Railroad west of Rock Springs. Three-fourths of a mile east of Lawrence Section House the railroad passes with an abrupt curve around a ledge of rocks, where the junction of the Bitter Creek series and the Lower Green River can be plainly seen. Here you may place your forefinger on a limestone of the Lower Green River and your thumb on a bad-land sandstone of the Bitter Creek Group. In the escarped hills on either side, the line between the limestones and buff and pink sandstones can be plainly seen. These rocks dip to the west at an angle of about four degrees, and as you go eastward this dip gradually increases, and bed after bed of the Bitter Creek Group can be seen well exposed by passing back and forth among the hills until reaching a point about a mile and a half west of Blair's coal mine, you come to a high ridge or hogback where the series ends. This hogback is composed of the upper sandstone of the Point of Rocks Group; the junction of the two groups on this line can be very well seen. The gray sandstone of the Point of Rocks Group is massive and indurated. The brown, ferruginous shales of the Bitter Creek Group yield readily to atmospheric degradation, and have been swept away back of the ridge or hogback, leaving broad, naked surfaces of gray sandstone.

Another fine section can be obtained by commencing on the southern face of the Quien Hornet Mountain and passing over the escarped ledges in a southwesterly direction along the bluffs of Red Creek until you reach the foot of the great hogback which is composed of beds of the Point of Rocks Group.

Vermilion Creek in its upper course runs through beds of this group. Its many wet-weather tributaries have carved the country with deep but flaring channels, and the naked beds can be seen on every hand; and the bad-land hills are filled with fossils; but the lower members of the group cannot well be studied by reason of some complicated but interesting displacements that are observed a little north of the Vermilion Cañon. These displacements will be discussed hereafter.

To the southward this group of rocks is developed over broad areas. The Cañon of Desolation for much of its course is cut through these rocks, and in its high walls this group can be studied to advantage. The Pink Cliffs of Southern Utah are of this age.

POINT OF ROCKS GROUP.

A good section of this group can be obtained at Point of Rocks Station. There is a series of cliffs and abruptly escarped hills extending from a point northeast of the station in a westerly direction for several miles. These escarpments face Bitter Creek and the Union Pacific Railroad. In the cliff immediately back of the depot at Point of Rocks the junction between the Bitter Creek and Point of Rocks Groups is well seen. As I have already described, the lower members of the upper groups are brown, friable, arenaceous, ferruginous shales, with occasional beds of soft sandstone, all weathering easily; and the line of junction between that and the massive gray sandstone which forms the summit of the Point of Rocks Group can be plainly seen. In these shales immediately overlying the massive sandstone there are beds and seams of coal. The first massive sandstone is the Upper Hogback Sandstone. These rocks all have an easterly dip, and as you go westward you soon reach the base of the Upper Hogback Sandstone, then pass the beds of irregularly bedded shales and sandstones until you reach a second massive, gray sandstone, which in many places is broken into two or more beds. This is the Middle Hogback Sandstone. Still going westward, massive and thinly bedded sandstones of yellowish-buff color alternating with massive beds of light gray or white sandstone, are seen. About six miles from the station the railroad turns southward and debouches from the narrow cañon valley of the Point of Rocks into the broad open valley of the Salt Wells. To reach the base of the Point of Rocks Group it is necessary to diverge from the railroad, which passes along the foot of the cliffs, and continue in a westerly direction until the last massive gray sandstone is reached. It will then be noticed that the massive beds, both yellow and gray, have been passed, and that another series of more thinly laminated beds underlie the massive series. These alternating beds of gray and buff belong to the Golden Wall Group. The separation between these two groups at this point is not as plainly marked as at many other regions. The whole thickness at this locality is about 1,800 feet.

When Messrs. Meek and Bannister made their section along this line, or their Point of Rocks Section, they commenced a few hundred feet below the summit of the group and ended about 300 feet above its base, which was not seen by them; for in turning southward with the railroad they crossed two great faults having their throw to the north. The lines of faulting pass along a valley showing no rock exposures, and when they passed out into Salt Wells Valley they were on beds of the Salt Wells Group at a horizon of six or eight hundred feet below the summit.

Another good section of this group can be obtained at Rock Springs. A few hundred yards west of the mineral spring known as Rock Spring, a great, massive sandstone stands in a ledge, the beds dipping to the west at an angle of about 16 degrees. The brown shales and sandstones of the upper group have been stripped from this sandstone over broad areas, and the junction between the two can be plainly seen. Starting from this point and going eastward, a series of gray sandstones above, interrupted by carbonaceous shales and beds of coal, are passed; then gray and buff sandstones are seen until the Van Dyke Mine is reached. A little east of this point we come to the base of the Point of Rocks Group, and reach the summit of the Salt Wells Group. I have never examined this point with sufficient care to enable me to indicate the exact junction, but as described in the Point of Rocks Section above, the junction is not very well defined.

Fine sections can be obtained on either side of the Green River two miles above Flaming Gorge where this group of beds was measured and found to be 2,000 feet in thickness. Here they stand on edge, and their stratification can be well seen.

The foot of Desolation Cañon, and Gray Cañon on the Green River affords another fine section, and the group can be well studied in the Wasatch Cliffs at the head of the Escalante River, and in the hills at the foot of the Pink Cliffs, in Southern Utah.

SALT WELLS GROUP.

Standing south of the debouchure of the Point of Rocks Cañon into Salt Wells Basin, and looking eastward, lines of cliffs and escarped hills are seen. Climbing these hills until the first massive, light gray sandstone is found, you reach the summit of the Salt Wells Group and the base of the Point of Rocks. Then, turning westward you descend from this eminence, and still continuing in a westerly direction you pass along the foot of an escarpment which faces the railroad, the beds of which dip at an angle of about 8 degrees to the east, and hence you are passing from higher to lower strata. Still continuing in this direction for several miles, and crossing the broad valley of Pretty Creek, you reach at last the axis of the upheaval near Baxter Section House. Here we find an escarpment facing the north, the rocks of which are light colored, arenaceous shales above and dark, argillaceous shales below. The arenaceous shales are at the base of the Salt Wells Group; the black shales below are believed to belong to the summit of the next group. No examination of the section has been made along this line nor have the beds been studied in detail, but the upper and lower limits of the group are tolerably well defined. On the Green River, about two miles and a half above Flaming Gorge, the junction between the black shales of the lower group and the yellow shales of the upper can be well seen, and the junction between this group and the Point of Rocks Group is also well seen. Here the beds stand on edge and were measured, and a thickness of nearly 2,000 feet obtained. This group can be well studied in narrow zones along the northern flanks of the Uinta Mountains. Fine exposures occur in the Pink Cliffs and at Gunnison's Butte on the Green River south of Gray Cañon, and north of the point where that river was crossed by Captain Gunnison on his trip to Utah in 1853.

SULPHUR CREEK GROUP.

This group of black shales can be well seen in the hills near Hilliard Station on the Union Pacific Railroad. Here Sulphur Creek cuts through them for several miles. In Professor Meek's "Section on Sulphur Creek near Bear River," his "No. 1" is the summit of the group. The locality does not present a good type from the fact of the great displacements to which the beds have been subjected. Their relation to underlying beds cannot be determined with certainty; but on the north and south sides of the Uinta Mountains many fine exposures are found. I have already mentioned the point where the junction of this group with the overlying can be seen, north of Flaming Gorge; the beds dip to the north at an angle of nearly 90 degrees, and on the south side of Henry's Fork the junction of the black shales with the next group is plainly seen. Here the beds were measured and found to be 2,050 feet in thickness.

Farther eastward between the head of Dry Lake Valley and Vermilion Creek the beds dip to the north at an angle of about 25 degrees and are truncated with the great Uinta flexure. Still farther south in the Escalante Valley, Paria Valley, Kanab Valley and many other localities, the entire group is well exposed.

HENRY'S FORK GROUP.

This group can be well studied at the typical locality which is on the south side of Henry's Fork, commencing about two miles above its mouth and extending for many miles to the westward. These beds stand on edge and are well exposed. Their junction with the black shales can be plainly seen and the base of the group is the second conglomerate below the teliost shales; the teliost shales themselves constitute a conspicuous datum point from which to study the stratigraphy of this district. Many sections can be obtained on either side of the Uinta Mountains. Perhaps no better place can be found than on Ashley's Creek, where the group stands in a hogback near Dodd's Ranch. Many other localities could be mentioned on the Price, Escalante, Dirty Devil, Paria and Kanab Rivers.

FLAMING GORGE GROUP.

This group can be well studied at the typical locality, viz, in the vicinity of Flaming Gorge. Commencing at the conglomerate above mentioned as forming the base of the Henry's Fork Group, you pass southward over the upturned edges of the beds, crossing the bad-land sandstones, then the Mid-group Limestones, then the bad-land indurated sandstones, until the White Cliff Limestone is reached. The massive, cross-bedded sandstones beneath, is a very conspicuous feature of the landscape, and forms the summit of the next group.

In mentioning the typical and other localities of the foregoing groups I have not given detailed sections, as in a following chapter, on the descriptive geology of the Uinta Mountains and adjacent country, it will be necessary to describe more minutely the stratigraphy of all these groups. These typical localities excepting that of the Sulphur Creek Group all fall within the area that is to be described. The typical localities of the remaining or lower groups are without the region described in this volume, and hence I shall give sections of the groups as they occur at the typical localities.

WHITE CLIFF GROUP.

The locality selected as representing the typical series of this group is in Southern Utah. Here a long irregular escarpment or line of cliffs is seen facing southward, from which the geologist may overlook two other subparallel lines of cliffs and see in the distance the walls of the Grand Cañon of the Colorado. The Paria, Kanab and Rio Virgen, with their many tributaries that head in the Pink Cliffs above and to the north, have cut many cañons and cañon valleys through these escarpments, and here the structural geology and stratigraphy are plainly revealed; not only of the White Cliff Group but also of the Vermilion Cliff and Shinarump Groups. The section which I shall give of these three groups was made along the course of the Kanab in the winter of 1871.

The escarpment known as the White Cliffs presents to the mid-day sun a bold wall of pure white or golden sandstone reflecting its rays with a shimmering, brilliant light. At such a time the traveler toiling over the arid sand-dunes below, sees before him to the east or west a long stretch of pink and vermilion hills—hills of shifting sands, with no promise of spring or brook at which his thirst may be quenched; the precipice of the Vermilion Cliffs to the south, and the White Cliffs a wall of fire to the north. A more conspicuous or well defined topographic feature could not well be imagined.

On top of the wall and usually a little back from the edge the limestones which form the base of the Flaming Gorge Group is seen. This limestone has been traced from point to point along the intermediate country for the entire distance from Flaming Gorge to the White Cliffs.

The following is a section of the White Cliff, Vermilion Cliff, and Shinarump Groups from the base of these limestones to the summit of the Upper Aubrey Group.

FIG. 9.—SECTION OF WHITE CLIFF, VERMILION CLIFF, AND SHINARUMP GROUPS.

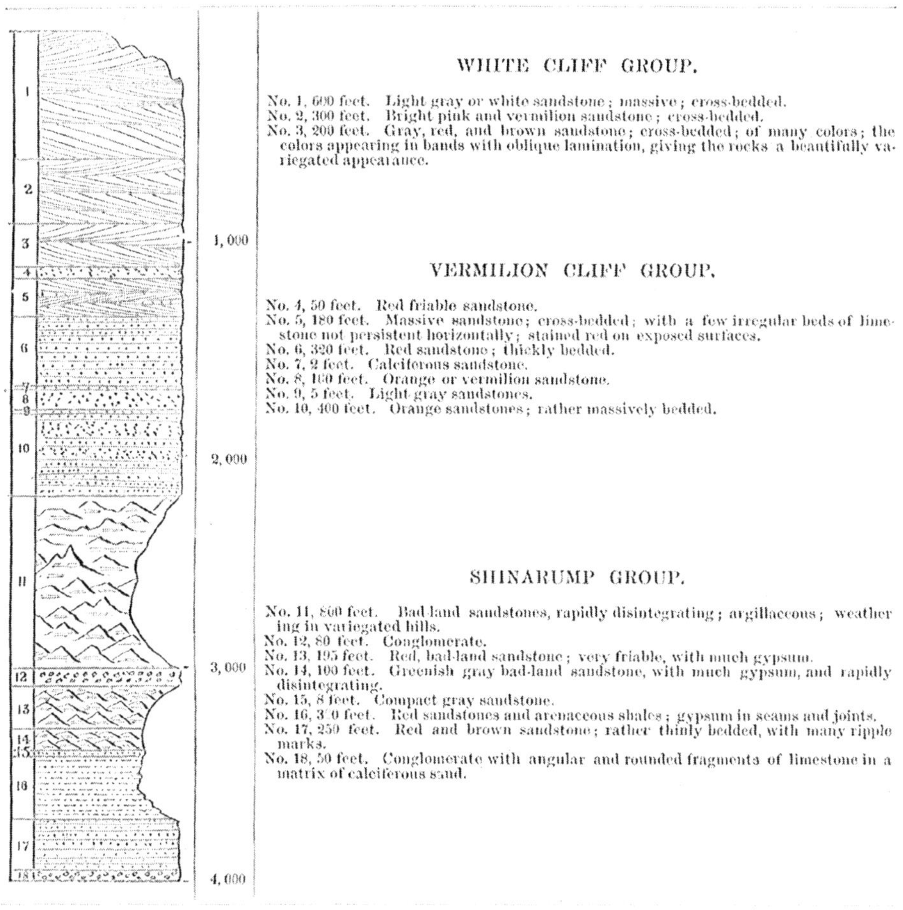

The sandstones of this group are well seen in the vicinity of Flaming Gorge on the south side of the Green River; again between Dry Lake and Vermilion Creek north of Po Cañon, and in a narrow zone on the south side of the Uinta Mountains, and in many other places on the tributaries of the Green and Colorado Rivers; and everywhere the lithologic characteristics are more or less persistent. The cross-bedded sandstones usually form a conspicuous landmark.

VERMILION CLIFF GROUP.

The wagon road from Toquerville to Paria, a little town on the Paria River, soon after climbing the Hurricane Ledge reaches the foot of the Vermilion Cliffs, and continues at this geological horizon until it commences to descend into the valley of the Paria. For seventy-five miles the road lies under this great ledge, whose salient buttes, deep alcoves, terraced and buttressed walls, towering pinnacles, all brightly colored in orange, vermilion and purple, and dotted here and there with straggling cedars and nut pines, constitute a grand panorama to the passing traveler.

Flaming Gorge on the Green River is cut through beds of this group and receives its name from the bright colors of vermilion sandstone; Labyrinth Cañon is cut through vermilion sandstone; Glen Cañon for the greater part of its course also, and fine exposures are seen along the Colorado Chiquito.

SHINARUMP GROUP.

South of the Vermilion Cliffs a low ledge or escarpment is seen capped with conglomerate. This is the Shinarump Conglomerate.

The variegated beds above and below the conglomerate are seen in many places on either flank of the Uinta Mountains, and from time to time this horizon is brought up by faults or flexures in all the stretch of country which intervenes between the Shinarump Cliffs and the Uinta Mountains.

UPPER AUBREY GROUP.

Mr. Gilbert, as geologist of the Wheeler expedition, described certain groups of limestones, sandstones and shales as the Aubrey Group. Previous to his publication I had in manuscript divided these beds into two groups and given them names; but in carrying out my determination to use the names of groups which had been adopted by others so far as such names were available, I have decided to call the two groups into which I wish to divide the Aubrey beds of Mr. Gilbert, the Upper and Lower Aubrey Groups.

The beds of the Upper Aubrey are exposed for thousands of miles along the Grand Cañon of the Colorado and its lateral cañons, everywhere forming the summit of the walls of these gorges. They are also well exposed along Marble Cañon; and Cataract Cañon at the junction of the Grand and Green furnishes another good section. Good sections are obtained at Horseshoe Cañon, the Cañon of Lodore, Whirlpool Cañon, and Split Mountain Cañon in the Uinta Mountains. Its junction with the Shinarump Group above, in all these places can be plainly seen, and in like manner its junction with the Lower Aubrey Group is apparent. To the southward in the Grand Cañon country these beds are a series of cherty limestones. At the junction of the Grand and Green they are a series of sandstones with intercolated cherty limestones, with a homogeneous sandstone at the summit 150 feet in thickness. In the Uinta Mountains we have a homogeneous gray sandstone which we call the Yampa Sandstone, from 1,000 to 1,200 feet in thickness, capped by a bed which is believed to be the equivalent of the one mentioned as found at the summit of the series at the junction of the Grand and Green, and varies from 150 to 200 feet in thickness. On the south side of the Uinta Mountains it is an indurated, calciferous sandstone, but on the north side of the mountains it is a cherty limestone, and on both flanks of these mountains it is characterized by a species of bellerophon. Here we have called it the Bellerophon Limestone.

LOWER AUBREY GROUP.

The Lower Aubrey Group is seen underlying the Upper Aubrey at all the localities mentioned for that group. In the Grand Cañon it is a conspicuous group, its relations to the Upper Aubrey and the Red Wall Groups being well marked. At the junction of the Grand and Green the lines of demarkation cannot be so closely drawn but they appear again very clearly in the Uinta Mountains.

RED WALL GROUP.

The Red Wall Group is the most conspicuous feature of the Grand Cañon of the Colorado and its tributary gorges. It often stands in a vertical wall 2,000 feet high or more, and is everywhere carved into a series of grand amphitheaters, which I have elsewhere tried to describe. There are two well defined members in the Grand Cañon country; the upper one thousand feet is a massive, homogeneous, saccharoid limestone; the lower one thousand feet is composed chiefly of thin beds of indurated limestones of very irregular stratification surfaces. These beds are somewhat argillaceous. The group is not well exposed in Cataract Cañon, as the river has not yet cut through the beds at that point, and some very curious displacements along the river serve to obscure the characteristics of the beds that are exposed. In the Uinta Mountains the two members seen in the Grand Cañon are represented by two massive, indurated limestones, often containing chert and separated by arenaceous shales.

TONTO GROUP.

I have elsewhere called these the rust colored beds, but Mr. Gilbert has called them the Tonto Group, and I accept his name. These beds are seen to overlie unconformably the beds of the Grand Cañon Group and of the Grand Cañon Schists. They are seen well exposed along or near the bottom of the Grand Cañon, where the river makes its double detour around the Kaibab Plateau, and again farther westward, where the river makes another detour around the Shí-wits Plateau.

A group of sandstones and arenaceous shales is found below the Red Wall horizon in Lodore and Whirlpool Cañons, where the Green River cuts through the Uinta Mountains. In the beds of this latter place I have discovered Carboniferous fossils, and suppose them to be of the same age as the Tonto Group; yet, as Mr. Gilbert has considered the Tonto beds to be of Silurian Age, I have called the latter Lodore Group provisionally. From geological considerations, I am inclined to consider the Tonto Group as forming the base of the Carboniferous series. The supposed *Cruziana* and metamorphosed corals discovered by Mr. Gilbert are not deemed by me to furnish sufficient evidence of their greater age. Their geological relations being apparently the same as the Lodore series, I am inclined to refer them to the same horizon; the latter have been demonstrated to be Carboniferous. My opinion is strengthened by the fact that I find in the Grand Cañon 10,000 feet of sandstones, shales and limestones, underlying them unconformably, and hence separated by a long period of erosion, and at the base of this latter series I have found Silurian fossils. I

FIG. 10.—Comparative sections of Carboniferous strata.

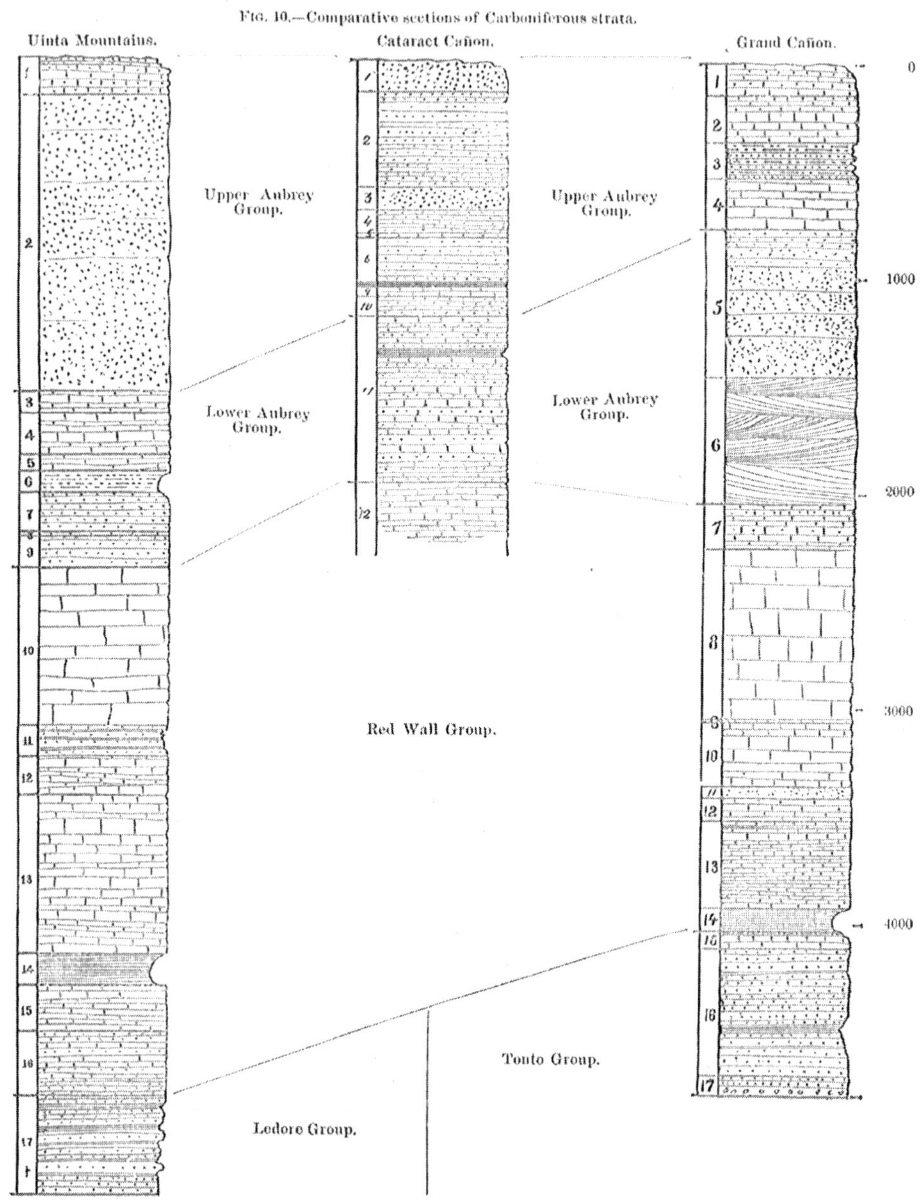

consider the Tonto, Red Wall, Lower Aubrey, and Upper Aubrey Groups to represent the Carboniferous time from base to summit.

In Figure 10 I give a Uinta Mountain, Cataract Cañon, and Grand Cañon section of these groups, side by side, for comparison. The Uinta Mountain and Cataract Cañon Sections were made by Mr. J. F. Steward.

UINTA MOUNTAIN SECTION.

By J. F. Steward.

UPPER AUBREY GROUP.

No. 1, 175 feet. Calciferous sandstone, containing *Bellerophon*, conchifers, &c.

No. 2, 1,400 feet. Massive buff sandstone.

LOWER AUBREY GROUP.

No. 3, 90 feet. Limestone, mottled dark, drab, and buff; very hard; cup corals and *Productus* abundant.

No. 4, 200 feet. Buff limestone, very fossiliferous; *Spirifer*, *Athyris*, &c., abundant.

No. 5, 75 feet. Heavy bedded, bluish-drab limestone; lower portion buff colored. This bed is filled with nodules of chert, (red, pink and purple chalcedony;) also abounds in remains of cyathophylloid corals, *Spirifer*, and *Productus*, all siliceous.

No. 6, 90 feet. Thinly bedded rocks, often shaly; texture variable; composition calcareous, arenaceous, and argillaceous.

No. 7, 180 feet. Compact buff sandstone; very hard.

No. 8, 20 feet. Dark bluish-drab limestone; very hard.

No. 9, 150 feet. Light pinkish-buff, fine grained sandstone.

RED WALL GROUP.

No. 10, 750 feet. Heavy bedded limestone, of pinkish-drab color, becoming arenaceous toward the top, and of a bright red color.

No. 11, 150 feet. Reddish, compact, and shaly sandstones.

No. 12, 185 feet. Pinkish, purple, brown, and bluish limestone, colored pink on the surface by oxide of iron from the overlying sandstone.

No. 13, 750 feet. Very compact, bluish-drab limestone, containing numerous seams of chalcedony.

No. 14, 150 feet. Purplish and drab argillaceous shales.

No. 15, 225 feet. Buff limestone, not well exposed.

No. 16, 300 feet. Limestone and sandstone, thinly bedded; only upper members exposed.

LODORE GROUP.

No. 17. 465 feet. Thinly bedded sandstones, lying unconformably on the Uinta Group.

CATARACT CAÑON SECTION.

By J. F. STEWARD.

UPPER AUBREY GROUP.

No. 1, 150 feet. Friable, buff colored, homogeneous sandstone.

No. 2, 450 feet. Red sandstone, thickly and thinly bedded.

No. 3, 105 feet. Fine grained sandstone, ending in a foot of very brown, shaly sandstone.

No. 4, 95 feet. Brownish-buff sandstone.

No. 5, 25 feet. Compact, bluish-drab limestone, containing *Productus nebrascensis, Athyris subtilita*, crinoidal stems, nodules of red chert, &c.

No. 6, 210 feet. Mostly massively bedded, coarse sandstone, almost a conglomerate at top, but gradually becoming fine textured; dark red and shaly at base; *Bellerophon.*

No. 7, 4 feet. Hard, compact, dark blue limestone.

No. 8, 6 feet. Fine buff sandstone.

No. 9, 50 feet. Blue limestone, divided into three parts by arenaceous members.

No. 10, 92 feet. Drab sandstone, very coarse at top, but becoming fine at base.

LOWER AUBREY GROUP.

No. 11, 721 feet.. Sandstone and limestone in alternation.

a, 70 feet. Drab, compact limestone, containing in great numbers *Allorisma, Myalina*, &c.; also a large *Pleurotomaria.*

b, 12 feet. Fine grained, light gray sandstone, very friable.

c, 3 feet. Compact limestone, same as *a*.

d, 50 feet. Fine grained, incoherent, ochre-brown sandstone.

e, 43 feet. Light colored, arenaceous shale.

f, 10 feet. Dark gray limestone, very compact and hard, containing crinoids.

g, 40 feet. Soft, friable, drab sandstone.

h, 30 feet. Compact, drab, fossiliferous limestone.

i, 75 feet. Fine grained, heavily bedded, friable, lavender-buff sandstone.

j, 12 feet. Drab, argillaceous, arenaceous shales, containing vermiform concretions of chalcedony.

k, 18 feet. Friable limestone, largely composed of crinoid stems, &c.

l, 10 feet. Buff and lavender, fine grained, incoherent sandstone.

m, 15 feet. Very low, compact, drab limestone, heavily bedded, and filled with fragmentary fossils.

n, 12 feet. Marly, buff, crinoidal sandstone; *Productus*, *Spirifer*, &c.

o, 42 feet. Fine grained sandstone, buff to drab at top, brown at base.

p, 6 feet. Dark gray limestone, containing *Productus*, *Spirifer*, *Chætetes*, &c.

q, 40 feet. Fine, light brown sandstone, massively bedded, changing to shale at base.

r, 25 feet. Very hard, compact, blue limestone.

s, 4 feet. Blue, argillaceous shales, containing a branching *Chætetes*, *Productus*, &c.

t, 2 feet. Hard, buff limestone.

u, 60 feet. Friable, fine grained, buff sandstone.

v, 22 feet. Hard, bluish drab limestone, with concretions of red chalcedony.

w, 75 feet. Light buff sandstone, very fine and incoherent; in part calciferous.

x, 50 feet. Hard, concretionary limestone, with nodules and thin seams of chalcedony.

y, 15 feet. Fine buff sandstone.

z, 50 feet. Very hard, dark drab limestone, containing siliceous concretions.

RED WALL GROUP.

No. 12. Thickness not determined. Buffish-lavender, friable, fine grained sandstone; base not seen.

GRAND CAÑON SECTION.

UPPER AUBREY GROUP.

No. 1, 145 feet. Limestone and sandstone, not very thickly bedded.

No. 2, 220 feet. Massive limestone, brecciated and cherty, and weathering in columnar forms.

No. 3, 170 feet. Gypsum and gypsiferous sandstone, irregularly bedded, contorted and broken, stained brown in patches.

No. 4, 240 feet. Massive limestone.

LOWER AUBREY GROUP.

No. 5. Bright red sandstones, thinly and thickly bedded, very red, weathering in long slopes.

No. 6, 600 feet. Red and buff sandstones, heavily bedded, exhibiting composite structure, (cross bedding,) with irregular and inconstant beds of limestone.

RED WALL GROUP.

No. 7. Limestones and calciferous sandstones; heavily bedded; gray and brown; much chert in limestone; chert red and vitreous; sandstone friable.

No. 8, 800 feet. Massive granular limestone; in some places cherty; sometimes running horizontally into thinly bedded rocks.

No 9, *a*, 10 feet. Friable, greenish sandstones. *b*, 6 feet. Purple sandstones, thinning out in places; has the appearance of having been eroded.

No. 10, 300 feet. Thinly bedded limestone, with layers and nodules of chert.

No. 11, 50 feet. Sandstones; gray and buff; sometimes mottled; probably calciferous.

No. 12, 100 feet. Heavily bedded limestone, with calciferous sandstones at summit.

No. 13, 400 feet. Thinly bedded, bluish limestone, with intercolated, thinly bedded sandstones and clay shales below. The limestones are concretionary and brecciated, and have many cavities filled with calcspar.

No. 14, 100 feet. Greenish, micaceous shales, with beds of gray and brown sandstone, containing iron concretions.

TONTO GROUP.

No. 15, 75 feet. Limestones; a good marble; often mottled; sometimes containing concretions of chert.

No. 16, 600 feet. Rust colored sandstones; thinly bedded; indurated; greenish above.

No. 17, 100 feet. Brown sandstone.

* * * * * * *

UINTA GROUP.

The Uinta Mountains are chiefly composed of Uinta Sandstone. The western end of this range where it abuts against the Wasatch Range, I have not carefully studied; but to the eastward the broad, massive range is a grand sandstone structure. Other groups are turned up on their flanks, and in Red Creek Cañon a lower group is seen. On the southeast margin of the range a line of peaks may be seen extending across the Cañon of Lodore, composed of groups of Red Wall Limestone.

In the many deep cañons and gulches by which the range is cleft, in the many amphitheaters that are found along the crest of the range, and in the mural faces of its lofty peaks, everywhere the sandstones are made bare to the eye of the geologist; but the best sections can be made along the cañons. In a subsequent chapter some of these sections will be given.

GRAND CAÑON GROUP.

This group is exposed in the great southern bends of the Grand Cañon, where the Colorado River passes the end of the Kaibab Plateau. The best exposure can be seen about ten miles below the mouth of the Little Colorado. Many of the lateral streams coming in from the west and north cut through this group and afford fine exposures. The best one probably is in

Kwá-gunt Valley. Some of the members are again exposed at the bottom of the Grand Cañon, where it passes the Shí-wits Plateau.

Lower Silurian fossils have been found at the base of this group.

RED CREEK GROUP.

The Red Creek Quartzite, with its intercolated beds of hornblendic, micaceous and chloritic schists, is well seen in Red Creek Cañon. Other exposures can be seen at the head of Willow Creek, a little stream that comes down from the O-wi-yu-kuts Plateau, and empties into the Green River midway in Brown's Park.

GRAND CAÑON SCHISTS.

This group is revealed in the depths of the Grand Cañon in all its great southern bends.

EPOCHS SEPARATING THE GROUPS.

BISHOP MOUNTAIN CONGLOMERATE.

The Bishop Mountain Conglomerate is found at different places to lie unconformably upon every group of the table which is represented in the Uinta Mountains and adjacent country. Its plane of demarkation represents a cessation of the movements of displacement in the region over which it is found, and that the same region was planed down to a base level of erosion, which base level was continued during the accumulation of these beds, for it is believed to be a subaërial conglomerate; but should further evidence prove it to be a subaqueous accumulation the plane of separation would then represent an epoch of change from a period of erosion to a period of deposition. This point will be more fully discussed hereafter.

BROWN'S PARK GROUP.

This group in Brown's Park is seen to lie unconformably on the Uinta Sandstone, and all the other Paleozoic, Mesozoic and early Cenozoic groups; the plane of demarkation, therefore, represents an epoch of change from a dry land to a submerged condition. The area over which it was deposited within the region of my study is of small extent, but the beds are known to continue farther eastward beyond the belt examined; and it may be found as examination is carried farther in that direction to be conformable with the next lower.

BRIDGER GROUP.

The plane of demarkation between this group and the next in order is not always well defined. The change from the green sands or bad-land rocks to the indurated sandstones and limestones of the Upper Green River is transitional; yet the epoch of change is important, for the Upper Green River attenuates both to the east and west, and in the latter direction it entirely disappears, so that the Bridger beds lie with an apparent conformity, but actual unconformity, on the beds of the Lower Green River. This is seen in the vicinity of Carter Station.

UPPER GREEN RIVER GROUP.

These beds are interpolated between the Bridger and Lower Green River, as described above, only in a portion of the country where the latter two occur. The Tower Sandstone which forms the base of the Upper Green River Group is laid down unconformably on the Lower Green River, the unconformity being represented by gentle valleys of erosion; and there seems to have been a period of erosion or dry land conditions separating the Tower Sandstone from the Plant Beds of the Upper Green River also, and during this dry land period the sands of the Tower Sandstone were eroded by rains and drifted by winds. After the deposition of the sands, the bottom of this great Green River lake was left bare for a time and the sands drifted in dunes.

LOWER GREEN RIVER GROUP.

The Lower Green River beds represent a period when minutely laminated bituminous shales and more massive limestones were deposited, the limestones prevailing as you descend in the series. These beds are all fresh water and are separated from those below by an abrupt plane of stratification which marks a change in the character of the sediments. The lower beds are soft, friable, and highly colored bad-land sandstones. But this plane of separation means something more. The conditions which prevailed during the deposition of the lower sandstones abruptly changed, leaving a part of the ancient lake dry and a part submerged, and in this submerged area the limestones and shales were deposited.

BITTER CREEK GROUP.

The Bitter Creek beds are chiefly bad-land sandstones. The area of lacustrine deposition had its greatest expansion during this time. The plane of demarkation separating it from the next group in order is one of great importance. When the beds of the underlying group had been laid down, and before these beds were formed, that movement began which, carried on through Cenozoic time, has given us the great Uinta upheaval. There seems to have been a widely spread dry land condition separating them, for on the flanks of the mountains the lower Bitter Creek beds rest unconformably on the next group, and this unconformity is by erosion and also by angle of dip. This is seen in several places. But the movement in upheaval in the Uinta Mountains was oscillatory, and we often find the upper members of the Bitter Creek series overlapping the older members, and in extreme cases all of the groups of Mesozoic Age also. The unconformity between the two groups away from the mountains is simply represented by erosion. The hard, gray sandstone, which is the upper member of the Point of Rocks Group, is often seen to have been eroded into gentle or more abrupt valleys, and the shales of the Bitter Creek Group were carried into and filled these valleys.

These facts are exhibited in very many places on either flank of the Uinta Mountains, and on either flank of the Aspen Mountain fold, or that fold the axis of which is seen in the Salt Wells Basin; yet there are many points where the conditions of recent erosion are such that the junction of the two groups are more or less masked, and where the unconformity is less apparent.

But this epoch of change has a more important significance. The group below I have classed with the Mesozoic, the group above with the Cenozoic, and the change was from marine to lacustrine conditions. But this change was not abrupt; brackish water fossils are found in the lower group associated with marine forms, and with these a few species of geophila; and brackish water fossils, in perhaps a very few instances of the same species with those below, are associated with fresh water fossils; hence the change from marine to fresh water conditions seems not to have been abrupt.

It will be noted that the epochs of change which separate the fresh water Cenozoic groups all represent a change in character of the sediments, and also represent more or less abrupt contraction of the expanse of fresh water. This was very great during the Bitter Creek period; somewhat less during the Lower Green River; somewhat less during the Upper; perhaps about the same, but less in some directions and greater in others, during the Bridger; and when we reach that point of time represented by the Brown's Park beds the area was quite small.

Those beds to which the name Wasatch Group has been given, and which are found on the eastern slope of the Wasatch Mountains, and stretching out to the eastward until they run under Lower Green River beds, are the western extension of the Bitter Creek beds, and hence the name Wasatch Group should be dropped. The conglomerate at the bottom of what was called the Wasatch Group is represented by the conglomerates of the Bitter Creek Group on both flanks of the Uinta Mountains.

The beds called the Washiki Group are the upper part of the Bitter Creek series. I have been unable to carry any line of demarkation between these beds over such an extent of country as would warrant their separation from the Bitter Creek series, yet this may be done, and in such a case the name of Washiki Group should be retained. In the region near Washiki Station, where they were first seen by Dr. Hayden, they are exceedingly conspicuous by reason of their brilliant colors. Professor Cope, who saw them a little farther to the southwest, thus appropriately describes them: "Several miles to the south we reach another bench whose bluffy face rises four or five hundred feet in buttress-like masses, interrupted at regular intervals by narrow terraces. This line is distinguished by its brilliantly colored strata, extending in horizontal bands along the escarpment. They are brilliant cherry-red, white, true purple with a bloom-shade yellow and pea-green, forming one of the most beautiful displays I ever beheld. The lower portions are of bright red, which color predominates toward the west, where the bluffs descend to a lower elevation. I found on them the remains of a turtle (*Emys euthnethus* Cope), and some borings of a worm in a hard layer. On top of these are clay and slate-rocks of a muddy-yellow color, with their various ledges rising to perhaps five hundred feet" (*vide* United States Geological and Geographical Survey of Colorado, page 437).

These latter beds are Lower Green River limestones.

In the same article, and immediately preceding this quotation, Professor Cope says: "At a short distance to the southward another line of white bluffs extends across the line of travel. This is not more elevated than the preceding one; I only found remains of tortoises in it."

On either flank of the Aspen Mountain fold this group of beds weathering white is seen, and I have several times at first confounded them with the Lower Green River, but the shales of these beds are carbonaceous, and often contain more or less lignitic coal; those of the Lower Green River are bituminous and yield oil. The limestones of the former are aggregations of shells or shell-marls.

THE CRETACEOUS GROUPS.

Planes of demarkation in the Cretaceous groups are not easily drawn. The three great, massive sandstones of the Point of Rocks Group are in many places broken into thinner beds, and then it becomes impossible, with our present knowledge at least, to say to which of these members particular beds may belong. The group below usually is very thinly bedded; sometimes, however, these beds are thicker and more indurated, and when this is the case and the Point of Rocks Group is broken up it is difficult to draw a line between the two groups. The same difficulty arises in separating the yellow arenaceous shales and the black argillaceous shales. Wherever the two groups are exposed side by side, above are seen thinly bedded sandstones and shales and below are black, minutely laminated shales, but it is very rare indeed that an exact line can be drawn. In the southern portion of the province the Salt Wells beds are massive, and there the separation is more easily made. The black shales of the Sulphur Creek Group are everywhere seen to rest upon a somewhat massive sandstone which is underlaid by bad-land sandstones, shales, conglomerates, &c., with a somewhat massive indurated sandstone at the bottom. There seems to be a very decided change in the paleontology of these groups from base to summit, but the fossils, so far as now known, do not afford definite lines of demarkation.

The relation of these groups to those established by Professors Meek and Hayden on the Upper Missouri, is not well determined. I have carefully tried to use their system of grouping and have failed. A very different lithologic series is observed, as must be apparent from a comparison of the two sections. Most of the fossils are of different species, and the few that can be referred to the species of Professors Meek and Hayden in that region present contradictory evidence. Those fossils that may be referred to "No. 2" are found above fossils which may be referred to "Nos. 3 and 4," and as we are tracing these beds over broad areas, and from time to time collecting new fossils, the stratigraphic relations of which should be given with their description, it seemed necessary that some grouping should be adopted, and I have given the best I could under the circumstances. Perhaps after the paleontology is more thoroughly studied the Upper Missouri groupings can be adopted here, but my present opinion is that all such attempts will prove futile. These opinions are based chiefly upon geological reasons, viz: All the evidence that has been published by Dr. Hayden and members of his corps concerning the Park Province, and all my own observations in that region, lead me to the conclusion that a long chain of islands stretched in a northerly and southerly direction through that region of country, separating the Cretaceous sea of the Plateau Province from the Cretaceous sea of the Upper Missouri; probably not forming a continuous wall between the waters of the two, but separating them in such a manner that very different physical conditions prevailed. It is manifest that the Cretaceous sea of the Plateau Province was fed chiefly with the sediments of the Basin Province, for all the Cretaceous sediments rapidly attenuate from that old shore line eastward, and many conglomerates and coarse sandstones of Cretaceous Age found there, are steadily replaced by finer materials in an easterly direction. It is much more probable that the Cretaceous sea of the Basin Province was continuous with that of Texas. The geological evidence seems to indicate this; the evidence derived from the fossils I leave for others to discuss.

FLAMING GORGE GROUP.

The epoch separating the Flaming Gorge Group from the Henry's Fork Group above was one which produced a change from bad-land sandstones to a conglomerate. The beds which overlie the conglomerate contain marine fossils, but all the fossils which we have obtained from the upper portion of the Flaming Gorge Group are of lacustrine habitat. The Mid-Group Limestone contains marine species, and this is true of the limestone at the base, *i. e.*, the White Cliff Limestone. The White Cliff period ended with the deposition of a massive cross-bedded sandstone; the Flaming Gorge period commenced with a deposition of limestone; thus we have an important epoch of change separating the two groups and this is widely spread, for it has been seen wherever the junction of the two groups has been studied.

WHITE CLIFF, VERMILION CLIFF, AND SHINARUMP GROUPS.

These groups can be separated only in a very general way. The upper group is characterized near the summit by a very persistent, massive, cross-bedded sandstone. The Vermilion Cliff Group is also a massive sandstone, and the base of the White Cliff Group is sometimes composed of massive sandstones, sometimes of thinly bedded sandstones, and often these beds are highly gypsiferous, in which case they disintegrate so rapidly that the bedding cannot be studied. The group has yielded no fossils.

The Vermilion Cliff Group as a great mass is easily recognized everywhere, but just where we should draw the line above is rarely plain. Often the massive sandstones of this bed are separated by very irregular and inconstant layers or aggregations of hard calciferous sandstones. These layers have yielded a few imperfectly preserved fossils.

The summit of the Shinarump Group is a series of gypsiferous sandstones exceedingly friable. They have often been called marls, and the separation between them and the massive vermilion sandstone is never very distinct. The difficulty is much greater where the gypsum disappears from the lower beds, as it does in places, where they are also found to be more indurated and more or less massive sandstones. The conglomerate which is found in the middle of the group is persistent over a very large area, and the whole group is characterized throughout the entire province by the occurrence of silicified wood in large quantities Sometimes trunks of trees from fifty to one hundred feet in length are found. The Shinarump Conglomerate is usually very hard, and weathers in such a manner as to form hog-backs or cliffs, and the softer gypsiferous beds above, when carried away by rains, leave behind fragments of this silicified wood, so that the Shinarump Conglomerate is often covered with great quantities of this material. Shinarump means literally "Shin-au-av's Rock." Shin-au-av is one of the gods of the Indians of this country, and they believe these tree-trunks to have been his arrows.

The plane of demarkation between the Shinarump Group and the summit of the Carboniferous is always well marked. Soft, gypsiferous shales are found at the base of the upper group, and either a pure limestone, a cherty limestone, or a homogeneous sandstone, at the summit of the Carboniferous. In places, however, a conglomerate is found at the base of the Shinarump Group, its coarser fragments being composed of cherty limestone which contains Upper Carboniferous fossils. So in some places, at least the epoch of change was a period of erosion. Flaming Gorge Group contains Jurassic fossils from its summit to its base, but the fossils found in the next three groups below are few and very imperfect; hence we cannot correlate these groups with the general geological succession which has been established throughout the world, but we know they lie between the Jura above and the Carboniferous below.

THE CARBONIFEROUS GROUPS.

The grouping of the Carboniferous beds is fully set forth in the section on page 57. The base of the Carboniferous series is not found in Cataract Cañon, but in the Uinta Mountains these beds rest unconformably upon the Uinta Group. In the Grand Cañon they rest unconformably upon the Grand Cañon Group and also upon the crystalline schists; hence in both places the plane of demarkation is important, and represents long periods of erosion.

UINTA GROUP.

The Uinta Sandstone rests unconformably upon the Red Creek Quartzite; ten thousand feet of its upper members are deposited unconformably against that metamorphic group. It is evident, also, that the metamorphism was anterior to the deposition of the Uinta Group, for the beds of the latter, especially near the junction, are chiefly made up of fragments of the former; hence the unconformity is very great.

The period of erosion separating the sandstones from the Carboniferous beds above was sufficient to carry away at least 3,000 feet of the Uinta Sandstone in some places. How much more was carried away we cannot say. To my mind this suggests that the Uinta Sandstone may be considered Devonian—an opinion which I would yield upon the slightest paleontologic evidence to the contrary.

GRAND CAÑON GROUP.

The Grand Cañon Group rests uncomformably upon the crystalline schists. The evidence of this is complete, for the lower sandstones and conglomerates first filled the valleys and then buried the hills of schistic rocks, and these conglomerates at the base of the group are composed of materials derived from the metamorphic hills about; and hence metamorphism was antecedent to the deposition of the conglomerates.

The plane of demarkation separating this group from the Tonto Group is very great. At least 10,000 feet of beds were flexed and eroded in such a manner as to leave but fragments in the synclinals. Then followed a period of erosion during which beds of extravasated material were poured over the fragments, and these igneous beds also were eroded into valleys prior to the deposition of the Tonto Group.

Fossils have been found at the base of the Grand Cañon series, but they are not well preserved and little can be made of them. Still, on geological evidence, I am of the opinion that these beds should be considered Silurian.

RED CREEK QUARTZITE AND GRAND CAÑON SCHISTS.

These are believed to be Eozoic.

* * * * * * *

The grouping which I have given above should be considered as merely tentative, and will probably need some modification hereafter; it may possibly need radical changes; it would be very unsafe with our present knowledge to assume otherwise; I know that it will need some interpolation in the Cretaceous groups in the southern part of the province. I should have been pleased to have delayed its publication until the entire province had been more thoroughly surveyed, but circumstances render it necessary that I should do something more than make general statements of the methods and results of the work which I have been doing. Congress has appropriated money from year to year for the work on the representation of a few leading scientific men of the country that the work was being done with reasonable skill and economy; but only the few who had time and were willing to examine the work in manuscript at the office could understand what we were doing, and it seemed but reasonable that a demand should be made for the publication of some specific results. Having concluded to commence the publication before the province was completely surveyed, it was absolutely necessary that some grouping of the geological formations should be used. The map must be colored to show the distribution of geological formations, and of course names must be given to the formations thus represented on the map, and a nomenclature is necessary for discussion; hence the publication of the table. But I shall be willing to modify it to any extent as facts are collected which seem to demand such a change, whether such facts are the results of my own labors or those of others. Still I present the table with some degree of confidence. The groups of rocks have been traced over broad areas, and in the district, the geology of which I am to describe in this report, the grouping fully represents the state of my knowledge. On account of the discussions which have arisen concerning the age of certain beds of lignitic coal, the plane of demarkation between the Cenozoic and Mesozoic may subject me to criticism; but, geologically, the plane is important, as it represents a decided physical change, and it certainly harmonizes with the opinion of paleontologists to a degree that is somewhat surprising. All of the plants described by Professor Lesquereux and collected by himself and others within this province have been referred by him to divisions in the Tertiary, and are found in strata above this physical break, and hence I agree with him in considering them Tertiary.

In subdividing the Cenozoic or Tertiary, Professor Lesquereux has attempted to draw very fine lines, dividing these beds into Eocene and Miocene, and further subdividing each of these two groups into upper, middle, and lower. In doing this he has done violence to the stratigraphy, and sometimes his upper, middle, and lower cross each other; but, in a general way, his Miocene is higher than his Eocene.

All of the fossils described by Mr. Meek which have been found above this physical break, he has referred unhesitatingly to Tertiary, and all of the fossils found below the physical break, he has referred, unhesitatingly with some, doubtfully with others, to the Cretaceous. There is a single exception to this in *Ostrea Wyomingensis*, which is a new species; and I am sure no paleontologist would insist that a new species of *ostrea* could be used as conclusive evidence in deciding the age of a group of beds. That Mr. Meek did not discover the physical break is not strange, for he did not see it. When he made his exploration in this region he was in ill health, and traveled by rail from station to station, stopping at these places and examining the rocks only in the vicinity of the stations. His health would not permit him to make long excursions in the country on foot, and it was impossible for him to obtain horses. He passed the physical break above mentioned on a railroad car, and his sections at Hallville and Point of Rocks are not connected by several hundred feet, as he states, and as I have since verified by passing over the ground; and the physical break is found in the gap. In like manner, on the opposite side of the Aspen Mountain uplift, he passed it in the cars between Point of Rocks and Green River Stations.

The conclusions reached from a study of the vertebrate paleontology by Professors Leidy, Marsh, and Cope entirely harmonize with this division of the Cenozoic and Mesozoic. There is a single exception to this; Professor Cope described a *dinosaur* found near Black Buttes Station as Cretaceous. I have verified the determination of the stratigraphic horizon by examining the place and finding other *dinosaur* bones; but this horizon is above the physical break, and the evidence of the *dinosaur* seems to be contradicted by the evidence furnished by many other species described by Professor Cope from about the same horizon.

LIGNITIC COAL.

An examination of the section will reveal the fact that lignitic coal is found abundant from the base of the Cretaceous through the recognized groups of that division, and in three of the groups of the Tertiary, giving a horizon of 11,500 feet. I know of no lignite bearing group in the Plateau Province which may be said to be richer in this product than others, and it would have led to confusion to characterize any group as the "Lignite beds."

While lignitic coal is found in great abundance through a long succession of formations or groups, it is rarely or never the case that any particular bed is persistent over a great area. In the Point of Rocks Group I have at one place found eleven beds, varying from ten inches to four feet in thickness, and three miles away where the exposure was complete so that no mistake could be made except by careless observation I have found each one of these beds represented by carbonaceous shales; and facts similar to this have been noted in all the other groups. It is frequently the case that, in studying the same group at two places separated by a few miles, a very different succession of coals will be observed. It seems that they were formed in small, irregular basins, from time to time, beginning with the Lower Cretaceous and ending high up in the Cenozoic.

Dr. C. A. White has prepared a catalogue of the species which, so far, have been collected in the Plateau Province, by myself and those assisting me in the work, and tabulated them in groups agreeing with the above scheme. He has also appended to each an additional list of fossils collected by others. The general correlation of the section to established successions elsewhere must at present rest on the evidence furnished by this catalogue.

CHAPTER III.

INVERTEBRATE PALEONTOLOGY OF THE PLATEAU PROVINCE,

TOGETHER WITH NOTICE OF A FEW SPECIES FROM LOCALITIES BEYOND ITS LIMITS IN COLORADO,

By Charles A. White, M. D.

Washington, D. C., *February* 1, 1876.

Sir: I have the honor to present the following preliminary report upon the paleontological collections made by parties under your direction during the years 1868 to 1875, inclusive; more especially upon the invertebrate fossils.

The collections are large and important, comprising, besides the invertebrate fossils noticed and described on following pages, vertebrate remains from strata of the Carboniferous, Jurassic, Cretaceous, and Tertiary periods; and plants from those of the Cretaceous and Tertiary periods. The plants, from strata of the last named period especially, are abundant and interesting, comprising as they do representatives of the classes Acrogens, Endogens, and Exogens, the latter being greatly in excess of the others.

Among the vertebrate fossils are the remains of fishes (Selachians, Ganoids, and Teliosts), reptiles, and mammals. Besides these, a small collection borrowed from Mr. W. Cleburn contains part of the skeleton of a Passerine bird which was discovered by him in the Lower Green River Group, near Green River Station, Wyoming Territory. Some of the other discoveries of vertebrate remains are also worthy of notice here, among which may be mentioned two or three species of teliost fishes at the base of the Cretaceous series of Wyoming and Utah, and fragments of the skeleton of a very large reptile in Jurassic strata of Northwestern Colorado. The collection of Mr. Cleburn also contains two or three species of insects.

The study of the collections as a whole, reveals many interesting facts bearing upon the physical conditions of the regions examined, during the deposition of the strata from which they have been collected, some of which are briefly discussed on following pages. Among the more important of these is the identification of the marine genera *Oculina*, *Phorus*, *Dentalium*, *Patella*, *Venus*, *Mesodesma*, *&c.*, from the Tertiary strata of Bijou Basin, forty miles east of Denver, Colorado. This indicates the extension of open-sea marine deposits much farther into the interior of the continent during the Tertiary period than has been previously known.

Upon following pages I present a classified catalogue of all the invertebrate species, following which are descriptions of the new species. This catalogue enumerates two hundred and sixty-two species in all, forty-eight of which are new to science, and described herein for the first time.

Very respectfully yours,

C. A. WHITE.

Professor J. W. POWELL,

Geologist in charge of the Second Division United States Geological and Geographical Survey of the Territories.

GENERAL OBSERVATIONS.

The fossils of the collections of which the following pages are occupied in large part by a classified and partially descriptive catalogue, have been obtained from strata of the Carboniferous, Triassic, Jurassic, Cretaceous, and Tertiary periods; very largely from the immediate vicinity of the Green and Colorado Rivers and from portions of Northern Utah and Southern Wyoming. The areas from which they have been collected are very small compared with that of the great Plateau Province, the study of the invertebrate paleontology of which the preparation of this report is only a beginning. It is, therefore, too early to draw final conclusions concerning the general lessons which full collections from that great region will be sure to teach us, or to deduce at present, any very satisfactory generalizations; but it may not be unprofitable to mention some of the facts, in their order, that have been observed while making the collections in the field and also during their more critical investigation in the laboratory. Some of these facts have an interesting bearing upon the characteristics of the fossil faunæ of the periods which the collections represent, the relation of those faunæ to each other, and to both fossil and recent faunæ of the whole Plateau Province as well as those of other regions.

For the purpose of facilitating reference to the groups of strata which have furnished the fossils, the following table is introduced. The classification of the formations used in this report is, for the geological ages and periods, the same as that of Dana's Manual of Geology (1874,) and for the groups of strata of the Pleateau Province, that of Professor Powell in his section of the Uinta Mountain region.

Table of the formations of the Uinta Mountain Region.

Thickness in feet.	Groups.	Periods.	Ages.
1,800.	Brown's Park Group	Tertiary	Cenozoic.
2,000.	Bridger Group		
500.	Upper Green River Group.		
800.	Lower Green River Group.		
3,000.	Bitter Creek Group		
1,800.	Point of Rocks Group	Cretaceous . . .	Mesozoic.
1,800.	Salt Wells Group		
2,000.	Sulphur Creek Group		
500.	Henry's Fork Group		
1,200.	Flaming Gorge Group	Jurassic	
1,100.	White Cliff Group	Triassic?	
1,100.	Vermilion Cliff Group		
1,800.	Shinarump Group		
1,000.	Upper Aubrey Group	Carboniferous .	Carboniferous.
1,000.	Lower Aubrey Group		
2,000.	Red Wall Group		
460.	Lodore Group		

In the following brief review of the faunal characteristics of the different groups represented in the collections it is well to consider how far any peculiarities they present, different from those which characterize their position in time, may have been occasioned by the then and there prevailing physical conditions under which the strata were accumulated. Some of those conditions were limited both in extent and duration, but others were of a more general and constant character. Almost all of the fossils of these collections are the remains of mollusks and other aquatic animals. It is a well-known fact that the character of the material composing the bottom upon which such animals live constitutes one of the most important elements in their habitat; that not only species, but even genera and families, are often separated from each other in the same waters by a difference in the character of the material composing the bottom. It is this gradually-accumulating bottom material that has constituted the strata from which we now obtain the fossil remains. The prevailing material of the strata which have furnished the greater part of the fossils of our collections, especially those of Mesozoic and Cenozoic ages, having an aggregate thickness of not far from three and a half miles, is sand. The bottom of the waters, salt, brackish, and fresh, of all the periods of both those ages, was almost constantly, either wholly or in very large part, composed of sand.

Such a condition as this, continued for so long a time, necessarily produced a marked effect upon the faunæ of those periods, giving them different or modified characteristics as compared with those of the same periods respectively in other parts of the world.

Again, the evidence afforded by both the vertebrate and invertebrate collections, and by those of the floræ of all the periods named in the section on a previous page, is in favor of the existence during that time of a warm-temperate and uniform climate. Furthermore, the labors of the field geologists have shown that there is a great degree of conformability of the strata of all the subordinate groups, from those of the Carboniferous to those of the Tertiary periods, inclusive; or at least that the cases of unconformability are few and of comparatively slight degree. So great a degree of uniformity in such important conditions as these having prevailed, it is not strange that the groups of strata of the different periods respectively are not in all cases clearly defined by faunal characteristics, even although they may be separated by sufficiently distinct physical characters by the field geologist.

The periods are, as a rule, very clearly separated from each other by faunal characteristics, there being a partial exception in the case of those of the upper group of the Cretaceous period and the lower group of the Tertiary. But these facts will be noticed under appropriate heads on following pages.

Our investigations further show that certain faunal characteristics which have hitherto been relied upon to fix the geological age of strata of marine, brackish and fresh water origin, respectively, are not parallel. In other words, our collections contain types or forms of fresh and brackish water origin that have been regarded as peculiar to the Tertiary period, which were obtained from strata that underlie those containing such marine types as are universally regarded as peculiar to Mesozoic age; showing conclusively, that so-called Tertiary fresh and brackish water types and Cretaceous salt water types co-existed. The land shells also that have been obtained from strata herein classified as Cretaceous, are of Tertiary or even of still more recent type. These facts have made it especially difficult to fix the period of our terrestrial, and fresh and brackish water fossils with satisfactory precision, if they were new species and obtained from unique and isolated localities.

A striking peculiarity of the strata of the Plateau Province, is the large proportion among them of fresh and brackish water deposits. So far as at present known, all the strata of Carboniferous age are of marine origin, the first unmistakably fresh water accumulations yet discovered in the Plateau Province being of Jurassic age. The only species obtained from these fresh water strata is a *Unio*, which is one of ordinary recent type; as is also another species of *Unio* and some Viviparine shells, described by Meek and Hayden, from the valley of the Upper Missouri River. These facts again illustrate the comparatively small value that can be placed upon fresh water invertebrate forms as indices of the passage of geological time.

Most of the Mesozoic strata were evidently deposited in water that was salt by virtue of having been a part of, or in communication with, the open ocean; but it is not improbable that many of the brackish water accumulations, especially those of late Cretaceous and early Tertiary age, may have been made in land-locked waters which had their saline character continued from former times by the leachings of surface drainage, similar to that of Great Salt Lake, but in a far less proportionate degree. This idea is suggested by the fact that the final change to exclusively fresh water lacustrine deposits was so gradual that all the former brackish water species, among which no open-sea forms have been discovered, passed away without any perceptible physical change in the accumulating strata.

LOWER SILURIAN AGE.

The Lower Silurian age is represented in the collections only by a very few imperfect fossils from Kwagunt Valley, Grand Cañon of the Colorado, Arizona. The Brachiopod genera *Lingulella* and *Obolella* are recognized with a good degree of certainty, and, distributed through the small masses of rock which contain them, there are apparently fragments of two or three other species.

These specimens doubtless belong to the Primordial period, and possess much interest as regards the geological age of the rocks which underlie and overlie them.

UPPER SILURIAN AND DEVONIAN AGES.

The present collections contain no fossils from strata of either Upper Silurian or Devonian age, but it is not improbable that rocks of these ages will yet be discovered in the Plateau Province.

CARBONIFEROUS AGE.

The collections contain fifty species from strata of Carboniferous age, much the greater part of which are from the Lower Aubrey Group. A few are from the Upper Aubrey, and a still less number from the Red Wall Group, while none are reported from the Lodore Group.

A large proportion of all these fossils are specifically identical with well-known forms in the strata of the Carboniferous or Coalmeasure period in the States of the Upper Mississippi Valley; and all but two of them belong to such types as we might naturally expect to find in the equivalents of those strata. These two belong to the two genera respectively *Archimedes* and *Amplexus*, the former of which, especially, has been regarded as an exclusively Subcarboniferous genus; and yet they are found in the Lower Aubrey Group, nearly three thousand feet above the base of the Carboniferous series, and also above, and mingled with, types that have not hitherto been found in strata so low as the Subcarboniferous

Few or none of the fossils of the collections are of such a character as to suggest the Permian age of the strata from which they were obtained, not even those of the Upper Aubrey Group. I have elsewhere shown* that the prevalence of certain types which have been relied upon to prove the Permian age of the strata containing them may be due to peculiar physical conditions, and I therefore regard it as not improbable that the *time* of the Permian period may be represented in the Plateau Province by the Upper Aubrey Group, although the distinguishing types are wanting there. In view also of the mixture which we find, of Carboniferous and Subcarboniferous types in the same strata, it seems probable that the time of the whole Carboniferous age, including its three periods, Subcarboniferous, Carboniferous, and Permian, is collectively represented by the four groups recognized in the Plateau Province.

It seems probable, therefore, that, although some localities in Nevada and Montana have furnished collections of almost exclusively Subcarboniferous types, we shall not, as a rule, be able to define in this region, the three periods into which the age is divided in other parts of the world. It seems also probable that no divisions of the Carboniferous strata of the Plateau Province can be made that will represent geological periods, well defined upon paleontological grounds, either corresponding to those already established in other parts of the world, or differing from them.

MESOZOIC AGE.

TRIASSIC PERIOD.

Some small collections of fossils which possess peculiar interest were collected by Mr. E. E. Howell, in 1874, from the following localities in Utah: At Toquerville; Virgin River, south of Toquerville; near Workman's

*Geology of Iowa, 1870, vol. i, page 249.

ranch, ten miles east of Toquerville, and also two miles west of Kanab. They were obtained from the lower portion of the Shinarump Group, the lowest group of Triassic strata in the Plateau Province. The specimens are all very imperfect, but the following genera have been recognized: *Pentacrinus*, *Rhynchonella*, *Camptonectes*, and *Myalina*. Besides these there were fragments of other conchifers, the generic relations of which are not recognizable. The specimens of *Pentacrinus* consist only of joints of the column, like those of *P. asteriscus* Meek and Hayden, so common in the Jurassic strata of the same region, and, indeed, seem undistinguishable from those of that species. So far as can be determined, the fragments of *Rhynchonella* may be those of the Jurassic, *R. gnathophora* Meek, and those of *Camptonectes* may belong to any one of the several species known to exist in the Jurassic strata of the Plateau Province. In short, if the collections had been placed in my hands for determination, without any statement of their stratigraphical position, I should have referred them to the Jurassic period with no other doubts than those suggested by the imperfection of the specimens. If their stratigraphical position is correctly reported, which I know no reason to doubt, it seems certain that the strata containing them ought to be referred to the Jurassic rather than to the Triassic period. Before such an important conclusion as this is reached, however, it will be necessary to secure more perfect and complete collections.

JURASSIC PERIOD.

Twenty-seven species have been recognized among the Jurassic fossils of the collections, at least four of which are new. With the exception of two Echinoderms all the species are molluscan.

Considerable interest attaches to the fact that a species of *Unio* has been obtained from strata of this period at Flaming Gorge, Utah, indicating the presence of fresh water at that point at one time during the period. The fact is also of still further interest as indicating that the fresh-water molluscan types which became so prevalent in the Tertiary period were introduced early in Mesozoic time if not before.

CRETACEOUS PERIOD.

A much larger number of species, all of which are molluscan, have been obtained from strata of the Cretaceous than from those of any one of the other periods represented in the collections. The entire absence of all articulate and molluscoidean species from all the Cretaceous collections is quite remarkable. All four of the groups of strata are represented in the collections, those from the Henry's Fork Group containing the smallest number of species.

The groups as a rule appear to be separated by good paleontological as well as physical characteristics. Those of the Henry's Fork and Sulphur Creek Groups, however, are similar, and the dividing line between the Salt Wells and Point of Rocks Groups appears to be indistinct as regards generic and family types; but, with very few exceptions, the species have not been found to pass from one group to another. The exceptions thus far noticed are those of species that have a very wide geographical as well as an unusually great vertical range.

The Henry's Fork and Sulphur Creek Groups, so far as they have been examined, appear to have been wholly open-sea deposits, no genera of brackish water habitat, except *Ostrea* and *Anomia*, which are also open-sea forms, having been discovered in any of the strata. The Sulphur Creek Group is also remarkable for containing nearly all the Cretaceous Cephalopods of the collections; the only exceptions being a specimen of *Baculites ovatus* Say, from the Salt Wells Group in the valley of Red Creek, Utah, and species of *Scaphites* from the same group two miles northwestward from Salt Wells Station, Wyoming.

The Salt Wells Group is not only remarkable for its paucity of Cephalopods, but also in consequence of the fact that from among its strata we obtain the first Cretaceous fresh-water forms. Even among the fossils of some of its more distinctively marine strata, we obtain such forms as are usually found in the brackish and fresh water Cretaceous and Tertiary deposits of that region. The earliest of the fresh or brackish water Cretaceous deposits that have been discovered in the Plateau Province occurs among strata of this group near Coalville, Utah, a fortunate exposure of which afforded Mr. Meek, a few years ago, species of the genera *Unio*, *Cyrena*, *Physa*, *Neritina*, &c., all having a remarkably modern aspect; but the strata which contained them are immediately overlaid by those which contain *Inoceramus*, *Gryphea*, *Anchura*, and other distinctively Mesozoic forms.

The Point of Rocks Group is well represented in the collections by molluscan species, all of which are either Conchifers or Gasteropods. Among them are a few land shells, many fresh-water species, and all but a few of the remainder belong to genera of known brackish-water habitat. Furthermore, some species of these remaining few genera have been found associated with brackish-water forms. It thus appears that the formerly prevailing marine conditions over the region that we now call the Plateau Province began to draw to a close early in the epoch represented by this group, and had well nigh ceased at its close.

A good illustration of this gradual change is presented by the strata of the Point of Rocks Group at Upper Kanab, Utah, where, toward the base of the series exposed, the fossils are mostly marine; above these a greater proportion of brackish-water forms are introduced; still higher up fresh-water forms prevail, and the upper strata contain only fresh water and land shells; the deposition of all the strata having evidently been continuous and uninterrupted.

Among the more interesting observations that have been made in relation to the fresh water and land shells of this epoch of the Cretaceous period, are those concerning the great differentiation of types that had thus early taken place. To so great a degree had this differentiation then attained that the species of *Unio*, *Helix*, *Physa*, &c., seem to have been as diversified and well developed as they are at the present time. Indeed the species of these genera are so closely like some of those now living that they need only the fresh condition of recent shells to remove all suspicion of their great antiquity from the mind of the casual observer.

After the foregoing statements concerning the faunal characteristics of the Point of Rocks Group, one might naturally inquire for the reasons that have led to its reference to the Cretaceous rather than to the Tertiary period. Laying aside all considerations suggested by the vertebrate and floral remains that have been collected from its strata, the reply may be briefly stated thus: There is no physical break between this group and the Salt Wells Group below it. Its strata contain at least three species of Inoceramus, which genus has never been known in strata of later date than the Cretaceous period. *Odontobasis*, a species of which has been obtained from near the summit of the group, is regarded as a Cretaceous genus; and in view of the facts before stated, that land and fresh and brackish water mollusks are comparatively valueless as indices of the passage of geological time, the presence of no known forms in its strata forbid the reference of this group to the Cretaceous period.

CENOZOIC AGE.

TERTIARY PERIOD.

The collections of Tertiary fossils contain sixty species, exclusive of those that were obtained from localities beyond the limits of the Plateau Province. All of them are either brackish or fresh water species; the only truly marine forms of Tertiary age being those obtained at Bijou Basin, Colorado, which have already been noticed, and, as they are also described and catalogued on following pages, they will not be considered in the following general remarks, which are intended to apply mainly to that portion of the Province which lies north of the Uinta Mountains.

One-half of all these species were obtained from the Bitter Creek Group, the lowest group of the Tertiary series. This difference in the relative abundance of species in the different groups is of course due primarily to the conditions under which the species lived, but evidently in large part also to the very much greater geographical extent, as well as greater thickness, of this group than of any of the others. Among the primary conditions referred to, an obvious one was, the continuance of the brackish waters, so common in the last epoch of the Cretaceous period, into the first epoch of the Tertiary in some localities, although they seem to have given place to wholly fresh waters in other localities before the close of the Cretaceous period. Collections have been made from these brackish-water Tertiary strata at Black Buttes, Point of Rocks, and Rock Spring, all in the valley of Bitter Creek, Wyoming, and where they reach a thickness of from five to seven hundred feet above the base of the Tertiary series. The species are clearly distinct from all others, either of this or any of the other Tertiary groups; but it is not to be denied that, although they are also all specifically distinct from any of the species found in the underlying Point of Rocks Group of the Cretaceous period, there is a prevalent similarity of type between the fossils of the two groups that is apparent upon merely casual inspection.

No true or exclusively marine species have been discovered in these brackish-water Tertiary strata, and it is probable that the waters in which they were deposited were previously cut off from the open sea, but yet retaining to a great degree their former saltness. The genera thus far discovered are *Ostrea*, *Anomia*, *Corbula*, *Corbicula* (*Leptesthes*), *Cyrena* (*Veloritina*), and *Neritina*, besides the more exclusively fresh-water genera *Unio*, *Goniobasis*, *Viviparus*, *Tulotoma*, and *Leioplax?*

The final change to a wholly fresh, from the brackish water condition, which was never to be resumed, was so gradual that no physical difference appears in the strata accumulated under both conditions; but from and after that change a uniformity of molluscan type prevailed through all the subsequent epochs of the Tertiary period, as represented in the Plateau Province, that is really remarkable. It is especially so if, as Professor Powell has suggested from stratigraphical considerations, these Cenozoic groups represent the whole of what is generally known as the Tertiary period. Here and there, at different places in each of the Tertiary groups, except the Brown's Park group, which, because of its barrenness of fossils, is not included in this discussion, a few locally restricted species have been found, amounting to a considerable number in the aggregate. But prevailing at numerous horizons through all these groups after the brackish-water condition had ceased, and often in great profusion, are the three molluscan genera *Unio*, *Viviparus*, and *Goniobasis*, which are almost invariably immediately associated and almost as invariably without other faunal associates except occasionally a large discoid *Planorbis*.

The Unios are of several species, which are defined by characters similar to those upon which accepted recent species of the genus are established; but I have been unable to discriminate with entire satisfaction more than one species each of *Goniobasis* and *Viviparus* among these prevailing forms in the northern part of the Plateau Province, from the upper part of the Bitter Creek Group to the top of the Bridger Group, inclusive, with the possible exception of *Viviparus Wyomingensis* Meek, from the Bridger Group. The *Planorbis* just mentioned I have usually referred to *P. spectabilis* Meek, but in the Bitter Creek Group, especially south of the Uinta Mountains, a variety occurs with fewer and broader volutions, in which respect it corresponds with the description of *P. Utahensis* Meek. The *Viviparus* and *Goniobasis* I have, in the following catalogue, referred respectively to *V. paludinæformis* Hall sp. and *G. tenera* Hall sp. *Goniobasis nodulifera* Meek (= *Cerithium nodulosum* Hall) and *G. Carteri* Conrad, are regarded as synonyms of *G. tenera;* and from among the thousands of examples that have been collected from the strata under discussion, it would be easy to make selections that, if found separately, would be taken to indicate an equal number of species, as different from those as they are from each other. Fortunately, however, the specimens in all cases are so abundant that other selections may be made showing full intermediate gradations between all the species that have been, and doubtless all that may yet be, proposed from among them.

The character and extent of the variations of these species in their geographical distribution, vertical range, and local association will be discussed in a future report. It is, therefore, sufficient now to suggest that these forms will present some of the best opportunities for the zoölogico-historical study of certain species through a great lapse of geological time that paleontology has ever furnished.

This remarkable uniformity of molluscan types through all the groups, together with their almost exact identity with recent types of fresh-water mollusca, seems at first view to present an argument against the supposition that those Cenozoic deposits occupied the whole of Tertiary time, when considered only in relation to the invertebrate remains; but the slight value of fresh-water molluscan forms in such generalizations has already been shown. If relied upon at all, their modern aspect would seem to indicate late Tertiary time only, while, on the other hand, the physical connection of the lowest group with the uppermost group of Cretaceous strata is such as to leave no doubt that the former represents the earliest epoch of Tertiary time.

Besides this several of the species found in the brackish-water layers at the base of the Bitter Creek Group are closely related to species found in similar deposits in Slavonia and referred to the Eocene Tertiary by Brusina.* (*See* "Fossile Binnen-Mollusken aus Dalmatien, Kroatien, und Slavonien von Spiridion Brusina, Agram, 1874.")

* It is an interesting fact that these collections of Tertiary fresh water mollusks in Slavonia possess many Unione and Viviparine forms that are of living American, and not European types, while all the American fossil fresh water forms with which I am acquainted are of American recent types.

By comparing the invertebrate fauna of those fresh water Tertiary deposits with the faunæ of existing fresh waters we observe the entire absence from our collections of all articulates, except a species of *Cypris* and the insects discovered by Mr. Cleburn. The list of Molluscan genera found in those ancient lakes compares closely with those of the great existing American lakes, notwithstanding the fact that the floral remains of the former indicate a uniform and much milder climate than now exists in either of the two regions.

Thus far no well defined fluvatile deposits have been discovered, but it is probable that those fresh water species found among brackish water forms constituted portions of the molluscan faunæ of rivers that flowed into the ancient lakes or estuaries, because they are specifically different from, and more various than, those of the purely fresh water deposits. This suggestion is supported by the well-known fact that the molluscan types of lakes are fewer than those of rivers, while the differentiation is yet greater in brackish and greater still in marine waters.

In closing these remarks upon the Tertiary period a question arises similar to the one briefly considered at the close of the remarks upon the Cretaceous period, namely: Why has the dividing line between the strata of the Tertiary and Cretaceous periods been drawn where it is rather than at some horizon either above or below it?

The answer is nearly the same as in the former case There is no physical break in the Cretaceous strata, from the base of the series to the top of the upper, or Point of Rocks Group, at which horizon there is at all observed points, extending over a large region, considerable unconformability by erosion of the lower strata of the Bitter Creek Group, upon the upper strata of the Point of Rocks Group.

The separation of the two periods, as represented by the strata of the Plateau Province, is a physical rather than a paleontological one. Upon purely paleontological ground it is difficult to indicate precisely where the line should be drawn, but it should evidently be somewhere near the one indicated in Professor Powell's section. This being the case, and it being necessary to draw such a line, it is more rational to draw it upon a line of a physical break than through conformable strata either above or below it.

CATALOGUE OF THE FOSSILS COLLECTED BY THE VARIOUS PARTIES IN THE FIELD DURING THE YEARS 1868 TO 1875, INCLUSIVE.

CARBONIFEROUS AGE.

CARBONIFEROUS PERIOD.

RED WALL GROUP.

1. *Chaetetes milleporaceus* Troost.—Gypsum Cañon, Colorado River, Utah. The specimens have their characters obscured by silicification, but they doubtless belong to this species. It also occurs in the Lower Aubrey Group. (See No. 4.)

2. *Syringopora multattenuata* McChesney.—Gypsum Cañon, Colorado River, Utah.

3. *Campophyllum* ——— ?.—Cataract Cañon, Utah. A large species, larger than *C. torquium* Owen, but the specimens are too imperfect for full specific description.

LOWER AUBREY GROUP.

4. *Chaetetes milleporaceus* Troost.—Split Mountain Cañon, Green River, Utah. Also obtained from the Red Wall Group. (See No. 1.)

5. *Fistulipora* ——— ?.—Confluence of Grand and Green Rivers, Utah. Weathered specimens.

6. *Syringopora* ——— ?.—Confluence of Grand and Green Rivers, Utah. Specimens consisting of rather small, flattened, or subspherical masses. Tubes small and much distorted, but imperfect by silicification.

7. *Amplexus zaphrentiformis* White.—Near Echo Park and at Split Mountain Cañon, Utah. Described on a following page.

8. *Lophophyllum proliferum* McChesney.—Confluence of Grand and Green Rivers, Utah. Characters more nearly typical than those of the variety called *Sauridens* found near Santa Fé, New Mexico.

9. *Lithostrotion* ——— ?—York, Utah; west base of Wasatch range.

10. *Acervularia* ——— ?.—Split Mountain Cañon, Green River, Utah.

11. *Archæocidaris cratis* White.—Confluence of Grand and Green Rivers, Utah. Described on a following page.

12. *Archæocidaris trudifer* White.—Confluence of Grand and Green Rivers, Utah. Specimens consisting only of imperfect spines.

13. *Erisocrinus typus* Meek and Worthen.—Confluence of Grand and Green Rivers, Utah. The type specimens of Meek and Worthen were obtained from the Coal-measures of Illinois, and consisted only of calyces. Ours shows about two and a half centimeters in length of the arms, each of which consists of a double, interlocking series of pieces; the arms when closed lying so closely together as to leave only a linear suture between them.

14. *Scaphiocrinus carbonarius* Meek and Worthen.—Confluence of Grand and Green Rivers, Utah.

15. *Eupachycrinus platybasis* White.—Confluence of Grand and Green Rivers, Utah. Described on a following page.

16. *Polypora* ——— ?.—Confluence of Grand and Green Rivers, Utah. A large specimen, having unusually large fenestrules. Obverse side only shown.

17. *Fenestella* ——— ?.—Near Echo Park, Utah. Obverse side only shown.

18. *Archimedes* ——— ?.—Near Echo Park, Utah. Specimens consist of two axes only, one of which is dextral and the other sinistral in its volutions. They are, however, both referred to one species.

19. *Discina* ——— ?.—Bee-hive Point, near Horseshoe Cañon, Utah. A single lower valve.

20. *Productus punctatus* Martin.—Confluence of Grand and Green Rivers, Utah.

21. *Productus longispinus* Sowerby ?.—Near Echo Park and at the confluence of Grand and Green Rivers, Utah.

22. *Productus costatus* Sowerby?—Near Echo Park, Utah. The specimens consist of the ordinary American forms generally referred to that species, but are probably distinct from it.

23. *Productus costatus* var.—Near Echo Park, Utah. Like No. 22 in

essential characters, except that the radiating costæ are reduced in size to that of raised striæ.

24. *Productus Prattenianus* Norwood.—Confluence of Grand and Green Rivers, Utah. Some of the specimens possess the median row of spines or nodes upon the ventral valve, like those which Dr. Newberry named *P. nodosus*.

25. *Productus semireticulatus* Martin.—Confluence of Grand and Green Rivers, Utah. All the examples are of the variety named *P. Ivesii* by Dr. Newberry.

26. *Productus Nebrascensis* Owen.—Confluence of Grand and Green Rivers, Utah.

27. *Productus muricatus* Norwood and Pratten.—Near Echo Park, Utah.

28. *Productus multistriatus* Meek.—Confluence of Grand and Green Rivers, Utah.

29. *Chonetes granulifera* Owen.—Confluence of Grand and Green Rivers, Utah.

30. *Chonetes platynota* White.—Near Echo Park, Utah.

31. *Hemipronites crinistria* Phillips.—Near Echo Park and at the confluence of Grand and Green Rivers, Utah. It also occurs in the Upper Aubrey Group. (See No. 49.)

32. *Meekella striatocostata* Cox.—Confluence of Grand and Green Rivers, Utah.

33. *Spirigera subtilita* Hall.—Confluence of Grand and Green Rivers, and near Echo Park, Utah. Occurs also in the Upper Aubrey Group. (See No. 50.)

34. *Spirifer cameratus* Morton.—Confluence of Grand and Green Rivers, Utah.

35. *Spirifer Rockymontanus* Marcou.—Split Mountain Cañon and near Echo Park, Utah. Occurs also in the Upper Aubrey Group. (See No. 51.)

36. *Spiriferina Kentuckensis* Shumard.—Confluence of Grand and Green Rivers, Utah. Occurs also in the Upper Aubrey Group at the same locality. (See No. 52.)

37. *Aviculopecten occidentalis* Shumard.—Two miles above Belleview, Utah.

38. *Myalina* ———?.—Confluence of Grand and Green Rivers, Utah. The specimens have the aspect of *M. recurvirostris* Meek and Worthen, but all of them have lost their beaks. (See No. 53.)

39. *Allorisma subcuneata* Meek and Hayden?—Confluence of Grand and Green Rivers, Utah. The examples of the collection agree with those of this species from the typical localities, as given by Meek and Hayden, and they also agree very nearly with the description and figures given by Dr. Newberry of *A. capax*.

40. *Edmondia Aspenwallensis* Meek.—Confluence of Grand and Green Rivers, Utah.

41. *Pleurophorus* ———?.—Confluence of Grand and Green Rivers, Utah. The species is probably new, but the specimens are too imperfect for full description.

42. *Schizodus Wheeleri* Swallow.—Confluence of Grand and Green Rivers, Utah.

43. *Bellerophon* ———?.—Confluence of Grand and Green Rivers, Utah.

44. *Euomphalus* ———?.—Confluence of Grand and Green Rivers, Utah. The specimens are imperfect, but are probably those of *E. luxus* White.

45. *Pleurotomaria excelsa* Newberry.—Confluence of Grand and Green Rivers, Utah.

46. *Naticopsis remex* White.—Confluence of Grand and Green Rivers, Utah. Described on a following page.

47. *Phillipsia* ———?.—Near Echo Park, Utah.

UPPER AUBREY GROUP.

48. *Discina* ———?.—Bee-hive Point, near Horseshoe Cañon, Utah.

49. *Hemipronites crinistria* Phillips.—Bee-hive Point, near Horseshoe Cañon, Utah. Occurs also in the Lower Aubrey Group. (See No. 31.)

50. *Spirigera subtilita* Hall.—Bee-hive Point, near Horseshoe Cañon, Utah. Occurs also in the Lower Aubrey Group. (See No. 33.)

51. *Spirifer Rockymontanus* Marcou.—Bee-hive Point, near Horseshoe Cañon, Utah. Occurs also in the Lower Aubrey Group. (See No. 35.)

52. *Spiriferina Kentuckensis* Shumard.—Confluence of Grand and Green Rivers, Utah. Also occurs in the Lower Aubrey Group at the same locality. (See No. 36.)

53. *Myalina* ———?.—Confluence of Grand and Green Rivers, Utah. Occurs also in the Lower Aubrey Group at the same locality. (See No. 38.)

54. *Edmondia* ———?.—Confluence of Grand and Green Rivers, Utah.

55. *Bellerophon Montfortianus* Norwood and Pratten.—Confluence of Grand and Green Rivers, Utah. The specimens are imperfect, but have apparently the markings and other characteristics of this species as it occurs in the Coalmeasures of the Mississippi Valley, but the shell is evidently more elongate or less compact.

56. *Bellerophon carbonarius* Cox, var. *subpapillosus* White.—Bee-hive Point, near Echo Cañon and near Echo Park, Utah. Also at Junction Mountain and near Diamond Peak, Northwestern Colorado. This variety differs from the typical forms of the species in its larger size and in having that part of the last volution, which is plain in the typical shell, marked with distant, slightly-raised papillæ, arranged in rows corresponding to and continuous with the revolving striæ.

MESOZOIC AGE.

JURASSIC PERIOD.

FLAMING GORGE GROUP.

57. *Pentacrinus asteriscus* Meek and Hayden.—Flaming Gorge; Santa Clara River, two miles below Gunlock; Diamond Valley; Lower Potato Valley; "White Hills," south of Twelve-mile Creek, near Gunnison; three or four miles south of Kanara, Utah; and at the Vermilion Hog-backs, Northwestern Colorado. The specimens consist only of joints of the column, the only part of the species yet discovered.

58. Spine of Echinoid, too indefinite for either specific or generic recognition. Santa Clara River, two miles below Gunlock, Utah.

59. *Rhynchonella gnathophora* Meek.—Flaming Gorge, Utah, and Vermilion Hog-backs, Northwestern Colorado.

60. *Rhynchonella Myrina* Whitfield.—Vermilion Hog-backs, Northwestern Colorado.

61. *Ostrea strigilecula* White.—Island Park and Flaming Gorge, Utah; and Vermilion Hog-backs, Northwestern Colorado.

62. *Ostrea (Alectryonia) procumbens* White.—Vermilion Hog-backs, Northwestern Colorado. Shell of moderate size, irregularly ovate in marginal outline; margins coarsely dentate; valves moderately thick, usually attached by nearly the whole surface of the lower one.

63. *Camptonectes stygius* White.—Lower end of Long Valley; mouth of Thistle Creek, Spanish Fork Cañon; Upper Kanab; and three or four miles south of Kanara, Utah.

64. *Camptonectes bellistriatus* Meek and Hayden.—Three or four miles south of Kanara, Utah.

65. *Camptonectes platessiformis* White.—North base of Aquarius Plateau, Southern Utah. Resembles *C. platessa* White in its surface-markings, and *C. Stygius* White in its marginal outline.

66. *Gervillia* ———?.—North base of Aquarius Plateau, Southern Utah. Resembles *G. Montanaensis* Meek, but the axis of the shell is more oblique to the hinge-line, and the wing narrower than in that species.

67. *Pinna* ———?.—Mouth of Thistle Creek, Spanish Fork Cañon, Utah. Surface radiately ribbed both above and below the median angle; probably a new species, but the specimens are too imperfect for satisfactory description.

68. *Modiola subimbricata* Meek.—Vermilion Hog-backs, Northwestern Colorado.

69. *Myophoria* ———?.—Island Park, Utah.

70. *Trigonia Americana* Meek.—Flaming Gorge, Utah.

71. *Trigonia Montanaensis* Meek.—North base of Aquarius Plateau, Utah.

72. *Trigonia Conradi* Meek and Hayden.—Flaming Gorge, Utah.

73. *Trigonia* ———?.—Santa Clara River, two miles below Gunlock, Utah.

74. *Unio Stewardi* White.—Flaming Gorge, Utah. Described on a following page.

75. *Trigonella* ———?.—Island Park, Utah. Shells rather small-exterior nearly perfect, but the hinge is unknown, and they are referred to this genus provisionally.

76. *Undetermined Conchifers.*—Two species. Flaming Gorge; north base of Aquarius Plateau; Square-top Butte, east base of Aquarius Plateau, Utah.

77. *Undetermined Conchifer.*—Different from No. 76. Island Park, Utah.

78. *Myacites* ———?.—South base of Thousand-lake Mountain, Utah.

79. *Neritina* ———?.—"White Hills", south of Twelve-mile Creek, near Gunnison, Utah; and Vermilion Hog-backs, Northwestern Colorado.

80. *Neritina?? Powelli* White.—Mouth of Thistle Creek, Spanish Fork Cañon, Utah. Described on a following page.

81. *Undetermined Gasteropods.*—Two species, very small, and the specimens numerous. Mouth of Thistle Creek, Spanish Fork Cañon, Utah.

82. *Belemnites densus* Meek and Hayden.—Island Park and Flaming Gorge, Utah; and Vermilion Hog-backs, Northwestern Colorado.

83. *Ammonites cordiformis* Meek and Hayden.—A small fragment of the inner volutions. Vermilion Hog-backs, Northwestern Colorado.

CRETACEOUS PERIOD.

HENRY'S FORK GROUP.

84. *Ostrea prudentia* White.—Head of Water-pocket Cañon, Southern Utah.

85. *Gryphea Pitcheri* Morton.—Near Twin Mesas; Upper Pine Creek; near Last Chance Creek; head of Water-pocket Cañon and Lower Potato Valley, Southern Utah. The specimens are numerous, and show the usual extreme variations. It occurs also in the Sulphur Creek Group. (See No. 97.)

86. *Exogyra lævinscula* Roemer.—Lower Potato Valley and south base of Mount Hillers, Southern Utah. It occurs also in the Sulphur Creek Group. (See No. 98).

87. *Exogyra ponderosa* Roemer.—Head of Water-pocket Cañon, Southern Utah. It occurs also in the Sulphur Creek Group, in Utah, and was obtained from a locality in Middle Park, Colorado. (See Nos. 99 and 202.)

88. *Plicatula hydrotheca* White.—Head of Water-pocket Cañon, Southern Utah. Described on a following page.

89. *Inoceramus Howelli* White.—Lower Potato Valley and Upper Pine Creek, Utah. Described on a following page.

90. *Avicula linguiformis* Shumard.—Lower Potato Valley and Sink Spring, Utah.

91. *Camptonectes platessa* White.—Head of Water-pocket Cañon, Southern Utah.

92. *Undetermined Conchifers.*—Lower Potato Valley, Utah.

93. *Cardium* ———?.—Head of Water-pocket Cañon, Southern Utah. A rather large subspinous species, probably new, but the specimens are all imperfect.

94. *Callista Deweyi* Meek and Hayden.—Head of Water-pocket Cañon, Southern Utah. The specimens consist only of casts in sandstone.

95. *Arca* ———?.—Head of Water-pocket Cañon, Southern Utah. An elongate species, represented only by a cast in sandstone.

SULPHUR CREEK GROUP.

96. *Ostrea congesta* Conrad.—Fold, ten miles west of Black Bluff, Green River, and Island Park, Utah; base of Diamond Peak and near Vermilion Cañon, Northwestern Colorado. The specimens from the last-named locality are unusually large, and a few of them were found free, but most of them were, as usual, found attached to fragments of *Inoceramus deformis*. The species occurs also in the Point of Rocks Group, Utah, in Western Kansas, and in Middle Park, Colorado. (See Nos. 159 and 200.)

97. *Gryphea Pitcheri* Morton.—Near Black Bluff, on Green River; Upper Kanab; fold, ten miles west of Black Bluff and Sink Spring, Utah. It also occurs in the Henry's Fork Group. (See No. 85.)

98. *Exogyra læviuscula* Roemer.—Upper Kanab, and near Black Bluff, on Green River, Utah. Occurs also in Henry's Fork Group, Utah. (See No. 86.)

99. *Exogyra ponderosa* Roemer.—Upper Kanab, Utah. It occurs also in Henry's Fork Group, Utah, and in Middle Park, Colorado. (See Nos. 87 and 202.)

100. *Inoceramus deformis* Meek.—Fold ten miles west of Black Bluff on Green River, and Island Park, Utah. Base of Diamond Peak and near Vermilion Cañon, Northwestern Colorado. It occurs also at the base of the Point of Rocks Group, near Coalville, Utah; in western Kansas, and in Middle Park, Colorado. (See Nos. 167 and 203.)

101. *Lucina subundata* Hall and Meek.—Upper Kanab and Thistle Creek, Utah. A species probably identical with this occurs in the Salt Wells Group at Coalville, Utah. (See No. 132.)

102. *Leiopistha Meekii* White.—Upper Kanab and Sink Spring, Utah.

103. *Turnus sphenoideus* White.—Upper Kanab, Utah. Described on a following page.

104. *Lunatia concinna* Hall and Meek.—Sink Spring, Utah.

105. *Anchura ruida* White.—Upper Kanab, Utah. Described on a following page.

106. *Anchura prolabiata* White.—Upper Kanab and Sink Spring, Utah. Described on a following page.

107. *Turritella Uvasana* Conrad.—Upper Kanab, Utah.

108. *Cassiope Whitfieldi* White.—Upper Kanab, Utah.

109. *Pseudobuccinum Nebrascense* Meek and Hayden.—Upper Kanab, Utah.

110. *Baculites ovatus* Say.—Fold ten miles west of Black Bluffs, Green River, Sink Spring, near Twin Mesas, and Upper Kanab, Utah. Occurs also in the Salt Wells Group. (See No. 157.)

111. *Scaphites Warreni* Meek and Hayden.—Fold ten miles west of Black Bluff, Green River, Utah.

112. *Ammonites Woolgari* Mantell?.—Last Chance Creek, Utah.

113. *Ammonites* ——— ?.—Fold ten miles west of Black Bluff, Green River, Utah. This species is of the type of *A. Woolgari*, but the volutions are proportionally deeper and the umbilicus smaller than in that species.

114. *Ammonites* ——— ?.—Upper Kanab, Utah. Specimens imperfect, but they indicate a species quite different from any others in the collections.

115. *Buchiceras Swallovi* Shumard.—Upper Kanab, Utah.

116. *Helicoceras* ——— ?.—Near Twin Mesas, Utah. The specimens show two rows of long dorsal spines and a crenulated or transversely undu-

lated surface. They are so compressed in shale that the character of the coil is not shown, and may, therefore, probably belong to the genus *Crioceras*.

117. *Helicoceras* ——— ?.—Upper Kanab, Utah. A fragment, different from No. 116.

118. *Belemnitella* ——— ?.—Upper Kanab, Utah, and Sulphur Creek, Bear River City, Wyoming. The specimens are more or less imperfect, but they closely resemble, and are probably identical with, *B. mucronata*, so common in the Cretaceous strata of New Jersey.

119. *Serpula intrica* White.—Upper Kanab, Utah.

SALT WELLS GROUP.

120. *Ostrea soleniscus* Meek.—Coalville, Lower Salina Cañon, and near False Creek, Utah; Bear River City, and Hilliard Station, Wyoming.

121. *Ostrea* (*Alectryonia*) *sannionis* White. Weber Valley, near Coalville, Utah. Described on a following page.

122. *Ostrea* (*Alectryonia* ——— ?.—Near False Creek, Southern Utah. The specimens are fragmentary, but they indicate an unusually large species of this subgenus.

123. *Gryphea* ——— ?.—Coalville, Utah. The specimens are imperfect, but they seem to indicate a species materially different from *G. Pitcheri* Morton.

124. *Anomia* ——— ?.—Coalville, Utah.

125. *Inoceramus problematicus* Schlotheim.—Lower Salina Cañon and Coalville, Utah; Bear River City, Wyoming.

126. *Inoceramus* ——— ?.—Two miles northwestward from Salt Wells Station, Wyoming.

127. *Inoceramus Gilberti* White.—Near Last Chance Creek, Southern Utah. Described on a following page.

128. *Avicula* (*Pseudoptera*) *rhytophora* Meek.—Coalville, Utah.

129. *Modiola* (*Brachydontes*) *multilinigera* Meek.—Coalville, Utah.

130. *Arca Coalvillensis* White.—Coalville, Utah. Described on a following page.

131. *Macrodon* ——— ?.—Coalville, Utah. A rather large, elongate species, represented only by a sandstone cast.

132. *Lucina subundata* Hall and Meek?.—Coalville, Utah. Apparently identical with that species. (See No. 101.)

133. *Cardium curtum* Meek and Hayden.—Coalville, Utah.

134. *Cardium subcurtum* Meek.—Coalville, Utah.

135. *Cyrena* (*Veloritina*) *securis* Meek.—Coalville, Utah. Mr. Meek's types were from the Salt Wells Group, Sulphur Creek, Bear River City, Wyoming, but ours, although imperfect, seem to belong to the same species.

136. *Cyrena* (*Veloritina*) *erecta* White.—Upper Kanab, Utah, and Hilliard Station, Wyoming. Described on a following page.

137. *Tellina* (*Arcopagia*) *Utahensis* Meek.—Coalville, Utah.

138. *Tellina modesta* Meek.—Coalville, Utah.

139. *Mactra arenaria* Meek.—Coalville, Utah.

140. *Corbula nematophora* Meek.—Coalville, Utah.

141. *Corbula* ——— ?.—Coalville, Utah.

142. *Martesia* ——— ?.—Coalville, Utah.

143. *Physa* ——— ?.—Coalville, Utah. One imperfect example only was found. It was associated with shells of marine type only, but it nevertheless seems to possess the characters of a true *Physa*.

144. *Neritina Bannisteri* Meek.—Hilliard Station, Wyoming. The type specimens of this species were obtained by Mr. Meek from among brackish and fresh water forms near Coalville, Utah. No fresh, or exclusively brackish water forms were found associated with our examples, although the geological horizon is doubtless identical, or very nearly so, at the two localities.

145. *Neritina pisum* Meek.—Coalville, Utah.

146. *Neritina* (*Velatella*) *patelliformis* Meek.—Coalville, Utah.

147. *Lunatia Utahensis* White.—Coalville, Utah. Described on a following page.

148. *Anchura fusiformis* Meek.—Coalville, Utah, and Sulphur Creek, Bear River City, Utah.

149. *Turritella micronema* Meek.—Coalville, Utah.

150. *Turritella Coalvillensis* Meek.—Coalville, and ten miles southeast of Kanara, west of Cone Mountain, Utah.

151. *Eulimella funicula* Meek.—Coalville, Utah.

152. *Turbonilla* (*Chemnitzia*) *Coalvillensis* Meek.—Coalville, Utah, and Hilliard Station, Wyoming.

153. *Gyrodes depressa* Meek.—Coalville, Utah.

154. *Fusus* (*Neptunea*) *Gabbi* Meek.—Coalville, Utah.

155. *Fusus* (*Neptunea*) *Utahensis* Meek.—Coalville, Utah.

156. *Admetopsis gregaria* Meek.—Coalville, Utah.

157. *Baculites ovatus* Say.—Below "Wall Rock," basin of Red Creek, Utah. Occurs most commonly in the Sulphur Creek Group. (See No. 110.)

158. *Scaphites* ——— ?.—Two miles northwestward from Salt Wells Station, Wyoming.

POINT OF ROCKS GROUP.

159. *Ostrea congesta* Conrad.—Near the base of the group, Coalville, Utah. The species occurs most abundantly in the Sulphur Creek Group of the Plateau Province; but it has a wide geographical, as well as a great stratigraphical, range. (See Nos. 96 and 200.)

160. *Ostrea* ——— ?.—Upper Kanab, Utah.

161. *Ostrea* ——— ?.—Bear River Valley, near Mellis Station, where it is associated with fresh and brackish water mollusks.

162. *Ostrea Coalvillensis* Meek.—Coalville, Utah.

163. *Ostrea insecura* White.—Two miles west of Point of Rocks, Wyoming. Described on a following page.

164. *Anomia gryphorhynchus* Meek.—Two miles west of Point of Rocks, Wyoming.

165. *Inoceramus* ——— ?.—Top of Aspen Mountain, but near the base of the group, Wyoming. The species is nearly like *I. sagensis* Owen, but the specimens are too imperfect for specific identification.

166. *Inoceramus* ——— ?.—Upper Kanab, Utah. It has the general aspect of both *I. Howelli* and *I. fragilis*, but differs from both in essential details.

167. *Inoceramus deformis* Meek.—Near the base of the group, Coalville, Utah. This species is most common in the Sulphur Creek Group, but it has a wide geographical, as well as a great vertical, range. (See Nos. 100 and 203.)

168. *Unio gonionotus* White.—Sevier Cliffs, twelve miles above Panguitch, Utah. Described on a following page.

169. *Unio* ——— ?.—Associated with the last (168), but differs from it in its more convex beaks and in wanting the plications of that species.

170. *Unio belliplicatus* Meek.—Bear River Valley, near Mellis Station, Wyoming.

171. *Unio Vetustus* Meek.—Bear River Valley, near Mellis Station, Wyoming, and Cañon of Desolation, Utah.

172. *Cyrena* (*Veloritina*) *Durkeei* Meek.—Bear River Valley, near Mellis Station, Wyoming.

173. *Cyrena* (*Veloritina*) ——— ?.—Upper Kanab, Utah.

174. *Cyrena* (*Veloritina*) *cytheriformis* Meek and Hayden.—Two miles west of Point of Rocks, Wyoming.

175. *Corbula undifera* Meek.—Rock Spring, Wyoming.

176. *Corbula pyriformis* Meek.—Bear River Valley, near Mellis Station, Wyoming.

177. *Corbula tropidophora* Meek.—Two miles west of Point of Rocks, Wyoming.

178. *Limnæa* ——— ?.—Upper Kanab, Utah.

179. *Limnæa* ——— ?.—Bear River Valley, near Mellis Station, Wyoming.

180. *Planorbis* (*Bathyomphalus*) *Kanabensis* White.—Upper Kanab, Utah. Described on a following page.

181. *Physa Kanabensis* White.—Upper Kanab, Utah. Described on a following page.

182. *Physa* ——— ?.—Bear River Valley, near Mellis Station, Wyoming.

183. *Physa* ——— ?.—Upper Kanab, Utah. Associated with No. 181, but it is a larger species, and has a much shorter spire, the volutions of which are more broadly shouldered on the proximal side of the suture.

184. *Rhytophorus priscus* Meek.—Bear River Valley, near Mellis Station, Wyoming.

185. *Rhytophorus Meekii* White.—Bear River Valley, near Mellis Station, Wyoming. Described on a following page.

186. *Helix* ——— ?.—Cañon of Desolation, Utah.

187. *Helix Kanabensis* White.—Upper Kanab, Utah. Described on a following page.

188. *Goniobasis nitidula* Meek.—Bear River Valley, near Mellis Station, Wyoming.

189. *Goniobasis insculpta* Meek.—Rock Spring, Wyoming.

190. *Goniobasis chrysalis* Meek.—Bear River Valley, near Mellis Station, Wyoming.

191. *Goniobasis Nebrascensis* Meek and Hayden.—Cañon of Desolation, Utah.

192. *Goniobasis chrysaloidea* White.—Bear River Valley, near Mellis Station, Wyoming. Described on a following page.

193. *Goniobasis Cleburni* White.—Bear River Valley, near Mellis Station, Wyoming. Described on a following page.

194. *Goniobasis* ——— ?.—Upper Kanab, Utah.—It is associated with *Pyrgulifera humerosa* Meek, and bears some resemblance to *G. Cleburni*, but it has a proportionally much shorter spire. The specimens are all sandstone casts.

195. *Pyrgulifera humerosa* Meek.—Bear River Valley, near Mellis Station, Wyoming, and Upper Kanab, Utah.

196. *Viviparus Panguitchensis* White.—Sevier Cliffs, twelve miles above Panguitch, and Upper Kanab, Utah.

197. *Campeloma macrospira* Meek.—Bear River Valley, near Mellis Station, Wyoming, and Cañon of Desolation, Utah.

198. *Odontobasis buccinoidea* White.—Two miles west of Point of Rocks, Wyoming. Described on a following page.

199. *Turritella* ———?.—Upper Kanab, Utah. Near the base of the group.

CRETACEOUS FOSSILS FROM BEYOND THE LIMITS OF THE PLATEAU PROVINCE.

200. *Ostrea congesta* Conrad.—Western Kansas, and near Platte Cañon, Middle Park, Colorado.

201. *Ostrea* ———?.—Near Platte Cañon, Middle Park, Colorado. A large biconvex species.

202. *Exogyra ponderosa* Roemer.—Near Platte Cañon, Middle Park, Colorado.

203. *Inoceramus deformis* Meek.—Western Kansas.

204. *Inoceramus (Volviceramus) exogyroides* Meek. Three miles northeastward from Hot Springs, Middle Park, Colorado.

205. *Inoceramus Barabini* Morton?.—The specimens vary from the typical forms in being deeper from hinge-line to base.

206. *Avicula Parkensis* White.—South of Grand River, Middle Park, Colorado. Described on a following page.

207. *Heteroceras* ——— ?.—Three miles northwestward from Hot Springs, Middle Park, Colorado. The species is represented by a fragment only.

CENOZOIC AGE.

TERTIARY PERIOD.

BITTER CREEK GROUP.

208. *Ostrea Wyomingensis* Meek.—Point of Rocks, Black Buttes, and Rock Spring, Wyoming.

209. *Ostrea arcuatilis* Meek.—Black Buttes, Wyoming.

210. *Anomia* ——— ?.—Black Buttes, Wyoming.

211. *Unio propheticus* White.—Black Buttes, Wyoming. Described on a following page.

212. *Unio petrinus* White.—Black Buttes, Wyoming. Described on a following page.

213. *Unio* ———?.—Black Buttes, Wyoming. A large massive species, but much shorter than *U. petrinus*, with which it is associated.

214. *Unio* ——— ?.—Near Evanston, Wyoming. A large, elongate species, but the specimens are too imperfect for specific recognition or description.

215. *Unio Leanus* Meek?.—South Fork of Vermilion River, near Diamond Peak, Northwestern Colorado.

216. *Unio brachyopisthus* White.—Black Buttes, Wyoming. Described on a following page.

217. *Corbicula (Leptesthes) fracta* Meek.—Black Buttes, Wyoming.

218. *Cyrena (Veloritina) Bannisteri* Meek.—Point of Rocks, Wyoming.

219. *Pisidium saginatum* White.—Almy Coal Mines, near Evanston, Wyoming. Described on a following page.

220. *Corbula subundata* White.—Point of Rocks, Wyoming. Described on a following page.

221. *Corbula crassitelliformis* Meek.—Black Buttes, Wyoming.

222. *Planorbis Utahensis* Meek.—South base of Pine Valley Mountains, Utah. (See No. 245, and also general remarks on page 85.)

223. *Planorbis* ——— ?.—Almy Coal Mines, near Evanston, Wyoming.

224. *Planorbis (Bathyomphalus)* ——— ?.—Almy Coal Mines, near Evanston, Wyoming. The specimens consist of fragments only, but they indicate a large, well marked species of this subgenus.

225. *Physa pleromatis* White—Southeast flank of Quien Hornet Mountain, Wyoming; east base of Pine Valley Mountains, Utah, and many other localities.

226. *Physa* ——— ?.—Almy Coal Mines, near Evanston, Wyoming.

227. *Helix* ——— ?.—Almy Coal Mines, near Evanston, Wyoming.

228. *Helix* ——— ?.—Different from No. 227. East base of Pine Valley Mountains, Utah.

229. *Helix peripheria* White.—South base of Pine Valley Mountains, Utah. Described on a following page.

230. *Neritina volvilineata* White.—Black Buttes, Wyoming. Described on a following page.

231. *Goniobasis tenera* Hall sp.—Various localities. (See Nos. 247, 259, and 265, and also general remarks on page 85.)

232. *Goniobasis* ——— ?.—Almy Coal Mines, near Evanston, Wyoming. This species is related to *G. Nebrascensis* Meek and Hayden, but is more elongate.

233. *Goniobasis Wyomingensis* Meek.—Black Buttes, Wyoming.

234. *Hydrobia recta* White.—Almy Coal Mines, near Evanston, Wyoming. Described on a following page.

235. *Hydrobia Utahensis* White.—West base of Mu-si-ni-a Plateau, 1,000 feet below its summit, Utah.

236. *Viviparus plicapressus* White.—Black Buttes, Wyoming. Described on a following page.

237. *Viviparus trochiformis* Meek.—West base of Mu-si-ni-a Plateau, tain, 1,000 feet below its summit.

238. *Viviparus trochiformis* var.—Associated with No. 337.

239. *Viviparus paludinæformis* Hall sp.—Various localities. (See Nos. 248, 260, and 266, and also general remarks on page 85.)

240. *Tulotoma Thompsoni* White.—Black Buttes, Wyoming. Described on a following page.

241. *Leioplax? turricula* White.—Black Buttes, Wyoming. Described on a following page.

LOWER GREEN RIVER GROUP.

242. *Unio Shoshonensis* White.—West side of Snake River, six miles north of Junction Mountain; cliffs four miles northwestward from the head of Vermilion Cañon and Dry Mountains, Northwestern Colorado. Described on a following page. It occurs also in the Upper Green River Group. (See No. 249.)

243. *Unio* ——— ?.—Two miles east of Lawrence Station, Wyoming. Base of the group.

244. *Sphærium* ——— ?.—Four miles northeastward from the head of Vermilion Cañon, Northwestern Colorado.

245. *Planorbis Utahensis* Meek.—West side of Snake River, six miles north of Junction Mountain, Northwestern Colorado. It occurs also in the Bitter Creek Group. (See No. 222, and also general remarks on page 85.)

246. *Helix riparia* White.—Eight miles below Green River Station, Wyoming. Described on a following page.

247. *Goniobasis tenera* Hall sp.—Various localities. (See Nos. 231, 259, and 265, and also general remarks on page 85.)

248. *Viviparus paludinæformis* Hall sp.—Various localities. (See Nos. 239, 260, and 266, and also general remarks on page 85.)

UPPER GREEN RIVER GROUP.

249. *Unio Shoshonensis* White.—Henry's Fork and Alkali stage-sta-

tion, Wyoming. Described on a following page. It occurs also in the Lower Green River Group. (See No. 242.)

250. *Unio* ———?.—Henry's Fork, Wyoming.

251. *Sphærium* ———?.—Alkali stage-station, twenty-one miles northward from Green River Station, Wyoming.

252. *Planorbis spectabilis* Meek.—Henry's Fork, Wyoming. Occurs also in the Bridger Group. (See No. 263, and also general remarks on page 85.)

253. *Planorbis* ———?.—Henry's Fork, Wyoming. A small species, marked with fine revolving lines.

254. *Physa* ———?.—Henry's Fork, Wyoming.

255. *Succinea papillispira* White.—Alkali stage-station, Wyoming. Described on a following page.

256. *Helix* ———?.—Henry's Fork, Wyoming. A small species, somewhat resembling the recent *H. perspectiva.*

257. *Pupa incolata* White.—Henry's Fork, Wyoming. Described on a following page.

258. *Pupa arenula* White.—Henry's Fork, Wyoming. Described on a following page.

259. *Goniobasis tenera* Hall sp.—Various localities. (See Nos. 231, 247, and 265, and also general remarks on page 85.)

260. *Viviparus paludinæformis* Hall sp.—Henry's Fork and Alkali stage-station, Wyoming, and various other localities. At the first-named locality the specimens are below the usual average size. (See Nos. 239, 248, and 266, and also general remarks on page 85.)

261. *Cypris* ———?.—Henry's Fork, Wyoming. This species seems to be specifically different from *C. Leidyi* Evans and Shumard.

BRIDGER GROUP.

262. *Unio Haydeni* Meek.—Near Fort Bridger, Wyoming.

263. *Planorbis spectabilis* Meek.—Henry's Fork, east of Fort Bridger, and six miles west of Badland Mountains, Wyoming. Occurs also in the Upper Green River Group. (See No. 252, and also general remarks on page 85.)

264. *Physa Bridgerensis* Meek.—Henry's Fork, east of Fort Bridger, Wyoming.

265. *Goniobasis tenera* Hall sp.—Various localities. (See Nos. 231, 247, and 259, and also general remarks on page 85.)

266. *Viviparus paludinæformis* Hall sp.—Various localities. (See Nos. 239, 248, and 260, and also general remarks on page 85.)

267. *Viviparus Wyomingensis* Meek.—Near Fort Bridger, and six miles west of the Cameo Mountains, Wyoming. This seems to be specifically distinct from the prevailing form that I have referred to *V. paludinæformis*, being a larger, thinner, and more inflated shell.

BROWN'S PARK GROUP.

268. *Physa* ——— ?.—This is the only invertebrate species discovered in the strata of this group, and all the examples of it are too imperfect to serve as the basis of a specific description.

TERTIARY FOSSILS FROM BEYOND THE LIMITS OF THE PLATEAU PROVINCE.

269. *Flustra* ——— ?.—Bijou Basin, forty miles east of Denver, Colorado. The specimens are found incrusting the oyster, No. 270.

270. *Ostrea* ——— ?.—Bijou Basin, forty miles east of Denver, Colorado. The species is a very large one; the largest example is nearly a foot in length and proportionally broad.

271. *Cyrena* (*Veloritina*) ——— ?.—Fresh-water Tertiary deposits, Crow Creek, Colorado, where it was found associated with No. 278.

272. *Corbicula Powelli* White.—Bijou Basin, forty miles east of Denver, Colorado. Described on a following page.

273. *Venus* ——— ?.—Bijou Basin, forty miles east of Denver, Colorado. The specimens are fragmentary, but the hinge is shown.

274. *Petricola* ——— ?.—Burrows only. Bijou Basin, Colorado.

275. *Mesodesma Bishopi* White.—Bijou Basin, forty miles east of Denver, Colorado. Described on a following page.

276. *Dentalium* ——— ?.—Bijou Basin, Colorado. A small longitudinally striated species.

277. *Dentalium* ———?—Bijou Basin, Colorado. Much like No. 276, except that its surface is marked only by encircling lines of growth.

278. *Melania Larunda* White.—Crow Creek, Colorado, where it is associated with No. 271. Described on a following page.

279. *Patella* ———?—Bijou Basin, Colorado. A single small example.

280. *Phorus exoneratus* White.—Bijou Basin, Colorado, forty miles east of Denver, Colorado. Described on a following page.

281. *Cerithium* ———?—Bijou Basin, Colorado. A single, small, imperfect example.

DESCRIPTIONS OF NEW SPECIES OF INVERTEBRATE FOSSILS FROM STRATA OF THE CARBONIFEROUS, JURASSIC, CRETACEOUS, AND TERTIARY PERIODS.

CARBONIFEROUS PERIOD.

Radiata.

Actinozoa.

Genus AMPLEXUS Sowerby.

Amplexus zaphrentiformis (sp. nov.).—Corallum having the external aspect of *Zaphrentis* rather than of *Amplexus*, being elongate-conical in form, more or less curved and tapering to a point or small pedicil at the base; epitheca well developed, having its surface marked by the usual concentric wrinkles and lines of growth, and with longitudinal lines marking the position of the septa, the latter not being very distinct; calyx circular or subcircular, the plain portion of the surface at its bottom equal to one-third or more of the diameter of the corallum; septal fossette well developed, situated at the concave side of the corallum; septa thirty or forty in number, rather strong; transverse plates numerous, well developed, somewhat irregular, and ending exteriorly against a moderately well developed external wall, which is distinct from the epitheca proper. This external wall contains no vesicles and apparently consists of solid coralline substance.

The largest example in the collection is nearly nine centimeters in length, the calyx having a diameter of twenty-five millimeters; but the average size of nearly one hundred examples is considerably less.

This species differs from all other species of *Amplexus* known to me in its zaphrentoid form, but its plain calyx-bottom, its broad transverse plates, and the absence of a vesicular zone, leave no doubt as to the propriety of referring it to the genus *Amplexus*.

Position and locality.—Lower Aubrey Group; Split Mountain Cañon, and near Echo Park, Utah.

Echinodermata.

Genus EUPACHYCRINUS Meek and Worthen.

Eupachycrinus platybasis (sp. nov.).—Calyx nearly flat; basal pieces small, concealed by the first joint of the column, which is proportionally large; subradial pieces rather small or of medium size, their inner ends also covered by the first joint of the column; judging from the portion of them that is visible, they are all of nearly regular rhombic outline; first radials much broader than long, broadly convex from side to side and abruptly convex from within, outward, all of them ending with a regular obtuse angle between the subradial pieces except the left anterior one, the angle of which is made a little irregular by the interposition of the second anal plate; first anal piece of the same size and shape as the subradial pieces; second anal piece apparently nearly as large as the first, between which and the left anterior first radial piece it is interposed, reaching nearly as far inward as the first radial piece does, and at which point it ends with an acute angle; plates all massive. Remainder of the structure unknown. Sutures all linear; surface nearly or quite smooth.

Diameter of the calyx, eighteen millimeters.

This species differs from the typical forms of the genus in the extreme flatness of its calyx, but the arrangement, number, and general character of the pieces composing it leave no doubt as to the propriety of referring it to *Eupachycrinus*.

Position and locality.—Lower Aubrey Group; confluence of Grand and Green Rivers, Utah.

Genus ARCHÆOCIDARIS McCoy.

Archæocidaris cratis (sp. nov.).—Spines slender, gradually tapering from base to point; shaft ornamented with sharp, distant spinules, each about one and a half millimeters long and pointing strongly upward; basal ring prominent, plain, except the fine crenulation of its edges, and situated very near the proximal end of the spine. Surface apparently smooth.

Length about six centimeters; diameter just above the basal ring nearly three millimeters; diameter of basal ring about four millimeters.

The collections of the Geological Survey of Nebraska in the cabinet of the Smithsonian Institution contain a single spine of this species, which, together with that of these collections, is all that is known of the species. It may be readily recognized by its smooth, slender shaft, with its distant, sharp spinules.

Position and locality.—Lower Aubrey Group; confluence of the Grand and Green Rivers, Utah.

Mollusca.

Gasteropoda.

Genus NATICOPSIS McCoy.

Naticopsis remex (sp. nov.).—Shell of ordinary size, very oblique when adult, by the elongation and enlargement of the last volution; volutions about four, convex, increasing rapidly in size, the last one large and much produced; spire small and short; suture impressed. Surface marked by the usual lines of growth, and, although that of the specimens in the collection is not very well preserved, there are some indications of the presence of faint revolving striæ also.

Length across the longest diameter of the aperture and body volution of an average-sized specimen, twenty-three millimeters; short diameter of the same, seventeen millimeters.

Position and locality.—Summit of the Lower Aubrey Group; confluence of the Grand and Green Rivers, Utah.

JURASSIC PERIOD.

Mollusca.

Conchifera.

Genus UNIO Retzius.

Unio Stewardi (sp. nov.).—From the Jurassic strata at Flaming Gorge of Green River, near the northern boundary line of Utah, some portions of a moderately large *Unio* were obtained that belong to an undescribed species. The valves are broadly oval in marginal outline, broadly but somewhat uniformly convex; beaks very near the anterior end; test massive; surface apparently marked only by the ordinary lines and imbrications of growth; cardinal and lateral teeth both strong; the lower lateral tooth of the left valve, and also that part of the hinge of the right valve against which it shuts, both strong and rounded into the cavity of each valve respectively, and both end posteriorly by abruptly rounded ends.

Length of largest example, eight and a half centimeters; height, sixty-two millimeters.

Compared with *U. nucalis* Meek and Hayden, the only other species of the genus known to me from American Jurassic strata, it is larger, more massive, the beaks placed more anteriorly, and the cardinal and lateral teeth more massive.

Specific name given in honor of Mr. J. F. Steward, of Plano, Ill., its discoverer.

Gasteropoda.

Genus NERITINA Lamarck.

Neritini ? ? Powelli (sp. nov.).—Shell moderately large, obliquely subovate in outline; volutions about three or three and a half, rapidly increasing in size, the last one much expanded; spire depressed, the apex scarcely appearing by side view of the shell; suture slightly impressed; aperture large, broadly subcircular or subtetrahedral; a broad rounded revolving prominence extends around the volutions, nearer to their distal than proximal side, and another less prominent one between the first one and the suture; the first one, especially, gives a degree of angularity to the last volution and to the margin of the aperture.

Surface marked by ordinary lines of growth, and also by somewhat prominent folds parallel with them; the folds being stronger upon the revolving prominences before mentioned than elsewhere, and disappear upon the under surface of the shell.

Greatest diameter of the largest example, twenty-eight millimeters; breadth of the same, twenty millimeters; height, the aperture resting upon the table, fifteen millimeters.

By carefully digging out the stony filling I have been unable to find any trace of a thickened inner lip such as characterizes the Neritidæ, but the body seems to be small, simple, and without even a proper columella. The shell has the external aspect of a member of the family Neritidæ, but it is not without much hesitation that I refer it to the genus *Neritina*. Indeed, this reference of it is made only provisionally until further investigation can be made. This disposition of it is made partly because it seems properly referable to no other established genus, and partly in view of the facts published by Brinkhorst in his *Monog. Gast. et Ceph. de la Craie Sup.* du Limbourg, 1861. In that work he describes and figures two species, *Nerita rugosa* Hoeninghaus, and *N. parvula* Brink., which he shows to have been so fossilized that the callus which formed the thickened inner lip was entirely removed by a natural process of solution, leaving the remainder of the shell intact, and in a condition similar to that of the species here described as regards the absence of an inner lip, but natural casts of his species showed that they originally possessed a well developed one. No such casts have been found with our shells, and it is not improbable that they were originally without any thickened inner lip.

If so, our shell cannot be properly referred to any genus with which I am acquainted, and in case further investigation shall leave no doubt that the shells have not been changed from their original character, I propose for it the generic name of *Lyosoma*.

Specific name given in honor of Prof. J. W. Powell, geologist in charge of the Second Division United States Geological and Geographical Survey.

Position and locality.—Flaming Gorge Group; mouth of Thistle Creek, Spanish Fork Cañon, Utah.

CRETACEOUS PERIOD.

Mollusca.

Conchifera.

Genus OSTREA Linnæus.

Subgenus ALECTRYONIA Fischer.

Ostrea (Alectryonia) sannionis (sp. nov.).—Shell rather small, alate at both sides of the beak, irregularly subquadrate in marginal outline, its longitudinal axis curved, the convexity of the curve being forward, almost as wide across the alations as at the base, but constricted in the middle; beaks small, not prominent, directed slightly backward; lower valve moderately convex; scar of attachment at the beak small or absent; ligament-area short, rather broad; its longitudinal furrow shallow but well defined, transversely striated, and pointing obliquely backward; posterior alation narrower than the anterior one, and a little longer than the corresponding alation of the other valve; muscular scar comparatively large, situated nearly mid-length of the valve and near the posterior margin, curved-spatulate in outline, the broadest end being toward the base of the shell; upper valve nearly flat, but in other respects corresponding with the lower.

Surface of both valves marked by the ordinary lines and lamellations of growth common to the genus and by numerous crenulated radiating plications, four or five of which upon each valve reach the base of the shell, giving that margin a coarsely zigzag or toothed condition. The other plications are smaller and die out at the sides of the shell and upon the alations.

Length from base to beak of a large example thirty-eight millimeters; breadth near the front the same; across the wings, thirty-three millimeters.

This is one of the most distinctly defined species of the genus known to me, and numerous examples of it show that it was subject to comparatively little variation.

Position and locality.—Near top of Salt Wells Group; Weber Valley, near Coalville, Utah.

Ostrea insecura (sp. nov.).—Shell rather small, thin, elongate-suboval in outline when adult, suboval or subcircular when young; beaks and area small; scar of attachment usually small and sometimes absent; surface comparatively smooth for an oyster; a few faint radiating plications appearing upon some examples. Length of largest example nearly five and a half centimeters; breadth twenty-nine millimeters.

Position and locality.—Point of Rocks Group; two miles west of Point of Rocks, Wyoming.

Genus PLICATULA Lamarck.

Plicatula hydrotheca (sp. nov.).—Shell of ordinary size, irregularly subovate in marginal outline; beaks rather narrow; lower valve broadly convex; hinge teeth well developed; upper valve nearly flat, or slightly concave near the beak.

Surface of both valves marked by small, slightly raised radiating plications, which are crenulated, a little irregular and more or less distinct upon all parts of the surface of both valves.

Length, three centimeters; greatest breath, twenty-four millimeters.

Position and locality.—Henry's Fork Group; head of Water-pocket Cañon, Southern Utah.

Genus INOCERAMUS Sowerby.

Inoceramus Gilberti (sp. nov.).—Shell irregularly suboval in marginal outline, the transverse diameter being greater than the vertical; front flattened; valves nearly or quite equal, both being gibbous and sometimes quite ventricose; umbones broad and elevated; beaks very near the front, incurved but not projecting beyond the front margin; front nearly straight vertically, and forming nearly a right angle with the hinge; front margin rounded below to the basal margin, which is broadly convex for more than half the length of the shell; postero-basal margin extending obliquely upward, with a slight emargination to the posterior extremity, which is abruptly rounded to meet the downward-sloping postero-dorsal margin; dorsal margin straight, its length equaling more than half the long diameter of the shell.

Upon each valve there is an obscure radiating shallow furrow or depression extending from the umbonal region to the postero-basal border and ending at the emargination there, before mentioned.

Surface marked by the usual lines of growth, and also by numerous extravagant and irregular concentric folds or wrinkles.

This species belongs to the section of the genus that Brongniart has designated under the name of *Catillus*. It is a peculiarly well-marked species and easily distinguished from all others found in the rocks of the great Rocky Mountain region.

Transverse length of an average-sized specimen seven and a half centimeters; height from base to hinge, five centimeters. Specific name given in honor of its discoverer, Mr. G. K. Gilbert, geologist of one of the surveying parties.

Position and locality.—Salt Wells Group; near Last Chance Creek, Southern Utah.

Inoceramus Howelli (sp. nov.).—Shell of medium size, obliquely and irregularly suboval in marginal outline, the vertical diameter being greater than the transverse; both valves having considerable convexity, that of the left valve greater than the other; beaks narrowed, prominent, the prominence of the left one greater than the other, both of them elevated above the hinge line, and also curving forward beyond the front of the shell; front flattened, extending almost straight downward from the front end of the hinge, with which it forms nearly a right, or slightly obtuse, angle. Antero-basal margin abruptly rounded to the base; basal margin short; postero-basal margin extending obliquely upward to the posterior extremity, straightened or slightly emarginate; posterior extremity abruptly rounded to meet the almost straight postero-dorsal margin.

Between the axis of the body of the shell and the postero-dorsal margin there is upon each valve a rather broad, shallow, but more or less distinct furrow or depression, extending from the umbonal region to the postero-basal margin, and ending at the emargination before mentioned. There is also a distinct alation upon each valve, separated from the body portion by a tolerably well-defined auricular furrow.

Surface marked by the ordinary lines of growth, and also by moderately distinct concentric folds, but the surface has a rather smoother aspect than is usual with species of this genus. Height of an average-sized example, from base to beaks, seven and a half centimeters; greatest breadth, which is near the base, five centimeters; length of hinge, thirty-seven millimeters.

This shell somewhat resembles *I. fragilis* Hall and Meek, but differs from it in possessing the shallow radiating furrow upon the body of the valve, and also in having a distinct posterior ear, separated from the body of the valve by an auricular furrow. It also resembles an example of *I. striatus* Mantell, in the cabinet of the Smithsonian Institution, from Saxony, but the beaks of our species are more elevated and turned more forward than they are in that species. *I. striatus* is also without the shallow radiating furrow before mentioned. It differs from *I. flaccidus* White in its smaller size, its smoother surface and more gibbous valves, that species being coarsely and extravagantly wrinkled. Specific name given in honor of Mr. E. E. Howell, who discovered it while geologist of one of the surveying parties.

Position and locality.—Henry's Fork Group; Lower Potato Valley and Upper Pine Creek, Utah.

Genus AVICULA Klein.

Avicula Parkensis (sp. nov.).—Shell small, slightly inequivalve, very oblique, elongate, thin at all the margins except the cardinal; anterior wing of ordinary size and shape; posterior wing rather large and long; both valves broadly but regularly convex; body of the shell broadest behind the middle; antero-basal border broadly convex; posterior extremity regularly rounded; postero-dorsal border nearly straight from the posterior border to the base of the posterior wing; beaks of ordinary prominence; surface apparently smooth.

Length from the end of the anterior wing to the posterior extremity of the shell, thirty-four millimeters; breadth across the widest part of the body, fifteen millimeters.

This species resembles *A. lingulifera* Shumard, but differs from that species in its more elongate form and more oblique hinge line.

Position and locality.—Cretaceous strata; south of Grand River, Middle Park, Colorado.

Genus ARCA Linnæus.

Arca? Coalvillensis (sp. nov.).—Shell longer than high, moderately thick; test somewhat massive; beaks depressed, situated near the anterior end;

umbones broad; anterior end rounded or subtruncate; base nearly straight or very broadly convex, and often slightly emarginate about the middle; postero-basal border rounded upward to the posterior extremity, which is abruptly rounded to the downward sloping, nearly straight postero-dorsal border, the latter forming an obtuse angle with the hinge border; hinge equal in height to about two-thirds the entire length of the shell.

A slight depression or flattening extends from the umbo of each valve to its base, causing the straightening or slight emargination of the basal border before mentioned. Area nearly obsolete; hinge rather slender; two or three long, slender transverse teeth occupy its middle portion; seven or eight teeth cross the surface of its posterior end obliquely downward and inward, and about an equal number of smaller ones cross the anterior end almost vertically; the inner ones of the latter set of teeth being very small and situated nearly beneath the beaks.

Surface marked by ordinary lines of growth, and by fine radiating lines, which are often obscure. Length, five centimeters; height, thirty-three millimeters.

Position and locality.—Salt Wells Group; Coalville, Utah

Genus UNIO Retzius.

Unio gonionotus (sp. nov.).—Shell elongate-subelliptical in marginal outline; flattened and thin when young, but becoming gibbous or almost cylindrical with age; dorsal margin broadly convex; base nearly straight; front regularly rounded; the rounding of the posterior end somewhat irregular, in consequence of the plications of the valves at that part; beaks obsolete, the umbonal region of each valve so flattened that they form an acute angle at the dorsum in the young, the angle increasing with age, so that it is very obtuse in the adult shell.

Surface of the anterior portion of the shell marked by only the ordinary lines and lamellations of growth, but the posterior portion, comprising more than half the length, is marked by strong, more or less irregularly radiating plications, which begin faintly a little forward of the middle, and increase gradually in strength to the posterior and postero-basal margins, and increase in number by a few bifurcations toward those margins; curving upward and backward from the uppermost of the longer plications there are several smaller, short ones that end at the postero-dorsal margin.

Length of the largest example in the collection, sixty-three millimeters; height, thirty-five millimeters. Young examples have very different proportions, as well as a marginal outline of different shape.

This species differs conspicuously from any other fossil *Unio* known to me, although young examples of it have some resemblance to those of the recent species *U. multiplicatus*, but the adult specimens have a very different aspect. It differs from *U. belliplicatus* Meek, from equivalent strata in Southwestern Wyoming, in its general shape and in the position and distribution of the plications, they being most conspicuous on the anterior portion of that shell, while the corresponding portion of ours is plain.

Position and locality.—Point of Rocks Group; Upper Kanab, Utah.

Genus CYRENA Lamarck.

Subgenus VELORITINA Meek.

Cyrena (Veloritina) erecta (sp. nov.).—Shell of medium size, subovate in marginal outline when adult, but subcircular when young, gibbous, especially the upper median portion, but somewhat compressed laterally at the postero-basal portion; front and basal margins regularly and continuously rounded; postero-basal extremity somewhat abruptly rounded upward to the sloping, broadly rounded postero-dorsal margin; umbones elevated; beaks small, incurved, and pointing forward; postero-dorsal margin of each valve flexed strongly inward, so that the hinge-ligament is hidden from sight by side view of the shell.

Surface marked by the ordinary lines of growth.

Length, thirty millimeters; height from base to umbones, thirty-four millimeters.

Position and locality.—Salt Wells Group; Upper Kanab, Utah, and Hilliard Station, Wyoming.

Genus TURNUS Gabb.

Turnus sphenoideus (sp. nov.).—Shell elongate-cuneate, inflated in front, narrowed, and laterally flattened behind; beaks anterior, incurved, adjacent;

postero-dorsal margin sloping from behind the beaks to the posterior extremity, and apparently capped by a slender, accessory plate; posterior extremity abruptly rounded; basal margin nearly straight; front regularly rounded, both laterally and vertically; anterior gape consisting of a narrow, vertical slit that occupies the middle of a somewhat prominent projection at the antero-basal portion of the shell, which projection has the shape of a Norman shield, as seen by front view, when both valves are in their natural position; umbonal groove distinct and moderately deep, causing a distinct groove upon the stony internal casts of the shell, which is of about the same dimensions and character as that which is left by the radiating internal rib; besides these two grooves, there is another, somewhat broader furrow radiating from behind the beak of each valve to near the posterior end. A broad, cake-like accessory plate covers the beaks and the space between them; and, apparently, two others, one upon each valve, occupy the space between the umbonal plates and the top of the Norman shield-shaped projection before mentioned.

Surface marked by fine, concentric, raised lines, besides the radiating furrows before mentioned. The masses of rock from which our specimens were broken out, contained what appear to have been calcareous, siphonal tubes, but none of them were found to be unmistakably connected with the shells.

Length, thirteen millimeters; greatest height, seven millimeters; breadth at the front, six millimeters.

Position and locality.—Sulphur Creek Group; Upper Kanab, Utah.

Gasteropoda.

Genus RHYTOPHORUS Meek.

Rhytophorus Meekii (sp. nov.).—Shell subfusiform; spire moderately produced, nearly one-third as long as the entire length of the shell; volutions about six, convex, the last one somewhat large, elongate, convex, and tapering from the middle toward the anterior end; suture impressed, and upon the proximal side of it there is an almost equally impressed revolving line, having the aspect of a second suture; folds of the columella well developed.

Surface marked by the ordinary lines of growth and also upon the spire by numerous small longitudinal folds, parallel with the slightly oblique direction of the lines of growth. These folds appear upon the distal portion only of the last volution.

Length of the largest example obtained, twenty-five millimeters; diameter of the body volution, twelve millimeters.

This species differs from *R. priscus* Meek, with which it is associated in the less robust and more elongate form of the shell, its proportionally longer spire, more delicate and finer markings, and the less abrupt convexity of the volutions upon the proximal side of the suture.

The specific name is given in honor of the author of the genus.

Position and locality.—Point of Rocks Group; Bear River Valley, near Mellis Station, Wyoming.

Genus PLANORBIS Guettard.

Subgenus BATHYOMPHALUS Agassiz.

Planorbis (*Bathyomphalus*) *Kanabensis* (sp. nov.).—Shell rather small; spire flat or nearly so, suture impressed; volutions five or six, narrow, regularly increasing in size to the aperture, broadly convex upon the upper side; periphery abrubtly rounded to the broadly convex under side, the latter extending obliquely downward and inward to the well defined, moderately broad, and deep umbilicus.

Surface marked by ordinary lines of growth.

Diameter of coil, twelve millimeters.

Position and locality.—Point of Rocks Group; Upper Kanab, Utah.

Genus PHYSA Draparnaud.

Physa Kanabensis (sp. nov.).—Shell rather under the average size; very elongate; spire extended; volutions about six, broadly convex; aperture very narrow, ending sharply at its distal end and abruptly rounded at the proximal end.

The specimens of the collection are all imperfect, but the species is peculiarly distinguished by its very slender elongate form, its extended spire, spire, and its very narrow elongate aperture.

Position and locality.—Point of Rocks Group; Upper Kanab, Utah.

Genus HELIX Linnæus.

Helix Kanabensis (sp. nov.).—Shell having the general external shape and character of *H. palliata* Say, but, besides being considerably smaller, it presents some differences in its aperture. Like that species, its lip is reflexed, and it has a similar large tooth upon its parietal wall. In addition to the latter there are four short linear ridges upon the inner surface just within the upper and outer portion of the aperture, at the margin of which they terminate exteriorly, but extend inward in the direction of the whorl from two to three millimeters. The lowermost of these small ridges is shortest, but more prominent and tooth-like than the others. Only a single specimen was obtained, and that is very imperfect. It is described and named here because of its value as showing the great differentiation of Helecine types so early as the Cretaceous period.

Position and locality.—Point of Rocks Group; Upper Kanab, Utah.

Genus ANCHURA Conrad.

Anchura ruida (sp. nov.).—Shell rather small; spire moderately elongate; volutions about seven, convex; suture impressed; wing moderately large, contorted, bearing at its extero-posterior corner a falciform process which points backward in the direction of the spire; the outer border of this process and also that of the body of the wing continuously and broadly rounded to the extero-anterior corner of the wing, which is abruptly rounded; thence the anterior border of the wing extends nearly straight inward to a somewhat broad curved sinus adjacent to the columella, which sinus corresponds to the anterior canal in other species; inner border of the falciform process broadly concave; and between that process and the spire the distal border of the wing is shortly concave and a little reflexed, suggestive of a broad posterior canal, especially as the anterior canal is more than usually broad; inner lip provided with a distinct callus, which in some cases at least extends beyond the distal end of the aperture across the next volution; columella not much produced in front; volutions of the spire marked by many longitudinally oblique folds, which extend to the suture on the proximal side of the volutions, but not much beyond the middle on the distal side, and do not appear at all on the body volution or wing.

The whole surface marked by fine revolving striæ, which are more distinct upon the last volution and wing; last volution also marked by a moderately strong revolving carina, which extends outward upon the wing and is continued to the point of the falciform process.

Length, sixteen millimeters; breadth across the body volution, including the wing, twelve millimeters.

This species resembles *A. Americana* Meek and Hayden in general form and surface markings, but it differs from that shell by its large anterior sinus, the inflection of the anterior border, and the reflexion of the posterior border of the wing, and also in the general shape of the wing.

Position and locality.—Sulphur Creek Group; Upper Kanab, Utah.

Anchura prolabiata (sp. nov.).—Shell rather above medium size, subfusiform; spire elongated and tapering, with nearly straight sides, to a point; volutions, nine or ten, convex, the last one proportionally more enlarged than the others; suture impressed; wing large, broad, its outer border nearly straight or slightly convex, its anterior and posterior corners abruptly rounded; posterior border bearing a strong, broad, blunt process about midway between the spire and the outer margin of the wing, the outer margin of the process having a direction parallel with that of the outer margin of the wing; posterior border of the wing concave between the outer corner and the base of the process, and also regularly and continuously concave from the spire to the end of the process; anterior border of the wing broadly and regularly concave to the base of the anterior canal, which is apparently rather short.

Inner lip unknown.

Surface of the volutions of the spire marked by numerous vertical or slightly oblique folds or ridges, which disappear upon the body volution and wing; these folds are crossed by numerous fine revolving raised lines, which are hardly visible without the aid of a lens, except those adjacent to the sutures, which are stronger; these revolving lines are perceptible upon the body volution, but are very faint upon the wing. No revolving ridge passes out upon the wing from the body volution, such as is common upon shells of this genus.

Length about four and a half centimeters; breadth, measured across the wing and body volution, twenty-nine millimeters; diameter of the body volution, fifteen millimeters.

This species differs from all others known to me by the projection of the outer border of the wing beyond the posterior process.

Position and locality.—Sulphur Creek Group; Upper Kanab and Sink Spring, Utah.

Genus LUNATIA Gray.

Lunatia Utahensis (sp. nov.).—Shell globose; spire small, acute, but not much extended; volutions about eight, the last one much inflated, suture moderately impressed; aperture semilunar, somewhat abruptly rounded anteriorly, callus of the inner lip apparently not much thickened, but thicker anteriorly than posteriorly. Surface marked by the ordinary lines of growth.

Length from the apex to the anterior end of the aperture about four centimeters; diameter about three centimeters.

Position and locality.—Salt Wells Group; Coalville, Utah.

Genus GONIOBASIS Lea.

Goniobasis Cleburni (sp. nov.).—Shell large, gradually tapering from the last volution to the apex, the sides of the spire being only slightly convex; volutions apparently nine or ten, gradually increasing in size, the last one not being proportionally larger than the others; suture slightly impressed; sides of the volutions nearly flat or slightly convex, the outer and anterior sides of the last one broadly and regularly convex; aperture ovate; outer lip broadly sinuate.

Surface of the spire marked by strong longitudinal or slightly flexed and oblique ridges or folds which disappear toward the aperture of the last volution. Upon the anterior surface of the last volution beyond the distal end of the aperture, there are several slightly raised revolving lines, and the edges of the vertical plications are also sometimes seen to be faintly crenulated as if by incipient revolving lines.

The specimens of the collection have all lost the apex, but the length of a full grown one is estimated at five centimeters; diameter of the last volution, nineteen millimeters.

This is the largest species of *Goniobasis* known to occur at the locality where it was found, and which has furnished three other distinct species.

The specific name is given in honor of Mr. W. Cleburn, division engineer of the Union Pacific Railroad.

Position and locality.—Point of Rocks Group; Bear River Valley, near Mellis Station, Wyoming.

Goniobasis chrysaloidea (sp. nov.).—Shell of medium size, gradually tapering from the last volution to the apex; volutions about seven or eight, those of the spire slightly convex, the last one broadly rounded to the anterior end; suture impressed, the apparent impression being increased by the projecting fold of the distal edge of each volution, which is appressed against the proximal edge of the next preceding one.

Surface marked by more or less distinct longitudinal, slightly bent folds, which are crossed by several revolving lines that appear only upon the folds and not between them, giving them a knotted or crenulated appearance; anterior surface of the last volution also marked by distinct raised revolving lines.

Length twenty-eight millimeters; diameter of the last volution, nine millimeters.

This species differs from *G. chrysalis* Meek in its much larger size, much greater apical angle, straighter sides, and in the details of its ornamentation.

Position and locality.—Point of Rocks Group; Bear River Valley, near Mellis Station, Wyoming.

Genus VIVIPARUS Montfort.

Viviparus Panguitchensis (sp. nov.).—Shell elongate-trochiform; spire considerably produced in the case of some of the examples, but less so in others, convex-conical, diminishing more rapidly near the apex than at the proximal half of the shell; apex acute; volutions about six, flattened upon the outer side, especially the last two volutions; anterior side of the last volution broadly rounded and forming a more or less distinct angle with the outer side; the distal side of each volution concave to receive the convex proximal side of the next preceding one, but projects a little beyond it so that an angular shoulder is formed upon the proximal side of the suture.

Aperture subtrihedral in outline.

Surface marked by the ordinary lines of growth, and also by numerous minute, raised revolving striæ, upon both the outer and anterior sides of the volutions.

There is considerable variation in the flattening of the outer side of the volutions in different examples and in different parts of the same example. The volutions near the apex of all the shells are usually convex and not much if at all flattened; in some cases the outer side of the last volution is broadly convex, while in others it is not only flattened but a little concave, especially the part nearest the suture.

Length of an average sized example, thirty millimeters; diameter of the last volution, twenty millimeters.

Genus ODONTOBASIS Meek.

Odontobasis buccinoidea (sp. nov.).—Shell of medium size somewhat robust; volutions six or seven, regularly convex; suture faintly impressed; surface marked by somewhat strong longitudinal folds which end at the suture upon the proximal side of the volutions of the spire, but do not quite reach the suture upon the distal side, and upon the last volution they die out before reaching the anterior end of the shell; the whole surface also marked by somewhat coarse revolving raised lines, which in crossing the longitudinal folds give them a crenulated appearance. The revolving lines upon a narrow space on the proximal side of the suture, and also upon the space in front of the revolving furrow of the columella, are finer than the others. Odontoid process not very prominent, forming a small angular projection at the end of the revolving furrow of the columella.

Length, thirty-seven millimeters; diameter of the last volution, twenty-two millimeters; but these proportions vary considerably in different shells of the species.

Position and locality.—Point of Rocks Group; two miles west of Point of Rocks, Wyoming.

TERTIARY PERIOD.

Mollusca.

Conchifera.

Genus UNIO Retzius.

Unio petrinus (sp. nov.).—Shell very large, transversely elongate, moderately thick; test massive; basal and dorsal margins subparallel; the latter broadly but slightly convex and the former nearly straight or faintly emarginate about, or a little behind the middle; front abruptly rounded; postero-dorsal and postero-basal margins somewhat abruptly rounded to the posterior margin, giving, in some cases, a subtruncate appearance to the posterior end of the shell; beaks depressed, situated near the anterior end; umbones broad; hinge massive, both cardinal and lateral teeth being very strong.

Surface apparently marked in no other manner than by the ordinary lines and imbrications of growth. The outer prismatic layer is well preserved, and the umbones, like those of all the species of *Unio* I have examined, from the Mesozoic and Cenozoic strata of that region, appear to have suffered, while living, no erosion, such as is common in the case of the recent Unionidae of the Mississippi and its tributaries.

Length of the largest example in the collection, fifteen centimeters; height of the same, seven and a half centimeters. In the case of young examples the length is proportionally greater.

This species may be readily distinguished from all others at all likely to be confounded with it by its great size, elongate form, and its subparallel dorsal and ventral margins.

Position and locality.—Bitter Creek Group; Black Buttes, Wyoming.

Unio propheticus (sp. nov.).—Shell small or of medium size, obliquely subovate in marginal outline, moderately thick, the greatest thickness being a little below the umbones; test rather thick; umbones prominent, directed forward; beaks curved inward and forward, reaching as far as, or a little farther than, the front of the shell; front broad, nearly perpendicular; front margin slightly convex above, but abruptly rounded to the basal margin below; basal margin broadly rounded, or sometimes a little straightened at the middle; posterior extremity abruptly rounded; dorsal margin broadly rounded obliquely downward to the posterior extremity; the dorsum of each valve elevated and its margin flexed inward and downward to the cardinal ligament, so that the latter is hidden from sight by side view of the shell.

Surface marked by the ordinary lines of growth and by numerous fine radiating striæ, which appear also in the substance of exfoliated portions of the test.

Length, five centimeters; height from base to umbones, thirty-seven millimeters.

This species is of the type of *U. clavus* Lamarck, which it much resembles in general aspect. It is so different from any other known species of *Unio* in the Tertiary rocks of America that it cannot be mistaken for any of them.

Position and locality.—Bitter Creek Group; Black Buttes, Wyoming.

Unio brachyopisthus (sp. nov.).—Shell small or of medium size, somewhat gibbous, subcircular in marginal outline, the length and height being about equal; umbones broad, not prominent; beaks depressed, situated near the middle of the dorsum; postero-dorsal portion broad, depressed so that rounded umbonal ridges are formed, which extend to the postero-basal extremity, and the hinge ligament is hidden from sight by side view of the shell.

Surface marked only by the ordinary lines and lamellations of growth.

Length and height of the largest example discovered, each forty-four millimeters.

This species may be readily distinguished from all others by its subcircular, marginal outline and its extremely short and abruptly-rounded posterior. The shortness of the posterior portion does not appear so conspicuously in the young shell as in the adult, because the additions by growth are made more rapidly upon the basal and antero-basal borders than elsewhere.

Position and locality.—Bitter Creek Group; Black Buttes, Wyoming.

*Unio Shoshonensis** (sp. nov.).—Shell of ordinary size, broadly subel-

* The so-called tribal name is applied by the Indians themselves to their *country* or land, not to the tribe.

liptical or subovate in marginal outline; valves moderately and somewhat regularly convex; test not massive; dorsal margin broadly arched; front margin regularly rounded; basal margin broadly and regularly rounded; posterior margin somewhat abruptly rounded, the postero-dorsal portion sometimes obliquely truncated and sometimes sloping to a more prominent posterior extremity; beaks well defined, but not prominent; umbones broadly convex.

Surface marked by the ordinary lines and lamellations of growth.

Length of the largest example in the collection, nearly seven centimeters; height of the same, five centimeters.

This species bears some resemblance to *U. Haydeni* Meek, from the Bridger Group, but differs from that species in its larger size, its convex instead of straight dorsal margin, its rather more prominent umbones, and its greater proportionate height.

Position and locality.—Upper Green River Group; Henry's Fork and Alkali Stage Station, Wyoming; also in Lower Green River Group; west side of Snake River, six miles north of Junction Mountain; Cliffs, four miles northeastward from Vermilion Cañon; and Dry Mountains, Northwestern Colorado.

Genus CORBICULA Mühlfeldt.

Corbicula Powelli (sp. nov.).—Shell rather small, subelliptical in marginal outline; valves thin, slightly but somewhat uniformly convex; beaks small, not prominent; cardinal and lateral teeth well developed; both anterior and posterior lateral teeth finely crenulated transversely; middle cardinal tooth of each valve having a shallow vertical groove along its middle; a very faintly-raised ridge extends downward from beneath the beak on the inner surface of each valve, and dies out before reaching the base. Surface nearly smooth, but marked by fine lines of growth.

Length, twenty-three millimeters; height, from beak to base, fifteen millimeters; thickness, eight millimeters.

This shell differs from typical forms of *Corbicula* in its elliptical outline, slight thickness, and in the delicacy of the test. All the species associated with it, except an oyster, are exclusively marine forms.

Specific name given in honor of Prof. J. W. Powell, geologist in charge of the Second Division United States Geological and Geographical Survey.

Position and locality.—Tertiary strata, probably late Eocene; Bijou Basin, forty miles east of Denver, Colorado.

Genus PISIDIUM Pfeiffer.

Pisidium saginatum (sp. nov.).—Shell small, subcircular in marginal outline; anterior side slightly longer than the posterior; valves inflated, the convexity from beak to base being sometimes irregular in consequence of one or more abrupt concentric flexures.

Surface marked by ordinary lines of growth.

Length, five millimeters; height, five and a half millimeters; thickness, five and a half millimeters.

Position and locality.—Bitter Creek Group; Almy coal mines, near Evanston, Wyoming.

Genus MESODESMA Deshayes.

Mesodesma Bishopi (sp. nov.).—Shell small, subovate or subtrihedral in marginal outline, moderately gibbous; umbonal ridges somewhat distinct, the posterior pair more so than the others; umbones prominent; beaks small; both anterior and posterior lateral teeth well developed and transversely striated, as in *Corbicula;* cartilage pit beneath the beak small; cardinal tooth in front of it rather small and V-shaped; pallial sinus deep; muscular scars distinct; right valve unknown.

Surface nearly smooth, and marked by very fine lines of growth.

Length, about one centimeter; height, about six millimeters.

This shell differs from typical forms of *Mesodesma* in its V-shaped cardinal tooth, transversely striated lateral teeth, and deep pallial sinus.

Specific name given in honor of Prof. F. M. Bishop, of Salt Lake City, Utah.

Position and locality.—Tertiary strata, probably late Eocene; Bijou Basin, forty miles east of Denver, Colorado.

Genus CORBULA Bruguiere.

Corbula subundifera (sp. nov.).—Shell of ordinary size; marginal outline subtrihedral or subovate; valves only slightly unequal; beaks contiguous; umbones moderately prominent; beaks incurved and directed a little forward; front obliquely truncate, concave, producing indistinctly, defined anterior umbonal ridges; abruptly rounded below to the basal margin, which is broadly rounded; posterior extremity low, prominent, and sharply rounded; postero-dorsal margin sloping from the dorsum to the posterior extremity; this margin of each valve is bent abruptly inward and downward, producing a narrow, shallow furrow, bordered at each side by a somewhat prominent ridge, which extends from behind the beak to the posterior extremity of the shell.

Surface marked by numerous, more or less strongly elevated, concentric folds, which disappear before reaching the anterior and posterior margins. Between these folds, and upon those parts of the surface unmarked by them, the surface is marked by ordinary lines of growth.

Length, twenty-five millimeters; height, eighteen millimeters.

This species closely resembles *C. undifer* Meek, from the Point of Rocks Group at Rock Springs, Wyoming, but differs from that species in its less extended posterior extremity, its less angular posterior umbonal ridges, its less sharply elevated, concentric folds, and in wanting the peculiar flattening of the umbones between the posterior and anterior umbonal ridges which that species possesses.

Position and locality.—Bitter Creek Group; Point of Rocks, Wyoming.

Gasteropoda.

Genus SUCCINEA Draparnaud.

Succinea papillispira (sp. nov.).—Shell rather small, ovate or subelliptical in lateral outline; spire minute but prominent; last volution much expanded and broadly convex.

Surface marked by the ordinary lines of growth, and, under a lens, faint, close-set, revolving striæ are to be seen.

Length, eleven millimeters; breadth of aperture, six millimeters.

This species possesses peculiar interest from the fact that it is the first *Succinea* that has been discovered in the Tertiary strata of that great region. Although there are so few salient, specific characters in any species of the genus, this shell may be readily recognized by its minute spire, the length of which is only a very small part of the full length of the shell, and also by its broadly convex last volution.

Position and locality.—Upper Green River Group; Alkali Stage Station, twenty-two miles northwward from Green River Station, Wyoming.

Genus HELIX Linnæus.

Helix riparia (sp. nov.).—Shell of medium size, subconical; volutions about five, moderately convex; suture slightly impressed; spire considerably produced for a species of this genus, equal in length to about three-sevenths of the entire length of the shell; proximal side of the last volution broadly and continuously rounded from the outer side; umbilicus small, rather deep; outer lip unknown; aperture oblique, broadly subovate in outline.

Surface marked by the ordinary distinct lines of growth.

Position and locality.—Lower Green River Group; eight miles below Green River Station, Wyoming.

Helix peripheria (sp. nov.).—Shell of ordinary size, sublenticular in form; spire low and broadly convex; volutions about five, each broadly convex between the sutures; the last volution abruptly, almost angularly, rounded at the periphery of the shell; under side broadly convex and rounded sharply into a small, deep umbilicus. Lip apparently not reflexed.

Surface marked by the ordinary distinct lines of growth.

Peripheral diameter, about fifteen millimeters.

Position and locality.—Bitter Creek Group; south base of Pine Valley Mountains, Utah.

Genus PUPA Lamarck.

Pupa incolata (sp. nov.).—Shell small, turreted, regularly tapering to the apex; volutions about six, convex, regularly increasing in size to the aperture, the last one not being contracted; suture impressed; aperture subovate in outline, its length a little more than one-third that of the whole shell; outer lip thickened, reflexed.

Length, five millimeters; diameter of last volution, two millimeters.

This species is of about the same size as the recent species *Pupa fallax* Say, and closely resembles it in form and general character.

Position and locality.—Upper Green River Group; Henry's Fork, Wyoming, where it is associated with the following species:

Pupa arenula (sp. nov.).—Shell minute, ovate; volutions five or six, convex; suture impressed; aperture contracted; teeth of the aperture unknown.

Length, two millimeters.

This shell is of about the same size and shape as *Vertigo ovata* Say, and in general aspect it closely resembles that species. It appears, however, to be a true pupa; at least the characters which should separate it from that genus are not apparent.

Position and locality.—Upper Green River Group; Henry's Fork, Wyoming.

Genus NERITINA Lamarck.

Neritina volvilineata (sp. nov.).—Shell small, subovate in lateral outline; volutions three and a half or four, regularly convex; spire short, as is common in this genus, but somewhat prominent; suture slightly impressed; aperture semilunar; inner lip broad, plain, flat, its inner edge not clearly seen, but if crenulated at all, it is not conspicuously so.

Surface marked by numerous raised, revolving lines of unequal size, which increase in number by implantation as the volutions increase in size; the revolving lines crossed by the usual lines of growth, which give the surface, upon some parts, at least, an indistinctly cancellated appearance under the lens.

Greatest diameter of the largest example discovered, nine millimeters; height, lying with its aperture upon the table, five millimeters.

Position and locality.—Bitter Creek Group; Black Buttes, Wyoming.

Genus MELANIA Lamarck.

Melania Larunda (sp. nov.).—Shell large, elongate; volutions apparently eleven or twelve, uniformly increasing in size, moderately convex, bearing a revolving row of prominent, strong, outward projecting, laterally sharpened tubercles, which extend from the apex to the aperture; suture linear;

surface of the volutions on the distal side of the row of tubercles without revolving striæ, or having one or two indistinct ones; surface upon the proximal side of the row of tubercles marked by numerous elevated, slightly waved, revolving striæ, which are more distinct about midway of the space than elsewhere, and are very close together near the columella. Only three or four of these striæ appear upon the volutions of the spire, because the remainder are covered by each succeeding volution. Aperture oval or subelliptical; outer lip having a broad, shallow notch, the retreating angle of which is opposite the row of tubercles, anterior portion moderately extended and abruptly rounded to the columella.

Length, about nine and a half centimeters, when entire; diameter of the last volution, twenty-two millimeters.

This species is more nearly like a true *Melania* of Old World type than any of the so-called Melanians of North America with which I am acquainted.

Position and locality.—Tertiary strata ; Crow Creek, Colorado, where it was obtained by Mr. W. Cleburn.

Genus HYDROBIA Hartmann.

Hydrobia recta (sp. nov.).—Shell small, very slender, sides of the spire straight; volutions convex, apparently twelve or more, increasing regularly and uniformly in size from apex to aperture. Surface marked by the ordinary lines of growth.

Length of one example in the collection, nine millimeters; diameter of the last volution of the same, one and a half millimeters. Other examples indicate a length nearly twice as great as that here given.

Position and locality.—Bitter Creek Group; Almy coal-mines, near Evanston, Wyoming.

Hydrobia Utahensis (sp. nov.).—Shell rather small, elongate-conical, spire moderately produced, its sides straight or nearly so; volutions about six, convex; suture impressed; aperture ovate, a little longer than wide, its distal extremity slightly angular, its anterior end prominent and rounded. Surface marked by the ordinary lines of growth.

Length, about five millimeters; diameter of the last volution, nearly two millimeters.

Position and locality.—Bitter Creek Group; west base of Mu-si-ni-a Plateau, 1,000 feet below the summit, Utah.

Genus VIVIPARUS Montfort.

Viviparus plicapressus (sp. nov.).—Shell rather under medium size; spire, conical; sides nearly straight; volutions about seven, convex, the outer and anterior convexity of the last one continuous and uniform; suture impressed. At the distal side of each volution there is a small, more or less distinct, revolving groove or furrow, by which that part is folded and closely appressed against the proximal side of the adjacent volution, the fold forming a slight projection upon the proximal side of the suture. Surface marked by the ordinary lines of growth, and upon some examples there appears a faintly raised revolving line or incipient angulation near the middle of the outer side of the volutions.

Length, about twenty-five millimeters; breadth of last volution, twelve millimeters.

Position and locality.—Bitter Creek Group; Black Buttes, Wyoming.

Genus LEIOPLAX Troschel.

Leioplax ? turricula (sp. nov.).—Shell of ordinary size, elongate conical; volutions about eight, gradually increasing in size; convex angular, the angle being sharp, prominent, and situated a little in advance of the middle of the side of the volutions of the spire; suture slightly impressed; last volution broadly rounded from the revolving angle to the umbilicus; umbilicus narrow, deep and marked within by two or three revolving lines. Surface upon both sides of the revolving angle of the volutions marked more or less distinctly by two or three revolving raised lines.

Length, thirty millimeters; diameter of last volution, fifteen millimeters. This shell has the aspect of some forms of *Goniobasis*, but the presence of an umbilicus excludes it from that genus. It also varies from the typical forms of *Leioplax*, but appears to be more nearly related to this than to any other established genus and is accordingly referred to it provisionally.

Position and locality.—Bitter Creek Group; Black Buttes, Wyoming.

Genus TULOTOMA Haldeman.

Tulotoma Thompsoni (sp. nov.).—Shell moderately large, having the general form of shells of this genus; spire elevated, its sides broadly convex; volutions six or seven, their outer side flattened or only slightly convex; proximal side of the last volution also flattened or slightly convex, producing a more or less prominent revolving angle between them; suture linear or faintly impressed; umbilical chink minute or wanting. Surface of the three or four first volutions of the spire convex and unmarked, except by the ordinary lines of growth, but the last two or three volutions are conspicuously marked by prominent tubercles in two or three revolving rows, extending to the aperture, and which sometimes seem to be connected in their respective rows by slightly raised revolving lines. The distal row of tubercles is strongest and is situated near the suture, on its proximal side. The proximal row is immediately upon the distal side of the suture, the tubercles of which are more elongated transversely than the others, but not so prominent. Between these two rows there is sometimes another obscure one, but upon some shells it is reduced to only a raised line.

Length of a large example, thirty-eight millimeters; diameter of the last volution, twenty-five millimeters.

This shell resembles the recent species *T. magnifica* Conrad, but differs from that shell in its more convex volutions, its faintly impressed suture, and the different arrangement of its tubercles. It also resembles *T.* (*Viviparus*) *Strossmayeriana* Pilar, as published by Brusina, but differs in the less convexity of its volutions, especially the proximal side, and in the different character and position of the tubercles that adorn its surface.

Genus PHORUS Montfort.

Phorus exoneratus (sp. nov.).—Shell small, concavo-convex, the convexity of the upper side being slight and nearly uniform; volutions one and a half or two; suture not distinctly shown; surface apparently quite plain or marked only by lines of growth; without extraneous bodies attached to the periphery; aperture very oblique and very narrow.

Diameter of the shell, thirteen millimeters.

Position and locality.—Tertiary strata, probably late Eocene; Bijou Basin, forty miles east of Denver, Colorado.

CHAPTER IV.

GEOGRAPHIC DISTRIBUTION OF THE GEOLOGICAL FORMATIONS IN THE UINTA MOUNTAINS

AND A DISTRICT OF COUNTRY ADJACENT THERETO.

I propose to give a brief description of the geology of a part of the Uinta Mountains and a district of country lying to the north, stretching beyond the Union Pacific Railroad. The region is embraced within the meridians of 108° 30′ and 109° 52′.5 west longitude, and between the parallels of 40° 15′ and 41° 40′ north latitude. The Green River runs through the middle of the district, having a general northerly and southerly course, but from which it deflects in great curves.

The Uinta Mountains are composed of elevated valleys, tables, and peaks, the latter having a very irregular distribution, due to geological structure. The axis of the range is the axis of a great flexure, having a total displacement (or exhibiting an upheaval) of more than 30,000 feet. This flexure terminates on the east in the little valley separating the Uinta Mountains from Junction Mountain. The latter represents a short, abrupt, anticlinal flexure, having a north and south axis The Uinta uplift has brought up all of the Mesozoic and Carboniferous Groups with the Uinta Sandstone, and in one locality a still older group of rocks, viz, the Red Creek Quartzite, is exposed. On the flanks of the range, both to the north and south, Cenozoic groups are found. The grand Uinta displacement is only a flexure in its general characteristics, as the down-throw on the north side of the axis is, in some localities, in part produced by faulting; while on the south side of the axis faults are found having throws on the north side of the fissure. Thus the faults, instead of being a part of the general flexure of the slope, are opposed to it, and the faults themselves, in a part of their courses, change to flexures. In addition to the complications thus mentioned, there are other minor flexures within the greater. All of these complications will be spoken of further on.

Within the district which I undertake to describe, another great flexure must be mentioned. This has a north and south axis, and brings to view in the region north of Aspen Mountain the Sulphur Creek Cretaceous. On the flanks of this flexure we find the Salt Wells and Point of Rocks Cretaceous, and the Bitter Creek, Lower Green River, Upper Green River and Bridger Tertiaries, all of which groups took part in the movement which made this flexure; but there is no evidence that the Brown's Park Group or the Bishop Mountain Conglomerate was involved in the movement. The southern extremity of the flexure is well seen at the head of Red Creek, where the rocks dipping south from the end of the Aspen flexure become horizontal, and again are turned up by the great Uinta flexure, thus forming a synclinal between the flank of the greater flexure and the end of the lesser. The characteristics of this displacement also will be discussed hereafter.

I now proceed to describe the geographic distribution of the groups or formations in this district, and to give their general stratigraphic characteristics, and also to note some interesting facts concerning their conformities and unconformities.

All of the groups of rocks tabulated in Chapter II are found within this area except the Grand Cañon Group and the Grand Cañon Schists.

RED CREEK QUARTZITE.

The only locality where this group has been found within the territory embraced in the discussion is in the vicinity of Red Creek, a small tributary of the Green River, emptying into the latter at the head or western end of Brown's Park. Its geographic extension is well shown on the map, and needs no further description.

Red Creek separates Quartz Mountain and Mount Wheeler by a tortuous, flaring, craggy cañon whose sides rise to an altitude of about 2,000 feet above the creek, and here the interior structure of the group is revealed.

The group embraced under the name is the lowest horizon found within the region under discussion. It is composed in large part of a quartzite, very crystalline and white, and having the general aspect of virgin quartz. Only in a few places is the original granular structure apparent. Intimately associated with the quartzite are very irregular aggregations of hornblendic and micaceous schists, the latter sometimes bearing garnets. Originally these schists were perhaps argillaceous strata between the thicker strata of pure siliceous sandstone. The whole group has been greatly metamorphosed, producing a crystallization that in many places has quite, and in the remainder almost, obliterated the original granular or sedimentary structure, so far as it is apparent to the naked eye. Besides this recrystallization they have been profoundly plicated, or I should rather say implicated. It is only in a general way that any original stratification can be observed. This original structure can best be seen when standing at some distance from the beds to be studied.

Its relation to the Uinta Sandstone above it is exhibited in the lower end of the cañon of Red Creek and along the escarpment which faces Brown's Park on the south side of Mount Wheeler, up the cañon of an intermittent stream four miles farther west, and also up the cañon of Willow Creek. Other facts relating to the junction of the two groups are seen on the summit of Quartz Mountain. These facts are as follows: A part of the Uinta Group, which is later and higher, terminates abruptly against the quartzite. The thickness of the beds thus limited is about 8,000 feet, and as the beds are traced from the southward to this plane of junction they rapidly change from finer to coarser sediments, often appearing as conglomerates in the vicinity of the quartzite; but the total thickness of the beds is not increased by the transition from finer to coarser sediments, though particular beds may thicken, such thickening being compensated by the thinning out or disappearance of others. In these conglomerates the coarser materials are of quartzite, hornblendic rock, &c., similar to those of the Red Creek Group, held in a matrix of siliceous, hornblendic and micaceous sands, which are quite ferruginous. The position of the quartzite is on the flank of the great Uinta flexure, not its axis, and the junction of the lower two or three thousand feet of the Uinta Sandstone with the quartzite is not seen; while from two to three thousand feet of the upper members of the Uinta Sandstone were deposited over the summit of the quartzite.

From these facts we may safely infer that this was a great headland of quartzite standing out in the old Uinta Sea from some island, or perhaps from the mainland; that it rose above its waters as a lofty mountain, while from two to three thousand feet of these sandstones, whose junction with the quartzite is unseen, and while 8,000 feet of sandstone whose junction is seen, were deposited. Then this mountain headland was buried with two or three thousand feet of the upper members of the Uinta Group. During that great movement which began during Cenozoic time, and which has continued intermittantly unlil the present, and which has given us the Uinta upheaval, this quartzite behaved in a general way as an integral part of the sandstone, flexing when the sandstone flexed and faulting when the sandstone faulted. In the upper part of Figure 11 we have a diagram exhibiting

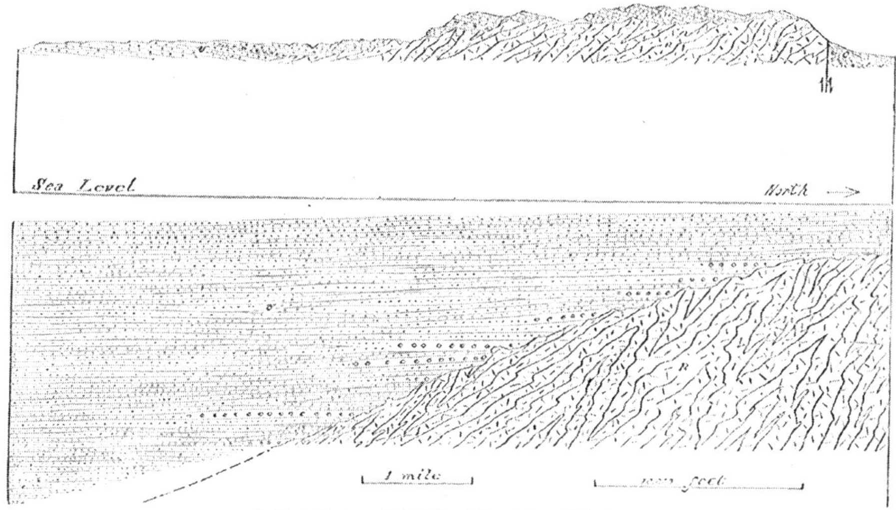

U. Uinta Group. *R.* Red Creek Quartzite. *C.* Cretaceous.

Fig. 11.—Section and diagram of the Red Creek Unconformity.

the relation of these two groups as now seen; the lower part of the same figure represents a restoration of the same section to the position these two groups held prior to the inception of the Uinta upheaval. It will be seen that the old shore line, in vertical outline, was now a bold cliff against which the waves of the Uinta Sea dashed, forming deep caverns in the mural rock, and then at other horizons was a retreating slope. A further study of the facts shows that on a horizontal plain the projecting rocks inclosed deep bays. But we must remember that as the beds were deposited denudation progressed; so that the slope seen does not represent it as it existed at any one time during the deposition of the beds, but only the slope which was finally produced. At the beginning of the Uinta epoch it must have been much steeper than it is represented in the diagram.

About 10,000 feet of the Uinta Sandstone is found to have been deposited against the old quartzite headland before it was buried by the upper members of the Uinta Group. Hence this headland must have been at least 10,000 feet high; but doubtless the quartzite itself was steadily denuded during this time, and we may suppose that it wasted away by erosion above quite as rapidly as it was buried below. Certainly this supposition is not violent; and this would lead to the conclusion that the great headland was 20,000 feet high at the time when the lowest known number of the Uinta Sandstone was formed. We may now with some degree of probability restore in imagination one feature of that ancient geography and see a mountain more gigantic in its proportions than any which now pierces the clouds floating over North America. Stand on the great plain by the Platte River and look at Long's Peak; on it pile all that can be seen of Pike's Peak from the banks of the Arkansas, and over these place all of Gray's Peak that stands above the same plain, and the mountain thus built up in imagination would not equal in altitude this quartzite mountain, whose feet were bathed in the old Unita Sea. Geologists have arrived at the conclusion that these quartzites and schistic rocks which appear over many portions of the earth were originally accumulated as sediments and subsequently metamorphosed. In the case of this group the metamorphism was anterior to the deposition of the sandstones as seen from the facts mentioned above, viz, that the sandstones are composed of material denued from the metamorphic group. But the sandstones have great thickness and underlie unconformably an extensive series of Carboniferous rocks. From this we infer that the quartzite is of great geological antiquity.

UINTA GROUP.

As shown by the map, the great mass of the Uinta Range is composed of sandstones of this group. Intercalated with the sandstones some shales are found, the latter being arenaceous, with a small portion of argillaceous material. In a few places the sandstones have assumed a crystalline structure, forming a quasi quartzite. The whole group is exceedingly ferruginous. Thin seams of clay ironstone are often seen to separate the strata of sandstone, and many of the shales contain large quantities of iron. Many of the sandstones are seen to be ferruginous on the interior when broken, but some of the beds are buff and light gray on fresh surfaces. The general color of the walls of the cañons and mountain escarpments is red and brown, due to the more complete oxidation of the iron. In the cañons and gulches, where bays of quiet water are formed, considerable accumulations of steel-gray iron sands may often be seen. These sometime form a pigment which the Indians of the region were accustomed to use as paint in former days.

The great mass of the sandstones are fine grained, but occasionally throughout the series strata of pebbles are found; near its junction with the Red Creek Quartzite these are conglomerates. Those peculiarities or markings of strata, known as ripple marks, are very abundant at many horizons from the top to the lowest known strata and mud rills, and rain drop impressions are sometimes found. A very few concretions have been found in the group. Weeks and months have been spent in the search yet no fossils have been found. Within the territory embraced in the description the base of the group is never seen. The Green River runs along the axis of the Uinta flexure for many miles but its bed is yet in the Uinta Sandstone so that it is impossible to determine the entire thickness of the group, but that which is exposed has a wonderful developement, no less than 12,500 feet of these sandstones and shales being seen.

I have already stated my reasons for considering this formation to be older than Carboniferous, and I have given it provisionally a Devonian color on the map. Professor Marsh in his article in the American Journal of Science and Arts, in the March number of 1871, "On the geology of the eastern Uinta Mountains," in speaking of these formations says, "* * * * and a subsequent examination of apparently a portion of the same series, on the western side of the river, rendered it probable that a part of them at least are of Silurian age." In that article the professor does not mention the finding of any fossils in the formation, and on what facts his statement is based I do not know; but his conclusion is entitled to great consideration, for, although his study of this region was of short duration, he fully appreciated the great series of formations brought into view by the Uinta upheaval, and in clear comprehensive language gives, in the article mentioned, a summary statement of the structural geology of the eastern Uintas.

The following section was made by Mr. John F. Steward in the summer of 1871. It commences at Beehive Point at the head of Red Cañon and ends at the foot of the cañon where the river debouches into Brown's Park. Lower members of the group are seen farther down the river but are not brought into the section.

Fig. 12.—SECTION OF UINTA SANDSTONE EXPOSED IN RED CAÑON.

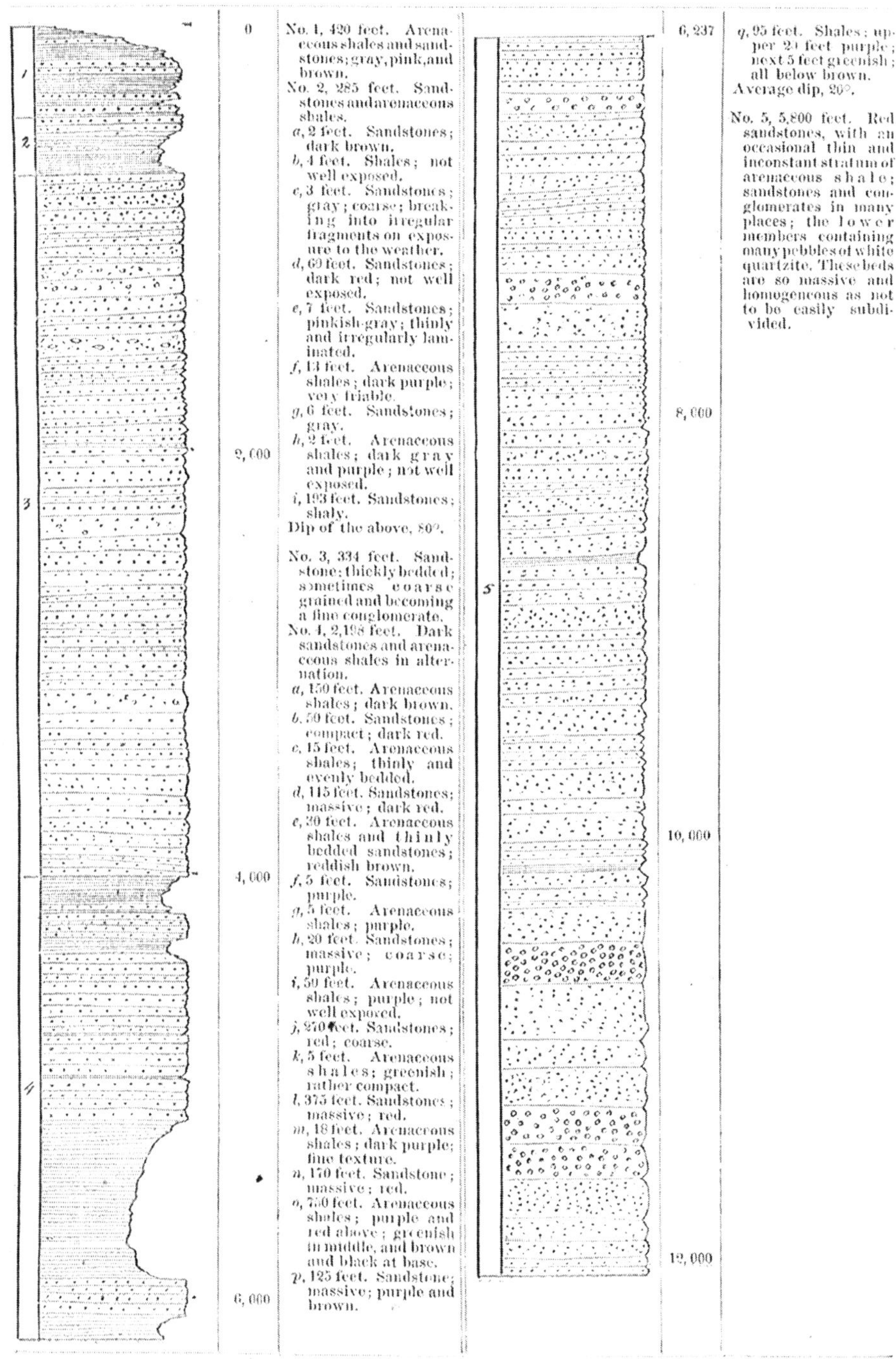

A good section can be obtained by passing over the Ó-wi-yu-kuts plateau. On the northeast, this plateau culminates in a high ridge of cherty and brecciated limestone which is the base of the Red Wall Group. By starting at the eastern extremity and foot of this ridge and going southwestward across the plateau and descending into Brown's Park until the axis of the flexure is reached, you pass over the upturned edges of the Uinta Sandstone. This section gives a thickness to the beds of more than 13,000 feet. The factors used in the measurement were the distance between the extremities of the line along which the section was made as determined by the topographers, and the observed dips along the line at subequal distances of about 200 yards. In 1871 we attempted to make a section from the axis, through the Cañon of Lódore, but the difficulty of navigating the river was so great that we could not perform the task with satisfaction; but the thickness of the beds found along this line was not less than 13,000 feet.

The Uinta Sandstone crops out along the base of the wall through the upper part of Whirlpool Cañon. On the north side of the Yampa Plateau, south of the Yampa River there is a monoclinal flexure and fault by which the Carboniferous rocks are uplifted several thousand feet. There are three cañons running across this displacement which cut through the Carboniferous rocks and reveal in their walls several hundred feet of the upper members of the Uinta Group. The anticlinal uplift which forms Junction Mountain is bisected by the Yampa River. The gorge through which the river runs is called Junction Mountain Cañon. In the heart of the cañon Uinta Sandstones are seen.

UNCONFORMITY AT THE SUMMIT OF THE UINTA GROUP.

A period of erosion or dry land condition intervened between the deposition of the Uinta Sandstones and of the Carboniferous Groups.

In Whirlpool Cañon the red sandstones of the Uinta Group are thrust up into the sandstones and shales of the Lodore Group, and in some cases almost sever them; that is, the Uinta Sandstones were deeply eroded into abrupt valleys with steep cliffs, some of them 400 feet high, anterior to the deposition of the Lodore Group. There is a difference of dip between the two groups of about four degrees, the lower group having the greater inclination to the south.

The following section illustrates the facts observed here:

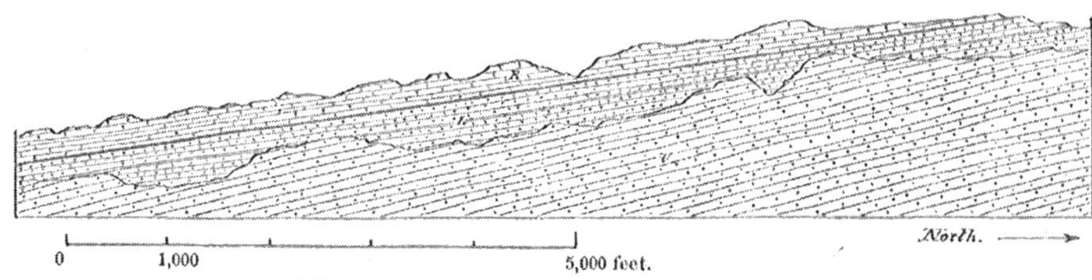

R. Red Wall Group. *L.* Lodore Group. *U.* Uinta Group.

Fig. 13.—Section showing the unconformity between the Lodore and Uinta Groups in Whirlpool Cañon.

At the foot of the Cañon of Lodore the unconformity is represented by a difference of dip of from 5 to 6 degrees, and the Lodore Group steadily overlaps the upper members of the Uinta Group, cutting off more than 2,000 feet of the latter. Here, also, the Uinta Sandstone is protruded into the Lodore shales. These facts are illustrated in the following section:

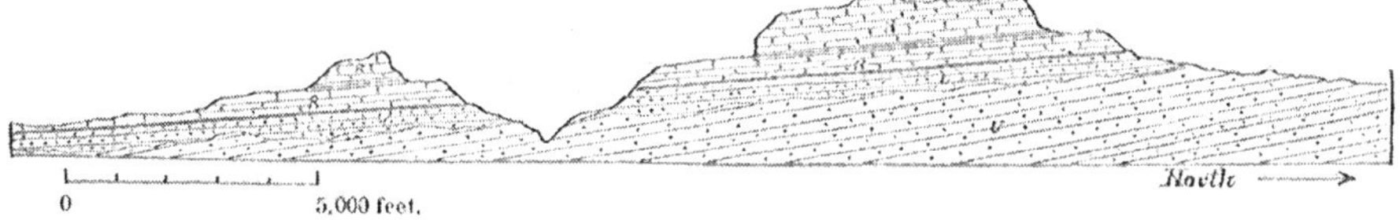

R. Red Wall Group. *L.* Lodore Group. *U.* Uinta Group.

Fig. 14.—Section showing the unconformity between the Lodore and Uinta Groups in the Cañon of Lodore.

On the northeast side of the O-wi-yu-kuts Plateau the Lodore Group is wanting, and the massive limestone at the base of the Red Wall Group rests upon the Uinta Sandstone. In passing from the northwest end of the ridge along the strike of the sandstone to the southeast, the upper beds of the Uinta Sandstone are seen to disappear, having been cut off by erosion before the deposition of the limestone, and there is from one to two thousand feet more of the Uinta Sandstone at the former end of the ridge than at the latter.

This unconformity can also be seen in the cañon of Junction Mountain, and it has been observed on the southern side of the Uinta Mountains, west of the district covered by the map, in the cañon cut by the tributaries of the Uinta River.

THE CARBONIFEROUS GROUPS.

CERTAIN GEOGRAPHIC DISTRICTS DESIGNATED.

In describing the geographic distribution of the Carboniferous and Mesozoic Groups it will be found convenient to designate under general terms certain districts of country, as follows:

FLAMING GORGE DISTRICT.

There is a belt of country, extending from Bruce Mountain westward to the border of the map, where most of the Carboniferous and Mesozoic and certain of the Cenozoic formations are turned up on edge, so that in a limited area nearly all these groups can be studied. The Green River enters the Uinta Mountains by a flaring, brilliant, vermilion gorge, a conspicuous and well known locality, to which, several years ago, I gave the name Flaming Gorge, and this name has been generally accepted. I shall call this the Flaming Gorge district.

PO CAÑON DISTRICT.

East of Bruce Mountain, for many miles, the Uinta displacement is chiefly by faulting, and with slight exception the Carboniferous and Mesozoic Groups have been carried down and are concealed. But southeast from Diamond Peak the displacement changes again into a flexure, and once more the Carboniferous and Mesozoic Groups are found turned up on edge. This region is at the eastern end of the O-wi-yu-kuts Plateau, the plateau itself culminating in a high monoclinal ridge at its eastern extremity, and the plateau is bounded on this side by a deep monoclinal cañon which divides it from a region of Mesozoic and higher Carboniferous hogbacks. This cañon is also a well marked and well known geographic feature. Some years ago I gave it the name Po Cañon, and that name has been accepted throughout the country. This I shall call the Po Cañon district.

YAMPA DISTRICT.

In the Yampa Plateau by a series of flexures and faults the whole Mesozoic and Carboniferous series are brought to view. East from the Yampa Plateau there is a simple anticlinal upheaval where all these groups are again seen. I shall call the Yampa Plateau and adjacent country, together with the region embraced in the Junction Mountain uplift, the Yampa district.

ISLAND PARK DISTRICT.

Finally, west of the lower end of the Cañon of Lodore and Whirlpool Cañon there is a zone stretching to the westward where all these groups are in like manner exposed. At the foot of Whirlpool Cañon lies the beautiful valley known as Island Park, which is embraced in this zone. I shall call this the Island Park district.

LODORE GROUP.

This group of rocks is seen in Lodore Cañon, from which locality it takes its name. Here it fills valleys in the Uinta Sandstone and buries the ancient cliffs and hills of the dry land period. These facts were set forth in the last section.

The group is composed of soft sandstones and shales with conglomerates at the base and against the ancient hill sides. Its outcrop on the northwest side of the cañon is of very limited extent and is not represented on the map, but on the southeast side of the cañon it mounts the wall for several miles and appears in Dunn's Cliff, where its thickness was measured and found to be 460 feet. Its outcrop is represented on the map by a narrow line. On the north side of the Uinta Mountains these rocks have been seen at but one point, viz, a little west of Beehive Point, and there is some uncertainty about this observation. Carboniferous fossils have been found in these beds.

The area of the outcrop at the bottom of Whirlpool Cañon is so narrow that the color has not been introduced on the map in that locality.

RED WALL GROUP.

Extensive outcrops of the Red Wall Group are found on the flanks of the Uinta Mountains. On the north side the entire group is composed chiefly of limestone, many of the beds being cherty. On the south side of the mountains many sandstones are intercalated with the limestone. About ten miles from Flaming Gorge in a southwestely direction, these beds are found dipping to the north, and as they are followed along the strike to the westward they are seen to rise in a high monoclinal ridge. This ridge is not well developed until we pass beyond the area embraced on the map. Another outcrop is seen on the northwest corner of the Ó-wi-yu-kuts Plateau; here the beds are standing vertically. On the eastern end of the same plateau, in the Po Cañon district, another outcrop appears where the beds dip a little north of east in a lofty monoclinal ridge. The central mass of Junction Mountain is Red Wall limestone, and the group crops out in an unbroken but irregular zone along the south side of the Uinta Mountains on the east side of the Cañon of Lodore, in the Escalante Péaks, and on the west side of the Cañon of Lodore in the Island Park district. The Ti-ra-yu-kuts like the Escalante Peaks are composed of the hard cherty limestones of the Red Wall Group and are true flanking peaks. Here the beds all dip to the south usually at a rather low angle, and along the northern margin of the outcrop the cherty limestones stand in peaks. Another outcrop is seen at the bottom of Split Mountain Cañon, and, last, these limestones are exposed on the Yampa Plateau on an escarpment formed by a fault or a monoclinal flexure which faces the Yampa River, and which is crowned by many towering peaks.

All these outcrops are well represented on the map.

LOWER AUBREY GROUP.

This group is made up of rather soft sandstones with intercalated limestones; altogether the rocks are much more friable than the last mentioned group, and they also yield much more readily to atmospheric degradation than the beds of the Upper Aubrey. Where the beds of the Red Wall and Upper Aubrey Groups stand in monoclinal ridges the beds of the Lower Aubrey are found in the inter-ridge or valley spaces. It is seen outcropping in the vicinity of Flaming Gorge and extending in a narrow zone westward beyond the region embraced on the map. On the east side of the O-wi-yu-kuts Plateau its outcrop can be traced along the eastern base of the monoclinal ridge, which is composed of Red Wall limestones as described above. Here the valley lies between the two monoclinal ridges and is known as Po Cañon. These beds are also found on both flanks of the Yampa Plateau and along the southern slope of the Uinta Mountains from its eastern extremity in a narrow zone to the western border of the region under discussion. These beds outcrop again in Split Mountain Cañon in a deep gulch running westward from its head, and again on the Yampa Plateau. Here some of its harder limestones are occasionally found standing in low peaks.

UPPER AUBREY GROUP.

In the Uinta Mountains the Upper Aubrey is composed of two members, a massive, homogeneous, light gray sandstone at the base, which I have called the Yampa Sandstone, having a thickness of a thousand feet or more; and above, a cherty limestone from 150 to 200 feet in thickness, which I have called the Bellerophon Limestone. These beds from their induration and homogeneity are well adapted to the formation of ridges.

The group is seen outcropping in the Flaming Gorge district, and in a zone stretching westward from Horseshoe Cañon for many miles. A little patch has been caught in the fault on the west side of Quartz Mountain and thrust between strata of Cretaceous Age, and its area is marked on the map. The monoclinal ridge on the east side of Po Cañon is of this age. It is seen on all sides of Junction Mountain. Yampa Cañon is carved through this sandstone. Here the rocks dip to the south and the homogeneous Yampa Sandstone on the north side of the cañon is cut by a multitude of little cañons, the channels of rainy day brooks. The entire slope is minutely carved in this manner and the spaces between the meandering cañons in many places are but narrow walls, and sometimes these walls are broken where the channels approach too closely, and by this process buttes with narrow bases, and towers and pinnacles are formed. Along the courses of these intermittent streams great numbers of pot-holes are found. This topography is too minute to be represented on the map. On the eastern end of the Yampa Plateau this sandstone forms the slope of the plateau where it descends into the valley, and is in like manner carved with innumerable gulches whose courses are interrupted by pot-holes.

This group has an extensive outcrop in the Yampa Plateau, and finally it has been traced from Whirlpool Cañon westward beyond the limits of the map.

*   *   *   *   *   *   *

The outcrop of these Carboniferous groups has been traced from point to point throughout the areas described above. In most places the exposures are complete and the relations of the beds can be well understood, and nowhere has any unconformity between its members been observed. Nor has any unconformity between the Upper Aubrey and the lower Mesozoic been observed; but as the lowest beds of Mesozoic Age are of very friable material, the exact junction is rarely seen.

In the line of the fault between the Flaming Gorge district and the Po Cañon district there is a fragment of Red Wall limestone, as seen on the map, on the northwest corner of the Ó-wi-yu-kuts Plateau, which was not carried down by the fault; i. e., the fault is to the north.

JURA TRIAS GROUPS.

SHINARUMP GROUP.

These beds are shales and soft sandstones, and hence in this region, which is plicated, they are found in valley spaces. The Lower Aubrey on one side and the Vermilion Cliff on the other stand in ridges. At the foot of the cliff on the south side of Flaming Gorge the Green River runs into the beds of this age and soon passes across them to enter the Upper Aubrey beds. Looking westward a towering cliff is seen on the right and a broken slope on the left and a narrow valley immediately in front, which may be followed until the bank of Sheep Creek is reached; then turning up Sheep Creek that stream is found to run nearly its entire course, as represented on the map, in beds of this age. The steep wall of vermilion sandstone on the north side of this valley is, except at one point, an impassable barrier. Eastward from Flaming Gorge the outcrop of the Shinarump Group is seen in a narrow valley between two ridges, for about six miles, until it is cut off by the great Uinta fault.

Outcrops are also found in the Po Cañon district. Here again the beds are found in the spaces between the ridges. The same is true along the foot of the Yampa Plateau to the east, south, and west; and also in a general way in its outcrop from the foot of Whirlpool Cañon through the Island Park district. But this topographic peculiarity is not shown on the map in the last mentioned region, as the area of the outcrop of all of the Jura Trias beds has its topography cut up so minutely by reason of many minor displacements and transverse lines of erosion that only a generalized representation could be given.

There is an island of Shinarump beds south of Echo Park, lying at the foot of the Yampa Plateau.

VERMILION CLIFF, WHITE CLIFF, AND FLAMING GORGE GROUPS

In this region the Vermilion Cliff and White Cliff Groups are massive sandstones, and hence stand in monoclinal ridges. Sometimes the base of the White Cliff Group is a series of softer beds, and two ridges are formed. Elsewhere the White Cliff Group rises high over the Vermilion Cliff beds in a wall which faces the axis of the Uinta upheaval on either side. Throughout this entire region the White Cliff sandstone is lighter colored than the Vermilion Cliff Group and everywhere exhibits that oblique structure known as false bedding.

The Flaming Gorge Group with its limestones and sandstones is of heterogeneous stratification and breaks down into comparatively low hills, which are found on the backs of the great White Cliff ridges. The area of outcrop is parallel and coextensive with that of the Shinarump Group, except in the region near Flaming Gorge and the district immediately south of Echo Park.

About four miles southeast from Diamond Peak there is a small outcrop of the Flaming Gorge beds standing on edge, with the summit of the group facing the plateau or axis of the Uinta upheaval.

It is an interesting fact that the bad-land sandstones of the Flaming Gorge Group, both above and below the Mid-Group Limestone, are of fresh-water origin.

The following is a section of the Jura Trias groups, made in the hills and cliffs west of Flaming Gorge and beginning above at the base of the conglomerate which underlies the teleost shales, and extending to the summit of the Bellerophon Limestone. In this region the limits of the section can be easily determined.

SECTION OF THE JURA TRIAS GROUPS.

FLAMING GORGE GROUP.

No. 1, 110 feet.—Gray, greenish gray, pink, purple, and chocolate beds; very friable; bad-land beds.

No. 2, 200 feet.—Bluish-gray limestone; Mid-Group Limestone.

No. 3, 500 feet.—Coarse red sandstone; (*unio* beds.)

No. 4, 250 feet.—Limestone; bluish-buff; compact; sometimes shaly and interstratified with orange shales and thin beds of gypsum.

WHITE CLIFF GROUP.

No. 5, 1,025 feet.—Massive sandstone; light gray and light orange, everywhere exhibiting false stratification in many directions and at many angles.

VERMILION CLIFF GROUP.

No. 6, 300 feet.—Sandstone; massively bedded; gray, drab, and brown within, but weathering with bright vermilion surfaces; well exposed on the summit of Flaming Gorge.

No. 7, 6 feet.—Shales, somewhat argillaceous.

No. 8, 359 feet.—Sandstones; rather friable, with intercalated shales; the latter containing much gypsum; weathering in variegated bright colors.

SHINARUMP GROUP.

No. 9, 1,095 feet.—Shales and sandstones containing much gypsum; weathering in many colors, but brown and chocolate tints prevailing; in many places constituting bad-land beds.

These beds all dip to the north at a great angle.

* * * * * * * * * * * *

It will be seen that the Jura Trias groups are exposed in outcrops on the north side of the Uinta Mountains in isolated patches, and these outcropping beds in the Flaming Gorge district dip to the northward. In the Po Cañon district they dip in a direction a little north of east. These two areas of outcrop are separated by a long space where these groups are carried down by the great Uinta fault, and their non-appearance at the surface is due chiefly to this cause, as they are not usually covered on this side of the range by unconformable Tertiaries. The exceptions will be noted hereafter.

On the eastern end of the Uinta Mountains, between the Po Cañon district and the Junction Mountain region, the upturned edges of Jura Trias rocks occasionally protrude through the overlying unconformable beds of Brown's Park age, but these protruding masses are too small to be shown on the map.

About the Junction Mountain uplift the eroded edges of the Trias are sometimes buried beneath unconformable beds of Brown's Park age.

On the south side of the Uinta Mountains the area of outcrop of the Jura Trias groups is very much greater. Near the head of Ashley's Creek the three upper groups of the Jura Trias are buried by unconformable rocks of Tertiary Age. Farther west, beyond the area covered by the map, these unconformable Tertiary rocks ride high up on the groups of Carboniferous beds.

THE CRETACEOUS GROUPS.

The Henry's Fork Group, which is the lowest Cretaceous formation, has an outcrop parallel and approximately co-extensive with the several groups of Jura Trias; that is, like those groups it was brought up by the great Uinta upheaval and the elevation of the Yampa Plateau. The same is true of the higher Cretaceous groups, but the latter are also brought into view in the Aspen Mountain upheaval; and hence, in the discussion of the geographic distribution of these formations it is necessary to refer to a district of country not heretofore mentioned in connection with the Carboniferous or Jura Trias groups.

I shall call this the Aspen Mountain district.

HENRY'S FORK GROUP.

Nothing further need be said of the geographic occurrence of this formation. The group is composed of sandstones, indurated arenaceous shales, and conglomerates. These shales ring under the hammer, and are of steel-gray color, and rarely afford footing to vegetation, and can be traced in a bright band everywhere through the outcrop of the formation. The conglomerates contain many gravels and bowlders of pre existing schistic rocks.

They have a much more extensive development on the south than on the north side of the Uinta Mountains.

On the south side of the Yampa Plateau, where the Fox Creek and Cliff Creek flexures unite, these conglomerates stand on edge with a dip of about 85 degrees to the southeast, and are firmly cemented, and stand as high walls, separated by a long, narrow valley, strewn with fragments of the conglomerate which have tumbled down from either side. Farther east, along the southern slope of the Yampa Plateau, they are very conspicuous features in the topography, as they are found standing in ridges and monuments. Here the topography is exceedingly complex, too much so to be represented on the map which presents but a crude generalization of the many wonderful features of this region.

SULPHUR CREEK GROUP.

These beds are soft argillaceous and arenaceous shales of dark color, but sometimes weathering a light gray. By reason of their exceeding friability the areas of outcrop are everywhere valley regions, often diversified with broad stretches of low, bad-land hills in many places quite naked of vegetation, but elsewhere covered with patches of *cactaceæ*. Conspicuous among these is a species of *opuntia*, with its minute, subtle thorns hedging the hills with a threat of festering wounds.

Its most extensive area of outcrop is in the Island Park sag, and it has a small outcrop in the northern portion of the Aspen Mountain uplift.

A fragment of these beds is seen southeast of Diamond Peak, which, with a fragment of the Flaming Gorge beds on one side and a fragment of Salt Wells on the other, is standing on edge. It will be noticed that these beds dip toward the axis of upheaval, that is, the highest beds are found nearest the mountain, and they all stand with an inclination from the horizon of 90 degrees.

SALT WELLS GROUP.

It is unnecessary to speak in detail of the outcrop of the Salt Wells beds, as the attention of the reader has already been called to the outcrop on the flanks of the Uinta Mountains and in the Aspen Mountain district. It is worthy of remark that in the Uinta Mountain region these beds are usually friable arenaceous and argillaceous shales, while in the Aspen Mountain district they are arenaceous shales and thinly bedded sandstones, and the greater induration of some of the beds in the last mentioned district causes the valley spaces, which are characteristic of this group, to be diversified with low ridges and cliffs.

POINT OF ROCKS GROUP.

The beds of this group can usually be divided into three somewhat well defined members, the Upper Hogback, Middle Hogback, and Golden Wall Sandstones, which are usually separated by a few feet of shaly sandstones, and these stratigraphic characteristics under conditions of upheaval and erosion usually result in the production of three ridges, which are the topographic features giving names to the several members. The upper sandstone is usually massive and of light gray color weathering unequally on exposed surfaces, which inequality is not determined by lines of stratification. Here an irregular mass tumbles down and a cave is formed; there an irregular mass is more indurated than the general body to which it belongs and stands in relief, often in some fantastic form; and such weathering gives the cliffs which are usually found along the outcrop of these beds a strange and weird appearance. The general structure is subconcretionary, and true concretions sometimes weather out. The same weathering is sometimes found in the Middle Hogback Sandstone.

The Golden Wall Sandstone is often homogeneous and of a bright yellow color in the Uinta region, and often stands as a sheer wall; hence its name; but in the Aspen Mountain district these yellow sandstones are broken into strata, and light gray sandstones and shales are intercalated. The ridge like topography characteristic of this group of beds so prevalent everywhere, renders it easy to trace every outcrop, and the peculiar and persistent characteristics of the upper member greatly facilitate the study of the relation between the Cretaceous below and Tertiary groups above. In the Uinta Mountains the unconformity at this horizon is everywhere apparent. The difference in dip is from two to fifteen degrees, and the evidence of intervening erosion is apparent; but in the Aspen Mountain country the difference of dip is not easily distinguished, but the evidences of erosion are usually apparent.

No evidence of unconformity between the Cretaceous formations has been discovered, and the planes of demarkation in many places are not well exhibited. In such a case the lines are drawn on the map only as approximations. Nor is there any evidence of unconformity between the lowest Cretaceous and the highest Jura. Here, also, the stratigraphic plane is sometimes obscure. The teleost shales contain the lowest Cretaceous fossils which have yet been found, and the bad-land beds below the conglomerates contain the highest Jurassic fossils found. The intervening conglomerates I have thought best to call Cretaceous.

In a general way the horizon of conglomerates can be easily traced; still, it is a variable one. Here the sandstones are found with conglomerates of small pebbles which cannot be easily separated from the sandstones as they merge into them by imperceptible gradations. Elsewhere well developed conglomerates are found, and sometimes heavy beds of coarse conglomerate prevail.

* * * * * * *

The following section of the Cretaceous Groups was made on the east side of the Green River above Flaming Gorge.

POINT OF ROCKS GROUP.

Upper Hogback Sandstone.—No. 1, 60 feet. Sandstones; indurated; light gray; stained in patches with iron.

No. 2, 60 feet. Sandstones; gray; on exposed surfaces stained brown with iron; containing fragments of coal.

No. 3, 25 feet. Sandstones; very massive; light gray.

No. 4, 5 feet. Carbonaceous shales, with seams of coal.

No. 5, 35 feet. Sandstones; indurated; gray.

No. 6, 18 feet. Carbonaceous shales, with seams of coal.

No. 7, 80 feet. Sandstones; indurated; dark gray.

No. 8, 60 feet. Sandstones; massive; light gray.

No. 9, 4 feet. Carbonaceous shales, with seams of coal.

No. 10, 110 feet. Sandstones; homogeneous; massive; light gray; indurated.

Middle Hogback Sandstone.—No. 11, 275 feet. Sandstone; buff; heavily bedded with intercalated shales and seams of ferruginous clay.

No. 12, 75 feet. Friable sandstones and carbonaceous shales.

Golden Wall Sandstone.—No. 13, 600 feet. Sandstones; yellow; rather massively bedded, with intercalated carbonaceous shales.

No. 14, 80 feet. Sandstone; massive; bright yellow.

All the beds of the above group dip to the north about 45 degrees.

SALT WELLS GROUP.

No. 15, 1,860 feet. Friable sandstones and arenaceous shales.

SULPHUR CREEK GROUP.

No. 16, 2,000 feet. Dark argillaceous and arenaceous shales.

HENRY'S FORK GROUP.

No. 17, 25 feet. Conglomerates; pebbles very small, the largest not being more than half an inch in diameter.

No. 18, 80 feet. Sandstones; mottled light gray and yellow; showing false stratification.

No. 19, 70 feet. Shales; (teleost shales.)

No. 20, 135 feet. Sandstones; rather heavily bedded above, but thinly bedded below; drab.

No. 21, 40 feet. Sandstones; coarse; buff.

No. 22, 100 feet. Sandstones; very friable; gray, greenish-gray, pink, purple, and chocolate.

No. 23, 50 feet. Sandstones; coarse; sometimes appearing as a conglomerate of fine pebbles.

No. 24, 100 feet. Sandstones; gray, greenish-gray, pink, purple, and chocolate; very friable.

No. 25, 75 feet. Conglomerate; dark; in some places a coarse sandstone.

*   *   *   *   *   *   *

Below I reproduce the section made by Professor Meek on Sulphur Creek to which reference has been made in a previous chapter. I copy his numbers and characterization of the beds, but group them in accordance with the scheme presented in this report. I also invert the order.

SECTION OF THE ROCKS EXPOSED ON SULPHUR CREEK, NEAR BEAR RIVER, WYOMING.

POINT OF ROCKS GROUP.

No. 1 (28), 200 feet.—Numerous thin seams and layers of dark carbonaceous shales, with harder thin bands of various colored argillaceous, arenaceous, and calcareous matter, including a few very thin streaks of coal; the whole being highly charged with vast numbers of fresh and brackish-water shells, such as species of *Unio*, *Corbicula*, *Corbula*, *Pyrgulifera*, *Viviparus*, *Melampus*, *&c.* Dip nearly east, about 75° below the horizon; thickness 175 to 200 feet exposed.

No. 2 (27).—A long space of perhaps 260 yards or more, with only a few low exposures of light-gray sandstone, showing a slight westward dip.

No. 3 (26), 80 feet.—Gray sandstone in place, apparently connected with some masses (that *may* not be in place) so as to include space enough for 60 to 80 feet,—forms crest of a hill.

No. 4 (25), 800 feet.—Brownish and reddish clays with a few distantly separated thin beds and layers of gray sandstone, altogether 750 to 800 feet in thickness.

No. 5 (24), 20 feet.—Conglomerate and some red clays.

No. 6 (23), 40 feet.—Whitish sandstone—forms crest of hill about 220 to 240 feet in height.

No. 7 (22), 110 feet.—Brownish clays and beds of sandstone, the latter light gray below.

No. 8 (21), 60 feet.—Brownish clays and sandy layers.

No. 9 (20), 40 feet.—Greenish white sandstone.

No. 10 (19), 600 feet.—Slope showing above some masses of conglomerate, like that of division 18, perhaps not in place, with, at places below this, some reddish clays; altogether space enough for 500 to 600 feet in thickness.

No. 11 (18), 40 feet.—Hard gray conglomerate, standing nearly vertical, and forming crest of hill about 350 feet high.

SALT WELLS GROUP.

No. 12 (17), 115 feet.—Brownish and bluish clays, with some beds of white, greenish, and brownish sandstones.

No. 13 (16), 45 feet.—Clays and sandstone below, (20 feet), and gray and brown pebbly sandstone above, (25 feet).

No. 14 (15), 125 feet.—Bluish laminated clays, with, at top (left or west side), a two-foot layer of sandstone, containing fragments of shells not seen in a condition to be determined.

No. 15 (14), 40 feet.—Ferruginous sandstone in thin layers, dipping northwest about 80° below horizon.

No. 16 (13).—A valley or depression showing no rocks, perhaps 150 yards across.

No. 17 (12), 150 feet.—Light gray sandstones and clays, including a bed of good coal, said to be 7½ feet in thickness; all dipping south-southeast 55° below horizon, and the sandstone above the coal containing many casts, *Inoceramus problematicus*, with a few casts of *Cardium* and undetermined univalves; altogether showing about 150 feet.

No. 18 (11).—Slope and unexposed space, perhaps 200 yards or more across.

No. 19 (10), 20 feet.—Light gray sandstone.

No. 20 (9), 255 feet.—Gray sandy shales with alternations of sandstone and clays.

No. 21 (8), 95 feet.—Heavy massive bed of light colored sandstone, about 90 feet in thickness, standing nearly vertical, with some 3 to 5 feet of sandy clay between it and the coal of division 7.

No. 22 (7), 7 feet 6 inches.—Bed of good coal, said to be 7½ feet in thickness.

No. 23 (6), 100 feet.—Greenish and bluish gray sandy clays, with some dark shale at places.

No. 24 (5), 100 feet.—Two or three rather heavy beds of light yellowish gray sandstone, separated by clays, probably occupying some of the space included in division 4. Near the lower part two layers 15 to 18 inches each, of sandstone, containing *Ostrea soleniscus, Trapezium micronema, &c.* Altogether 90 to 100 feet or more.

No. 25 (4), 300 feet.—Covered space, probably occupied by clays, but showing some sandstone that may or may not be in place; perhaps room enough for 250 to 300 feet.

No. 26 (3), 90 feet.—Soft light grayish sandstone, nearly vertical.

SUMMIT OF SULPHUR CREEK GROUP.

No. 27 (2), 100 feet.—Slope apparently occupied by clays, thickness perhaps 100 feet or more.

No. 28 (1).—Black shale, only seen in bottom of Sulphur Creek, thickness unknown.

* * * * * * *

BLACK BUTTE QUARTZITE.

Southwest of Black Butte Station on the Union Pacific Railroad there is a conspicuous topographic feature known as Black Butte. It is carved from beds of the Point of Rocks Group and is crowned with a dark indurated and exceedingly tough quartzite, which, in the distance, has the appearance of a bed of extravasated material, and even on closer examination I was deceived by its apparent similarity to some rhyolites.

Rocks having a similar appearance and structure are found on the summit of Aspen Mountain, and I unhesitatingly considered the latter to be quartzites; but, on visiting Black Butte, the general weathering and exceedingly dark appearance of these beds created the impression that they had been extravasated, though hand specimens had the appearance of quartzite, and I left the field with many doubts as to their nature. Captain Dutton has since made sections of this rock and examined them under the microscope and pronounces it a quartzite.

Such a conclusion in connection with the geological relations of these beds is very interesting Quartzites, from geological considerations of structure and erosion, are usually supposed to have been at some time deep seated and are often shown to have been involved in profound plication, or implication, and are usually considered to be metamorphosed sandstones, the metamorphism due to deep seated agencies; but this quartzite is of very late Cretaceous Age or may even belong to higher unconformable Tertiaries. In either case the same strata on every hand are soft, comparatively friable, granular sandstones; they are immediately underlaid by great thicknesses of sandstones of like characteristics. They have not been implicated or even plicated. No extravasated material is found in the immediate vicinity to which reference can be made as the origin of crystallization, and these beds on Black Butte are more than 200 feet in thickness, and metamorphism from contact with eruptive rocks, so far as my studies extend in this western country, is exceedingly slight, and indeed such slight change is rarely shown. There is nothing in the surroundings to suggest metamorphism.

Is it possible that conditions obtained here favorable to the deposition of silica by chemical precipitation? This question has been often suggested by facts observed at many other places in the Plateau Province. In my remarks on the Uinta Group I mentioned that some of the sandstones were quasi quartzites, and where such beds of quartzite are found the quartzite structure is invariably local. The same beds traced laterally are typical sandstones; and above and below, soft sandstones and excessively friable shales are found, and there is no local disturbance of these beds. They have simply been displaced in the grand upheaval in common with the sandstones and shales; and if this lithologic characteristic is due to conditions of deposition and have not been imposed by the agencies of metamorphism, at what place in the table of sedimentary groups shall we begin to consider quartzites to be products of metamorphism? At Black Butte the quartzite is as high at least as the very summit of the Cretaceous; in the Uinta Mountains the quartzites are low down in the Paleozoic series and these are separated by nearly 30,000 feet of sedimentary accumulations. May we go one foot farther down in the rocks, but across the great gap of unconformity, and say that the Red Creek quartzites were such from original constitution?

THE CENOZOIC GROUPS.

This description of the geographic distribution of the Cenozoic Groups will be confined to the region north of the Uinta Mountains, except in the case of the Brown's Park Group and the Bishop Mountain Conglomerate. A small strip of country on the south side of the mountains has been given a Tertiary color on the map for the purpose of presenting an interesting fact in the relation of the groups of that region; but this is only the border of a broad area through which Cenozoic formations are distributed, and to discuss this border with clearness it is necessary to enter into a consideration of the whole area, which can be done much better when we have the map of that country before us.

In the Uinta and White River basins, south of the Uinta Mountains, where these Tertiaries have a great development, the lower formations of this Age have been pretty thoroughly worked out, but there are higher beds not so well understood.

I now turn to a consideration of the country north of the Uinta Mountains.

BITTER CREEK GROUP.

Here the Bitter Creek beds have an extensive exposure on the flank of the Uinta upheaval and on either flank of the Aspen Mountain uplift.

In the Flaming Gorge district, west of the Green River, the beds of this group rapidly attenuate until they disappear, and here their lithologic character is changed, as the fine grained friable sandstones are replaced by conglomerates; and as the beds here are dipping at a great angle to the north, so that their upturned edges are well exposed, the harder conglomerates are seen to stand in high ledges and walls. Eastward from the Green River the beds rapidly thicken until, at Richard's Peak and Quien Hornet Mountain, a section of more than 5,000 feet is presented, and here at the base we have a great development of conglomerates. Richard's Peak itself is a monoclinal ridge of this conglomerate.

The disappearance of these beds by attenuation on the west side of the Green River and their increase above the normal thickness east of that stream, together with the change in their lithologic constitution, leads us to infer that we here have the beds exposed near the old shore line that was established by the upheaval of the Uinta Mountain region. Conglomerates are found at the base of the group in many places on the north side of the Uintas, and I suppose the conglomerates on the west side of the Green

River to be at the same horizon, namely, at the base of the series, and that the attenuation is due to the non-deposition of the upper beds over the area here brought to light. Of this, conclusive evidence was not obtained, and it may possibly be that these conglomerates represent higher beds which, farther from the shore, were sandstones of more thoroughly comminuted material. But, while I suggest this possible explanation, I am inclined to consider them as belonging to the lower members of the group, and that after their deposition the area was left as dry land, while the sands were accumulating in the bed of the lake farther from the axis of upheaval.

From the Green River eastward, nearly to the foot of Richard's Peak, the base of the group is composed of bad-land sandstones with more indurated beds intercalated; the latter are usually light gray, sometimes quite white; the former are exceedingly ferruginous and sometimes shaly; but from the western base of Richard's Peak, nearly to the outcrop of the Red Wall limestone, conglomerates are found, and here the whole thickness of the group is much increased. It is interesting to notice that these conglomerates are found opposite the outcrop of the Red Creek Quartzite. But the materials of which the conglomerates are composed seem not to have been derived from the quartzite, if I may trust my notes: and I should here state that the geographic relation between the quartzite and the conglomerate did not occur to me while in the field, and in my notes on the conglomerate I have mentioned that its bowlders are sandstones and limestones, and that some of the latter contain Jurassic fossils; but I have recorded observations at only two points—one at Richard's Peak, the other at Bruce Mountain. With the facts now at my command I am inclined to think that when this conglomerate was formed, erosion had not progressed through the Carboniferous groups and Uinta Sandstone so as to reach the quartzite on the upheaved side, but that the conglomerate is composed of sandstones from the Cretaceous groups, and limestones and sandstones of the Jura Trias, and possibly, to some extent, from Carboniferous beds. It would seem that the appearance of the conglomerate here is to be explained by geographic, rather than by geological, considerations—that is, the line of exposure of the base of the group in this region is near to the old shore line; for it is manifest that here was a headland projecting from the Uinta region into the old Bitter Creek lake, while westward, from Richard's Peak to the Green River, the present exposure of the strata is across the bed of an ancient bay.

West from Richard's Peak the plane of separation between the Bitter Creek and Point of Rocks Groups is masked to a greater or less extent on account of the exceeding friability of the lower beds of Bitter Creek age; still careful examination reveals the fact that they are unconformable, and this unconformity is very clearly exhibited at the eastern end of the monoclinal ridge, composed of the Upper Hogback Sandstone of the Point of Rocks Group, near the foot of Richard's Peak, in an amphitheater of erosion at the head of a dry gulch.

Between the western end of the outcrop of Red Wall limestone on the northwest end of the O-wi-yu-kuts Plateau and the Po Cañon district the base of the Bitter Creek series is not seen, as it has been carried down by the fault. On the north side of Diamond Peak the Bitter Creek beds are lying horizontal, and, studying this mountain from that side, it would seem to be composed of Bitter Creek beds, perhaps capped by beds of the Lower Green River, but on climbing the mountain its summit is seen to be composed of angular fragments of sandstones piled in an indiscriminate manner, the age of which was not fully determined; descending it on the south side this same confusion is observed. Of what the principal mass of this peak is composed I do not know.

In the Po Cañon district along the channel of Vermilion Creek and many of its lateral tributaries, deep corrasion has produced many steep escarpments of the Bitter Creek beds. Here we find the Point of Rocks Group standingon edge, and near by, and separated from the former only by narrow gulches, Bitter Creek beds of a horizon about midway in the group are found lying horizontally; but in a few places lower beds of the Bitter Creek series are turned up on edge with the Point of Rocks beds and the middle beds of the Bitter Creek Group lie over their upturned and eroded edges unconformably, and over some of the upper beds of the Point of Rocks Group in like manner. Thus the middle beds of the Bitter Creek overlap the lower beds, not because they were deposited over a broader area, but because the lower beds in a part of their extent were exposed to erosion and carried away prior to the deposition of the middle beds. These facts are illustrated in Fig. 15. I do not think that the base of the Bitter Creek series is found exposed in this vicinity. The displacement here has evidently been exceedingly complex, and its study is rendered difficult by unconformities, and it is not always easy to determine to which class of agencies certain

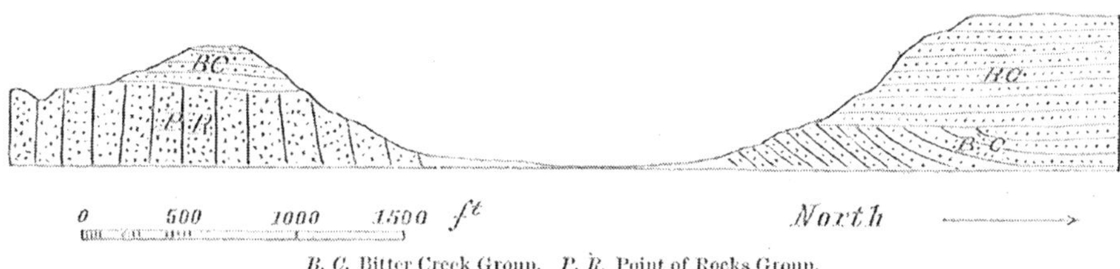

B. C. Bitter Creek Group. P. R. Point of Rocks Group.
Fig. 15.

phenomena are due. In some portions of the line of displacement the beds are marked by certain late Tertiaries of Brown's Park age as will be more fully explained hereafter.

West of Bishop Mountain, stretching across the many tributaries of the Vermilion, there is a broad expanse of country where the beds of this age are exposed in naked bad-land hills, and on either flank of the Aspen Mountain uplift they are seen usually forming regions sterile and desolate.

At the head of Little Bitter Creek there is a stretch of table land where beds of Bishop Mountain Conglomerate are found. In the late redistribution of this conglomerate its materials have been carried quite over the line separating the Bitter Creek from the Point of Rocks Group, so that the junction is completely masked, but in the escarpment south of the plateau which faces Quien Hornet Mountain the junction is well revealed; and the same is true farther to the north in lateral cañons along the upper course of Little Bitter Creek. The conglomerates found at the base of the series on the flank of the Uintas are not seen on the flanks of the Aspen Mountain uplift, and the Bitter Creek beds attenuate toward the north. From these facts I infer that the materials of the Bitter Creek Group were derived in large part at least from the Uinta region, that is that the bad-land rocks of Mesozoic Age were carried from the Uinta region and redistributed as bad-land beds of the Bitter Creek period.

In this great fresh water basin conditions favorable to the deposition of carbonaceous shales and lignitic coal obtained from time to time, now here now there, and such shales and coals are found distributed in great profusion throughout the entire area which has been studied. In a section made on the south side of the railroad between Lawrence Section House and Rock Springs more than 30 seams and beds of coal are noted. The coals of this horizon in the vicinity of Black Butte Station have been frequently described by other geologists.

It is not my purpose to discuss the distribution and character of the lignitic coals in this report.

LOWER GREEN RIVER GROUP.

In the Flaming Gorge district the Lower Green River Group overlaps the Bitter Creek Group, and farther westward disappears by attenuation.

The course of the Green River from the northern border of the area embraced on the map to the hogback six miles north of Flaming Gorge is through the beds of this group, and an irregular escarpment of these beds having deep reëntrant angles, and spaces broken into low hills, faces the axis of the Aspen Mountain uplift. The escarpment known as Pine Bluffs on the east side of the uplift is of this age. Another outcrop is found north of Dry Mountains and west of the Po Cañon district, where their upturned edges are exposed on the border of a basin of displacement or sag due to a downthrow.

This group is composed chiefly of bituminous shales and impure limestones, the latter being both arenaceous and argillaceous; but to the south, near the Uinta uplift, the group is much thickened and the shales are replaced by sandstones, and conglomerates of fine pebbles appear.

From this fact it is inferred that the beds of this group are derived from the Uinta region, and that the material was supplied from limestones and sandstones of Carboniferous Age. Conditions favorable to the accumulation of Carbonaceous shales and lignitic coal are less frequent than in the former period, but a fine bed of coal has been found at the base of this group on the bank of the Green River, about eight miles below the station, and Carbonaceous shales and thin seams of coal have been found at other horizons elsewhere.

UPPER GREEN RIVER GROUP.

The beds of this group are well exposed in high escarpments on either side of the Green River from the northern boundary of the district embraced on the map nearly to the hogback six miles above Flaming Gorge, and they stretch in a continuous but irregular belt on the west side of that stream for the same distance, and are exposed on Henry's Fork for many miles.

On the east side of the Green River they are found in outlying disconnected patches. The most important of the latter are colored on the map. They are also seen in the district east of Po Cañon with their edges upturned around the basin of displacement previously mentioned. It is probable that these beds are also found east of Pine Bluffs, but when that country was studied in 1868, I had not separated the Upper from the Lower Green River beds, and not having visited the country since, I am not prepared to give any facts concerning the matter.

In a former chapter I stated that the Upper Green River beds were interpolated between Bridger and Lower Green River only through a portion of the great Tertiary basin north of the Uinta Mountains. These beds have their greatest development in the region about Green River Station, extending for 20 or 30 miles to the north and south, and it is probable that the material of which they are composed was derived in part, at least, from other than the Uinta region, though doubtless this region yielded a share of the detrital matter. Carbonaceous shales and lignitic coal are found at this horizon on Henry's Fork. Two of the coal beds have been explored and when tested are said to have yielded fair coals.

I have already in a former chapter described the Tower Sandstone at the base of this group, and explained the nature of the unconformity between the Upper and Lower Green River Groups.

BRIDGER GROUP.

The Bridger beds are found outcropping on the western border of the district under discussion north of Henry's Fork, and again to the east of the Po Cañon district in the sag of displacement north of the Dry Mountains.

No unconformity has been discovered between the Bridger and Upper

Green River, and the plane of demarkation is obscure, or rather there is no plane of demarkation, but the separation is transitional; but the bad-land beds of the Bridger Group are very distinct from the limestones and sandstones of the Upper Green River. In the latter, sandstones usually rather massive, and in the case of the Tower Sandstone greatly so, have impure limestones intercalated. In the former, bad-land sandstones prevail, and these are largely green sands, but irregular beds and aggregations of chalcedony are abundant, and high in the series two well marked and persistent limestones are found. These beds of chalcedony afford the moss agates for which the region about Fort Bridger has been noted. I suppose them to have been deposited by chemical precipitation from waters highly charged with silica. The limestones are in many places crypto-crystalline, and break with a conchoidal fracture and often have the ring of phonolite. I consider these also to be chemical precipitates. Fresh water fossils are sometimes found imbedded in the crystalline masses, but can rarely be obtained in a perfect state, but fossils are more abundant in the arenaceous and argillaceous partings, and can be obtained in a good state of preservation. In the green sands vertebrate fossils have been found in abundance, and concerning them much has already been written by eminent paleontologists.

No coal has been discovered in the Bridger Group.

BROWN'S PARK GROUP.

These beds are found in the valley known as Brown's Park and a district of country stretching thence to the southwest beyond the Snake and Yampa Rivers. In Brown's Park they lie in a deep basin of erosion, the bottom and sides of which are composed of Uinta Sandstone. This basin is in the very axis of the Uinta uplift. Eastward, both on the north and south sides of the area of outcrop, the beds are seen to rest unconformably upon all of the Carboniferous, Mesozoic, and Cenozoic formations previously mentioned. Its unconformity with the Upper Green River, Lower Green River, and Bridger beds is well exhibited in the Dry Mountains in many fine exposures. Its structural relations to these beds will be discussed hereafter. Its sandstones are bad-land rocks of exceedingly fine texture. In some places these rocks are composed of thin laminæ of many delicate colors, but they do not readily part along the planes of stratification, but crumble easily and often break in large masses. Extensive beds and irregular aggregations of chalcedony are found and I suppose them to have been deposited by precipitation. Conglomerates are found, at the base, in some localities having a great development. The beds incline slightly from the wall of the park on the south side; this inclination may be due to the bottom on which they were deposited. On the north side the beds are turned up at a great angle, showing much displacement since they were deposited, and immediately outside of the irregular line of outcrop a fault has been observed with its throw to the south.

In Brown's Park the streams which come down from the mountains on either side have in many places cut through these beds and reveal in the depths of their channels the old floor of Uinta Sandstone. But a few hundred feet of these beds are left in Brown's Park, but eastward a much greater thickness remains preserved from denudation. It is probable also that this greater thickness is due in part to greater sedimentation.

In the northeast portion of the Po Cañon district there is another outcrop of this group. Here the beds rest unconformably on the Uinta Sandstone, the several Carboniferous groups, the several Mesozoic groups, on Bitter Creek beds, and also on the heterogeneous mass of sandstones of which Diamond Peak is composed.

BISHOP MOUNTAIN CONGLOMERATE.

This conglomerate is found only in isolated patches as remnants adventitiously preserved from the general erosion to which this widely spread formation has been subjected.

An outlying patch or fragment is found on the north side of Sage Creek overlying unconformably the beds of Lower Green River age. Another is found on the plateau where Sage, Little Bitter, and Pretty Creeks have their sources; here the conglomerate rests on Point of Rocks beds. Another is found on the summit of Quien Hornet Mountain resting on Lower Green River beds. Another is found on Bishop Mountain resting on Bitter Creek beds. On the south side of the Uinta Mountains a fragment is found west of Echo Park resting on Carboniferous beds. Another fragment is found ten or twelve miles west of the Cañon of Lodore resting on Carboniferous and Jura Trias beds. A fragment is found west of Brush Creek also lying on the Carboniferous and Jura Trias beds; and the Wa-ka-ri-chits are capped with this conglomerate, which here rests on Sulphur Creek beds.

These are the only fragments which I have discovered in the area embraced on the map, but to the westward, on both flanks of the Uinta uplift, this formation has a much more extensive geographic development and it is also found in greater thickness. On the north side of Connor Basin, at the head of Sheep Creek, this conglomerate has a thickness of more than a thousand feet.

There are some conglomerates on the peaks of the Dry Mountains which at one time I believed to belong to this period, but I now think they are of the Brown's Park age.

In the destruction and redistribution of this formation, the materials of which it was composed have been scattered in many places here and there on either flank of the Uinta uplift. The conglomerate is composed of bowlders and pebbles of sandstone, quartzite and crystalline schists, but sandstones and quasi quartzites probably of the Uinta period greatly prevail; but in the original beds and redistributed materials found so abundant north and northeast of Mount Wheeler where the Red Creek Quartzite is exposed, white quartz and crystalline schists are far more abundant than elsewhere. Sometimes at least the cement is calcareous. In the fragment west of Echo Park large and somewhat angular blocks of Uinta Sandstone are found.

I think that many geologists would ascribe this conglomerate to the action of ice, but throughout all that portion of the Rocky Mountain region which I have studied, I have so frequently found gravels and conglomerates of sub-aerial origin, and have in so many cases found reason to change my opinion concerning them, often having attributed a drift like deposit to glacial action, and afterward on further study abandoned the theory, being able to demonstrate its sub-aerial origin, and witnessing on every hand the accumulation of such gravels in valleys and over plains where mountains rise to higher altitudes on either side, and having in many cases actually seen the cliffs breaking down and the gravels rolling out on the floods of a storm, I am not willing to disregard explanations so obvious and so certain for an extraordinary and more violent hypothesis.

Irregular accumulations of clay, accumulations of sand, of gravels, and bowlders having in a general way all the lithologic characteristics of "drift" are very common in the Rocky Mountain region, and in many cases I am convinced that their origin can be traced to ordinary atmospheric agencies acting on the adjacent hills and mountains; and no glaciers or icebergs are needed for their explanation.

Nor need the thickness and extent of this Bishop Mountain Conglomerate serve to weaken this explanation, for the sub-aerial gravels in the valleys between the ranges in the Basin Province are of equal and often of greater development. Whenever a low plain, valley or basin is for a comparatively long period but little elevated above the base level of erosion, and during this time mountains and hills stand about the lowlands, there must be a great accumulation of drift, and where the highlands are areas of progressive elevation and the lowlands areas of progressive subsidence this accumulation may continue indefinitely.

Thus it is that I attribute the drift of the Rocky Mountain region to sub-aerial agencies, chiefly the action of rains and streams. Mountains are not degraded by the slow washing down of their surfaces but they are dug down by the corrasion of deep channels and the undermining of ledges and cliffs, and the materials thus loosened from the great rock masses to which they originally belonged are carried down to the lowlands by storms. In one hour of storm more material is carried to the lowlands than in days, weeks, or months when the mountain streams are clear brooks. Yet there has been glacial action in the Uinta Mountains, for there are found undoubted

MORAINAL DEPOSITS.

The deep valleys that lie at the feet of the axial peaks of this great range have been beds of now extinct glaciers. Morainal deposits, *roches moutonnées*, glaciated grooves, and morainal lakelets are found in very many of these elevated valleys. Often the valleys are so choked with the materials thus accumulated by the action of ice that travel across them is of great difficulty. From the crevices between these ice piled rocks high pines and firs are growing, and hundreds, thousands of little basins filled with clear, cold water are found. These glacial deposits are doubtless of much later origin than the Bishop Mountain Conglomerate; often they are mingled with and masked by drift which has been brought down from the heights by storms, and in many places it is impossible to separate that which is due to this latter agency from that which is due to the agency of ice; and as you descend the valleys away from the peaks where the glacial snow was accumulated the mingling of the two increases by an increase in the amount of drift until at last the glacial formation is lost and drift only appears; taken throughout the Uinta Mountains, the glacial material is far less in quantity than the drift material. What I have thus described as glacial action is exceptional or local and trivial as compared with drift agencies, which must always obtain in mountain regions alike when they are free from glaciers or when the elevated valleys are filled with ice.

Thus the glacial epoch in the Uinta Mountains was doubtless a reality; the evidences of such a time are abundant, but they are found only high up on the range, and the gravels and bowlders of the lowlands attest only to the ordinary action of drift agencies. I may remark here that the evidences of the same glacial epoch are abundant in the Park Mountains; but there also the glaciers were confined to the elevated ranges. The gravel beds on the lowlands are true drift.

LIGNITIC COAL.

But little reference has been made to the lignitic coals found in the Uinta region; it is expected that the coals of the Plateau Province will be discussed in a separate volume.

CHAPTER V.

STRUCTURAL GEOLOGY.

In the preceding chapters many of the facts relating to the structural geology of the region under discussion have been presented, but they were given only to serve purposes relating to the subjects of which I was then treating. In the first chapter it was necessary to refer to this region in characterizing the three provinces; in the second, other facts were presented in explanation of the grouping of the sedimentary rocks; and in the fourth, still other facts were given in discussing geographic distribution. I now propose to assemble these facts with others relating to structural geology, for the purpose of more clearly setting forth the geological structure of the Uinta Mountains, Yampa Plateau, Junction Mountain, Diamond Peak, the Dry Mountains, Brown's Park, and the Aspen Mountain district in the order thus indicated.

DESCRIPTION OF ILLUSTRATIONS.

For the purpose of more clearly setting forth these facts certain illustrations have been prepared and will be found in the atlas.

Structure Sections.—On Plate I is grouped a series of sections through the Uinta Mountains, from south to north, and six miles apart. In each section the structure observed has been projected below the line of sight to the level of the sea, that the facts observed might be represented in a more graphic manner. This hypothetic projection represents the most probable condition of underground structure to that depth, yet there may be unconformities unknown to us and of which no hint is given in the stratigraphy at the surface or in the structural geology of the surrounding country; but from the absence of these indications, such unconformities are rendered improbable.

As the Uinta upheaval began at the close of the Point of Rocks period, this gives us a datum point from which to measure displacement, degradation in the region of uplift, and sedimentation in the region of downthrow. For this reason the group is graphically accented in each section.

Displacement Diagrams.—On Plate II is grouped a series of diagrams designed to represent displacement and degradation. Each diagram corresponds to and is derived from a section in Plate I, and is composed of three lines: the sea level line and the surface line, which are the same as those in the corresponding section, and a third, a displacement line, which is the accented line of the section, projected in the region of uplift from the observed outcrop of the group which it represents (Point of Rocks Group), to the position it would have in the section had there been no degradation but displacement only.

We thus take the sea level as the zero from which to measure displacement; and by introducing the surface line, the accented line above becomes a zero for the measurement of degradation in the region of uplift; and as this accented line represents the position of the last bed deposited prior to the inception of the upheaval (which is the highest Cretaceous bed), it also forms a zero line from which to measure the sedimentation on the flanks of the upheaval which occurred subsequent to the inception of the displacement; or, in other words, a zero line from which to measure Post-Cretaceous sedimentation. Hence in the region of downthrow, with the accented line as the zero, the surface line measures the amount of Post-Cretaceous sedimentation, minus an unknown loss by degradation.

It may be well here to explain the method by which the position of the displacement line was determined. In the topographic survey the altitude of many points on the surface is fixed with a reasonable approximation to accuracy by the use of the barometer and theodolite. These points are the junction of drainage lines, the summits of peaks, and many other salient and conspicuous topographic features; and from these, contour lines are drawn by inspection. Hence the topographic map fixes the position of any bed appearing on the surface with all the accuracy necessary for the scale on which these sections and diagrams are drawn.

Another factor used is the general thickness of the beds. This is determined by measuring them where they outcrop on the flanks of the uplift.

The surface lines, the outcrop of the beds along these lines, and the thickness of the beds are factors sufficient for the construction of the sections and diagrams, but the observed dips and strikes afford many valuable checks in their construction.

A single diagram represents displacement and degradation in two dimensions; that is, in a vertical plane from south to north across the axis of upheaval. A group of these diagrams constructed on parallel planes, separated by equal intervals, and having the scale of these intervals in the group the same as the vertical and horizontal scale of each diagram, serves to represent displacement and degradation in three dimensions.

Stereogram.—To more fully bring the displacement into visual comprehension, the stereogram, Plate III, has been constructed. Here the lines representing the level of the sea, and those representing the present surface are omitted, leaving only the displacement lines; and between these others have been interpolated, so that the intervals are but 3,500 feet; and this has the effect of projecting the region in relief, as it would appear in a bird's-eye view had there been displacement but no degradation. To fully comprehend the meaning of this stereogram, it is necessary to remember that every deviation of a line from horizontality represents a corresponding inclination of the beds, and careful inspection will show that absolute horizontality very rarely occurs. The stereogram fails to represent the abruptness of flexure in some places, as the lines of displacement show the intersection of vertical parallel planes with the summit of the reproduced bed, and these planes have a north and south direction. Wherever they do not cross a flexure in the direction of the dip, but to a greater or less extent oblique to it, to such extent do the displacement lines fail to represent the abruptness of the flexure or angle of dip; in other words, the stereogram does not fully represent displacement in an east and west direction. But the axis of flexure in the Uinta Mountains has an easterly and westerly direction, and all other displacements are subsidiary to this; and as the displacement lines are drawn transverse to this axis, the general characteristics are well represented. It fails also to give the relation of the displacement to the level of the sea except in the case of the first line in the foreground.

I am indebted to Mr. Gilbert for this method of illustration.

It will be shown hereafter that *pari passu* with upheaval, degradation progressed, and with downthrow, sedimentation, and it is probable that degradation and sedimentation were necessary to upheaval and downthrow. Yet, for certain purposes, it is desirable that displacement be considered independent of the degradation with which in nature it must always be more or less complicated, and hence the stereogram has been constructed.

Bird's-Eye View.—The difference between upheaval and degradation in the region of uplift can be determined by examining the diagrams in Plate II; but to give a more graphic representation of this important fact in the Uinta uplift, the bird's-eye view, Plate IV, has been constructed.

Other sections, diagrams and stereograms are found in the atlas, to which reference will be made in appropriate place. All of these sections, diagrams and stereograms are constructed on symmetrical scales; that is, vertical and horizontal scales are the same and all agree with the map.

THE EASTERN PORTION OF THE UINTA MOUNTAINS.

DISPLACEMENT.

The Uinta Mountains have been produced by the degradation of a great upheaved block having its axis in an east and west direction. This axis is not a straight line; in that portion of the range under discussion it makes a great curve to the north; on the western border of the district the axis is found at Leidy's Peak. It runs a little north of Mount Lena, and in Brown's Park it passes about two miles north of Swallow Cañon, then it deflects southward and is found again on Vermilion Creek about four miles above its mouth. The total upheaval above the sea level, along its axial line, is about 30,000 feet. The method by which the amount of uplift is ascertained is as follows: It is in evidence that the upheaval began at the close of the Point of Rocks period. The thickness of the rocks exposed on both flanks of the uplift below that horizon is a little more than 25,000 feet, and the lowest bed seen is 5,400 feet above the level of the sea. The Uinta Sandstone has not been lifted as high at Leidy's Peak as it has at the mouth of the Vermilion by about 2,000 feet, but the Mesozoic groups attenuate from east to west, in the same distance, something more than 2,000 feet, and hence the summit of the Point of Rocks Group was carried about as high in the western as in the eastern region.

From the axis on either side the beds are flexed in a gentle curve to the north and south for many miles until the flanks of the range are reached, where the beds are seen to drop down by abrupt flexures or faults, and these lines of maximum displacement are subparallel with the axis. Thus a great block having its longest axis in an easterly and westerly direction was uplifted. In some places this block was severed from the adjacent country by fracture; in some places by more or less abrupt flexure; and it was itself flexed gently from the axis either way. Nothing more is needed to explain the character of this uplift between the lines of maximum displacement, but the latter present many interesting facts.

On Plate III, this portion of the Uinta uplift, together with the displacements of the Yampa district are represented in a stereogram. The general axis of the great uplift is easily recognizable, as is also the gentle flexure in either direction from this axis. Then the great Uinta fault *h*, *h*, *h*, *h* is seen on the north with the Flaming Gorge branch *i*, *i*. On the south side of the Uinta Mountains in the Island Park district we find the north Ti-ra-kav flexure *k*, *k*, *k* and the south Ti-ra-kav flexure *l*, *l*, *l*. In the Yampa district on its northern border the eastern extension of the north Ti-ra-kav flexure is scarcely seen, as there is an oblique area of upheaval between the Island Park sag *d*, *d* and the Echo Park sag *e*. The flexure of the Echo Park sag also becomes less abrupt in an easterly direction until it almost fades out. The displacements south of the Island Park and Echo Park sags need no further mention here, as they will be discussed in a subsequent portion of this chapter.

It will be seen in the Island Park district on the south side of the Uinta uplift that there are two lines of maximum downthrow approximately parallel, the north and south Ti-ra-kav flexures; the beds between these two flexures are nowhere horizontal. The south Ti-ra-kav flexure disappears toward the west until the region embraced in the stereogram is passed; a little farther westward it re-appears, sometimes as a flexure but usually as a fault. Passing the oblique uplift between the Island Park and Echo Park sags we again have two lines of maximum downthrow. The more northern, which is a continuation of the northern Ti-ra-kav flexure, is but faintly seen in the stereogram; the southern, which is the flexure of the Island Park sag, is more pronounced. All of these maximum flexures on the south side appear to be but slight from an examination of the stereogram, as its scale is very small and no exaggeration has been permitted; but they are very important characteristics in the structural geology of the region, and give rise to very remarkable topographic features. In the broad generalization necessitated by the scale of the illustration many minute displacements, parallel, oblique and transverse to these larger, disappear; that is, in the production of these greater flexures the beds were locally contorted and broken.

Turning now to the north side of the Uinta uplift, we find that the line of maximum displacement, beginning at the eastern extremity, is at first a gentle flexure with comparatively small uplift; but the flexure rapidly increases in abruptness and magnitude until at last we find that the beds are broken and we have a fault; but only a portion of the uplift is by faulting, and the beds on the thrown side are turned up at the edge. Farther westward the beds below lie nearly horizontal, and the beds on the upheaved side are flexed downward; and these conditions alternate so that we sometimes have the upheaved beds flexed downward only, while the thrown beds are nearly or quite horizontal. Again, we have the upheaved beds nearly horizontal at the edge and the thrown beds decidedly flexed upward; and another variation is found where the upheaved beds are flexed downward and the thrown beds upward.

It is probable that the displacement began by flexure, and continued until much of it was made in this way, and finally the beds broke, and the latter part of the displacement was by faulting. And when this faulting occurred, in some places the beds broke on the side of the flexure nearer the axis, in other places on the side of the flexure farther from the axis, and in still other places between the sides of the flexure; that is, the line of fracture meanders along the zone of flexure. As we approach the Flaming Gorge district we find that the faulting is greatly diminished, while the flexing is increased, the total throw or uplift, as we may please to consider it, remaining approximately the same. At last this line of abrupt displacement branches, and we have a faulted flexure to the south and an abrupt flexure to the north; the southern branch, farther westward, becomes a simple flexure, and the northern branch changes its course somewhat, so that the beds are greatly warped; then it becomes a faulted flexure, and finally a clean fault.

Thus the great Uinta block was uplifted, behaving in part as an integer to the extent that it was separated by flexure and fracture from the adjacent country, and as a body of minute parts as it was flexed along the axial line.

We are interested to know at what rate this great uplift progressed. The evidence bearing on this point is of three classes: first, that derived from the character of the displacement itself; second, that derived from degradation; and third, that derived from sedimentation.

The displacement is partly by faulting, partly by flexing. *A priori*, it would appear that whether any given displacement should be by faulting or flexing would be determined by four conditions, severally or conjointly: first, rate of displacement; second, constitution of the beds displaced, flexible and brittle beds being contrasted; third, the depth of the beds considered, for the deeply seated beds, being less free to move, would be more liable to bend, and beds nearer the surface, being more free to move, more liable to break; and fourth, the nature or application of the force producing displacement. Observed facts show that two at least of these *a priori* conditions, the second and third, are true conditions. Both Mr. Gilbert and myself have observed in the transverse section of a displacement that the hard beds have been broken and the soft beds bent, and I have elsewhere published such a section.

In a region of country visited by Mr. Gilbert during the past season, he found that the displacement in one district was by faulting, and in another by flexing. In the region of faulting there had been but little subsequent degradation; in the region of flexing, much subsequent degradation; and these conditions led Mr. Gilbert to the conclusion that the depth of the beds below the general surface at the time of the displacement had determined these characteristics, and in studying facts which had been collected in other regions by myself, he was able to show that they also lead to the same conclusions. The places where these facts were observed are so widely spread throughout the Plateau Province that it will not be convenient to assemble them here, but I am strongly disposed to accept Mr. Gilbert's conclusions.

The fourth condition is supposable, but that it is a *vera causa* I cannot say. I have often supposed it to be such in the study of particular faults, but on further study it has eluded my apprehension. We sometimes find a displacement of many thousand feet where the uplifted region is separated from the thrown by a broad zone of gently dipping beds, and it would seem *a priori* that where two regions were thus separated, the zone of change would be by flexure rather than by a series of ruptures, and such is usually though not invariably the case, and this seems to be a question of application of force, or in other words, character of strain, and it cannot be doubted that such a condition must be taken into consideration. Mr. Gilbert evidently recognizes it as a true cause, for in discussing the Basin Ranges, he says: "The displacement of comparatively rigid bodies of strata by vertical or nearly vertical faults, involves little horizontal diminution, and suggests the application of vertical pressure from below."

As to the first cause, rate of displacement, it is manifest that acceleration promotes rupture, retardation, flexure; but the other conditions which I have set forth so modify this rule, that rate of displacement cannot with any certainty be determined from facts of flexure and rupture alone.

The Uinta upheaval was partly by flexing, partly by faulting, and if there were no other conditions to determine these characteristics, we might say that so far as the beds were flexed they give evidence of slow movement; and so far as they were ruptured, evidence of a more rapid movement; and the twenty-five or thirty thousand feet of beds which are exposed to view and were involved in this uplift were chiefly of a character quite brittle, and this increases the evidence in favor of slow upheaval by flexing; but flexing may have been at great depths, and the superincumbent masses produced a condition favorable to flexing even in a rapid rate of movement. Many substances, especially metallic, are known to flow under great pressure, and it is probable that great pressure would produce in all rocks a quasi-fluid condition, and hence we cannot say that flexing attests to a slow rate. On the other hand, faulting, without considering other conditions, would seem to attest to rapid rate, but the character of the strain may have determined the rupture. Hence we may conclude that the characteristics of the displacement do not afford satisfactory evidence of the rate of its movement.

It will be seen hereafter that facts relating to degradation and sedimentation do give some satisfactory conclusions.

DEGRADATION.

EXTENT OF DEGRADATION.

The area of degradation which I have often for convenience called the region of uplift, represented in Plate II, embraces a little more than 2,800 square miles. From this about 8,300 cubic miles of rock have been carried away by rains and rivers—a mean degradation of about three cubic miles to the square mile. But a part of the region embraced on that plate will be discussed hereafter under the head of Yampa Plateau, and in what I have said concerning the Uinta Mountains above, this region has not been considered. Taking the Uinta Mountain region proper, then, we have an area of about 2,000 square miles from which about 7,100 cubic miles of rock have been taken, giving a mean degradation of 3½ cubic miles to every square mile of surface. But this has not been taken from all points equally; a greater amount has been carried from the axial region than from the districts along the flanks; and in the axial region a greater amount has been taken from the eastern than from the western end. Here where the displacement lines are carried highest, the surface lines are lowest, so that the degradation is more, not only by the amount of greater uplift but also by an additional amount in the deeper excavation of the valley. The region of highest uplift is the region of lowest degradation, and here more than 25,000 feet of beds have been removed.

To more fully comprehend the amount of degradation and its relation to upheaval, the bird's-eye view, Plate IV, has been constructed. Here we have represented a block from the Uinta Mountains forty miles in a north and south, and fifty miles in an east and west, direction. The one-half of the view in the foreground represents the degraded region, and the one-half in the background as it would appear had there been no degradation, but uplift only. It is believed that a careful study of the illustration will be amply repaid.

RATE OF DEGRADATION.

It would be interesting to know at what rate this degradation has progressed. We know of no means by which an absolute rate can be determined, but there are certain facts which lead to the conclusion that a maximum rate for this region was never established. These facts are found in the character of the topographic features produced by degradation, but in order that we may more fully understand them it will be well to briefly examine the agencies, methods, and conditions of degradation.

Degradation consists of disintegration and transportation, and they are mutually dependent parts of the general process. If disintegration is retarded, transportation is retarded, for the materials must be furnished ready for transportation. Again, if transportation is retarded, disintegration is retarded, as the beds to be disintegrated are to some extent protected by the accumulated products of the process; and if either is accelerated, the other must be accelerated.

DISINTEGRATION.

The rock masses which are brought above the level of the sea by upheaval are always found to be more or less coherent. Although these rocks are chiefly of sedimentary origin, the exceptions being extravasated masses, still they are usually found to have assumed a more or less crystalline structure, due either to the manner of their deposition or subsequent metamorphism, so that the minute parts, molecular or mechanical, of which these rocks were originally aggregated, cohere in great masses. There are many degrees of this coherence from bad-land sandstones or shales of extreme friability to schists and granites of extreme coherence; but whatever may be their degree of coherence, they must be disintegrated prior to their transportation to the sea.

PETROLOGY AS RELATED TO DISINTEGRATION.

The endurance of rocks as determined by their coherence depends on—

1. *Geologic Structure.*—The rocks may be irregularly massed or strati-

fied; the latter yield more readily than the former. The strata may be thick or thin; the latter yield more readily than the former. The strata may be horizontal or inclined, and the latter yield more readily than the former; and in each condition above mentioned heterogeneity promotes disintegration.

2. *Lithologic Structure.*—Under this head we may consider whether the beds are compacted crystals or cemented sediments; the latter yield more readily than the former, and heterogeneity promotes disintegration. Both in detrital and crystalline rocks there are certain conditions which may be grouped under the head of induration, including hardness and toughness, and the greater the induration the greater the stability; and the law of heterogeneity applies also to this condition.

3. *Chemical Structure.*—The principal condition of chemical constitution relating to endurance is solubility; the soluble yield more readily than the insoluble, and in chemical constitution the homogeneous is more stable than the heterogeneous.

It will thus be seen that in each particular mentioned above, the homogeneous is more stable than the heterogeneous, and these particulars in their correlations are themselves conditions of heterogeneity, so that the whole subject of petrology in its relation to disintegration, is one of degree of heterogeneity.

DYNAMICS OF DISINTEGRATION.

The principal forces of disintegration are gravity, heat, crystallization and chemical reaction. Gravity disintegrates the rocks directly where they break from cliffs and ledges partly by their own weight, and are further disintegrated by the fall, and indirectly through the agency of water in abrasion. Heat disintegrates the rocks by change of temperature, and probably by expansion of water permeating the rocks. Crystallogenic force also acts through the agency of water, for where the water which has permeated the rocks is frozen, the expansion due to this crystallization breaks them asunder. In chemical reaction the rocks are broken up through the agency of water which acts directly in dissolving them, or indirectly in promoting other chemical reactions.

In disintegration, therefore, we have an intricate plexus of forces acting on an intricate plexus of matter.

Now, so far as disintegration depends on the forces of heat, crystallization, and chemical change, the climate of the region is involved, aridity being contrasted with humidity, heat with cold, and great changes in either factor of climate promote disintegration; and so far as disintegration depends on gravity, the declivity of the surface exposed to degradation is involved, and a breaking up of the general declivity into greater and lesser slopes, promotes disintegration. We may, therefore, discuss the dynamics of disintegration as conditions of climate and declivity, and hence we may consider the factors of disintegration to be petrology, climate and declivity, and affirm that if the rate of transportation is sufficient to allow the forces of disintegration to act to their fullest extent, the rate of disintegration will depend on the heterogeneity of the rocks, heterogeneity of climate, and heterogeneity of declivity.

TRANSPORTATION.

Gravity is the force acting in transportation. It acts directly in transporting masses which fall from ledges and cliffs, and indirectly through the agency of water. In this indirect method there are two sources for the mechanical motion involved in the process: the one is the force of gravity inhering in the water, which is the vehicle of transportation, the other the force of gravity inhering in the rocks transported. Let us call the latter rock power, the former water power, and the rock material transported, load.

It is manifest that if the rocks on disintegration were in a fluid state, their own gravity would transport them. All of the rock material which is dissolved is placed in this condition, and its own gravity is the force which transports it; it does not float on the water, but behaves as an integral part of it, and with it obeys the laws of hydrodynamics. In this case the water is not the agent of transportation, but only the agent of disintegration.

When the rocks are disintegrated mechanically the water is properly the vehicle of transportation, and we have two cases, the one in which the load is driven by the water, the other in which it is floated on the water. When the transported matter is driven by the water along the bottom of the channel, both rock power and water power are employed, these two forces acting in inverse ratio with the specific gravity of water and load; that is, less water power is needed to drive the rock by the amount of the weight of the water displaced by the rock, for to this extent, rock power is used.

The amount of load which may be transported by the driving process, or in other words, by water power, plus an amount of rock power, begins with that degree of comminution which permits the load to be moved, and is limited by the power of the water on one hand and by friction on the other. And wherever the degree of comminution is such that the matter is transported partly or wholly by the agency of flotation to such extent as flotation is employed, the driving ceases and other limits are imposed.

We come now to the principal method of transportation; that is, that by flotation. Here the rock power is used in transportation, and the water is the vehicle. If the matter to be floated is of the same or less specific gravity than the water, a condition seldom obtaining, flotation is perfect, and the water power is not used either in transportation or to promote flotation. But when the floating matter is of greater specific gravity than the water, then the water power is used in promoting flotation. With a given amount of water and sufficient supply of load, the extent to which the water power will be utilized in promoting flotation will depend on two conditions: *First*, the power of the water, which is measured by fall into mass, or which may be expressed as velocity or again as declivity; *second*, it will depend on the relation which exists between the floating surface, or surface presented downward, and the mass of each particle of the load. In other words, it will depend on the specific gravity and comminution of the load. If the specific gravity of the load is but little greater than water, the velocity of the water becomes a very small factor, and the amount which can be transported will be chiefly limited by the containing capacity of the water, but this is a condition not actually found in nature. The difference between the specific gravity of water and load is great, and variable within such small limits that the variability may be neglected; but the relation between the floating surface and the mass of each particle of load may be determined by another condition than that of specific gravity, *i. e.*, size; for the ratio between the floating mass of a body, or the surface presented downward, and the mass of the body, increases with the diminution of a body. Then if the body is smaller, the ratio between the floating surface and mass is larger; and hence comminution promotes flotation. If this comminution is great, approaching complete or molecular comminution, the velocity of the water again becomes a small factor, and the amount of transportation chiefly depends on the containing capacity of the water; but as comminution is less and the size of the particles larger, some force must intervene to promote flotation, and this is derived from the water power; and to sustain the same amount of flotation more of this force must be utilized as the size of the particles increase. The amount of this force from which must be drawn the supply in supporting flotation depends, *cæteris paribus*, on the velocity or declivity, but practically the whole force is rarely utilized.

The extent to which this force is utilized depends upon many complex conditions by which the motion in the flowing water may be transmitted to the load. To float, the particles of rock must be suspended in the water, and as they fall from suspension during the process of transportation, they must be resuspended, so that the water power must be used in lifting, and this is done by the creation of secondary currents in regurgitation, eddying, boiling, &c., or movements in the water transverse or oblique to the direction of the flow, all of which impede the flow. If the flow is perfect no lifting can be done; so these secondary currents are produced by locally diverting the flow from its normal course, and this diversion to secure lifting must be directly or indirectly upward; the greater and oftener this diversion the more lifting will be done. In other words, we may say that water power is applied to the lifting of the particles and thus promotes flotation by heterogeneity of flow, and this heterogeneity of flow is induced by the heterogeneity of channel in both horizontal and vertical direction, but chiefly in the latter. And in obedience to well known laws of friction this heterogeneity of flow is greatly increased by intensifying the flow, or in other words, increasing the velocity of the water; and velocity is due to declivity. And that heterogeneity of channel, which by producing heterogeneity of flow utilizes the water power in lifting the load, is also due to declivity; and hence it remains, first, that the water power, *cæteris paribus*, is a function of declivity; and, second, the utilization of the water power, *cæteris paribus*, is a function of declivity; so that with a given amount of water and sufficient supply of load, the rate of transportation through the agency of flotation depends on declivity; and the amount of transportation through driving also depends on declivity. Therefore the rate of transportation of all mechanically comminuted matter is determined by declivity.

I have spoken of the containing capacity of water for load of the same or less specific gravity than water, but the amount of such load is so minute in comparison with the whole amount that we may neglect it. Again, I have spoken of the containing capacity of water for particles of load of greater specific gravity than water; the amount of matter transported in this way is great, but usually the supply is so limited that the containing capacity is rarely reached; but it seems probable from observations made on transportation of bad-land detritus that there are times when this containing capacity is actually reached, when the amount transported is limited by this condition, that is, containing capacity. Then what is this containing capacity? In matter of this character without water the rock power cannot overcome interstitial friction, and hence the matter is not transported. In order that it may be transported by rock power it is necessary, first, that the interstitial spaces shall be filled with water; and, second, that an amount of water be added sufficient to reduce interstitial friction so that it may be overcome by rock power. And it is possible that this can be determined mathematically for particles of any given form, size and weight; but in nature these forms are multifarious, and the determination of the containing capacity is a proper subject of experiment. I know of no such experiments having been made; but, from observations in nature, I am led to the conclusion that the containing capacity of water for particles of this nature is at least three times its own weight.

Again I must remark that the last mentioned condition of transportation is of very infrequent occurrence; and it remains, then, that in general transportation, the rate is determined by declivity.

Having now examined the processes of disintegration and transportation separately, we will examine them as combined in the

METHODS OF DEGRADATION.

These are, first, erosion or degradation of the general surface; second, corrasion or degradation of the stream channels; and, third, sapping or degradation of cliffs.

Erosion.—This is distributed over the general surface; the rocks are disintegrated by climatic agencies and transported into streams by the wash of rains, both by driving and flotation, and flotation is largely promoted by the beating of rains. In this method the rate of degradation depends on the rate of transportation. This is a fact of almost universal observation; for wherever there is soil or loose earth, the amount of such matter is the excess of disintegration over transportation.

We have already seen in the former analysis of transportation that with a given quantity of water, transportation will depend on declivity, but in the transportation belonging to this method of degradation the quantity of water is a factor of transportation only to a limited extent, for increased rainfall promotes the growth of vegetation which serves as a protection to the soil. Nor is this protection inconsiderable, for it preserves the rocks from the beating of the storms, and prevents the waters from gathering rapidly into rills and brooks, and strains the water of its earthy sediments. I have many times witnessed the action of a storm in an arid region where the disintegrated rocks were unprotected by forests, shrubbery, or turf, and as often have I been impressed with the wonderful power of the infrequent storm to gather up and carry away the land, as compared with the frequent storm in the prairie or forest of a land more richly clad. The same contrast may be observed in a region brought under the dominion of man by cultivation where the surface of a plowed field is swept away by a storm, and the furrows are the channels for floods of mud, while the meadow receives the rain with outstretched arms of verdure, which bear it gently to the earth, where it is gathered into quiet rills, which feed a stream made turbid it is true, but pure when compared with the stream of mud flowing from the field from which the plowman was driven by the storm.

Erosion, then, or surface degradation is not greatly promoted by increased rainfall, and it may be that its effect is rather to retard the process; but the difference between greater or lesser rainfall is plainly manifest in the topographic features produced—little rainfall giving angular reliefs; much, rounded reliefs.

Neglecting such a hypothetic condition as no rainfall, we have in nature to consider only *greater* or *lesser* rainfall. With greater rainfall we have a greater power, but a lesser utilization of the power; with lesser rainfall we have lesser power, but greater utilization; and in these varying conditions, just where maximum degradation is found I am not able to state. Hence, in the process of degradation which I have called erosion, we have simply to consider declivity, with exceptions so minute that they may be neglected.

Now, it must be taken into consideration that this is the most important method of degradation, as it acts everywhere on the dry land; but, because its operations are so greatly diffused, being universal in its action on dry land, it is so subtle and minute in its manifestations within any area which may come immediately under the eye that its efficiency is apt to be underrated.

Corrasion.—This is the action of waters gathered into streams where their operations are confined to more limited areas, that is, along the channels of such streams. Here the material supplied from the surrounding surfaces by erosion is further transported by the streams, and in the process of transportation becomes the instrument used in disintegrating the stream beds; and the material thus disintegrated is added to that furnished by erosion, and with it is transported by the streams, and this added material also becomes an instrument of disintegration.

The force used in disintegration is rock power and water power; load is the instrument, water the agent. All processes of solution are neglected.

The force of rock power and water power is measured by mass into fall, and this may be considered as declivity; the specific gravity of the instrument not being greatly variable may be neglected. There are other conditions of instrument, such as hardness and angularity of particles, which for any given particle might be of value in determining its efficiency; but, in the multifarious particles of diverse hardness and form, a general average will be established for streams, variable within such small limits that these conditions also may be neglected. The only condition of instrument of sufficient importance to be considered in this connection is size of particles, for the utilization of the particles as instruments is dependent, *cæteris paribus*, on their size. If the particles be too large they cannot be transported, and thus cannot be used as instruments; and within the limits of size transported, a greater amount of instrument will be used as the size of the particles diminish; that is, with a given stream, the instrument is increased with comminution of instrument, the instrument being the load, and load being increased by comminution as has been seen.

We have next to consider the beds to be corraded, and so far as their constitution is a factor in corrasion, it may be brought into the simple expression that heterogeneity promotes corrasion. But a part of the instrument of corrasion is derived from the rocks corraded; and as heterogeneity of these rocks promotes disintegration, and to the same extent promotes corrasion, it further augments the instrument of corrasion in the channel below. But it has been seen that in transportation the utilization of the water power in promoting flotation as a function of heterogeneity of flow is a function of declivity *cæteris paribus*. Hence, declivity not only increases the force, but it also utilizes the force, and, hence, multiplies itself as a factor of corrasion. A part of the instrument in corrasion is the load of the stream derived from erosion; and we have already seen that the amount of this load depends chiefly upon declivity; hence, the amount of instrument from this source depends on declivity of erosion, and the amount of instrument derived from corrasion depends on declivity; and the power of corrasion, that is, rock power plus water power, depends on declivity. Hence, with a given quantity of water and a given character of bed, rate of corrasion depends on declivity. Again, rapid corrasion increases the declivity of erosion, and hence increases erosion; and this increased erosion augments the instrument of corrasion, hence, increases corrasion; and declivity by the two methods of degradation enters the general problem of degradation as a factor with a rapidly increasing value.

Corrasion is a very important method of degradation, although its results are of much less magnitude than those of erosion. The evidence of this can be seen, and the results often strike the student of physical geography with great force. The deep channels in which the rivers run are grand topographic features. Deep river valleys and mountain gorges are everywhere seen to have been produced by this agency, and the power of the streams in carving their winding paths is readily comprehended. But the magnitude of this agency is more thoroughly brought into visual comprehension in the cañons that traverse the Plateau Province, for here erosion has not kept pace with corrasion. All the processes of erosion and sapping serve to obliterate the evidences of corrasion, and the latter appears more plainly as its progress exceeds that of the other methods; but still the evidences of corrasion rarely disappear until the land is buried by the sea; for wherever an area of land is above its base level of degradation, there corrasion will be manifest by deepening its channel; and wherever the dry land has been brought down near to its base level, there corrasion is manifest by widening its channel.

There is another method of degradation to be considered, viz:

SAPPING.—The walls that inclose the channels of corrasion are broken down by gravity, and when in the progress of corrasion the channel of a stream reaches beds which easily disintegrate, having passed through beds which disintegrate but slowly, degradation is increased by an undermining process, and as corrasion still continues through a series of yielding and unyielding beds, the walls of the streams are carried back in a series of steps, the tread of each step being the summit of a harder bed, the rise of each step the escarped edge of the harder bed above, underlaid by the softer. It is manifest that the conditions favorable to the continuation of this cliff degradation to any great distance back from the stream are found only where the beds are horizontally, or nearly horizontally stratified. But sapping is not confined to the undermining of walls produced by corrasion, but is carried on in simple anticlinal upheavals from the axis toward the flanks; in upheavals of the Uinta type, in like manner, and in the blocks displaced as integers, like those in regions having the Kaibab and other structures, from the elevated to the depressed portions. In these cases the cliffs are produced by the unequal erosion of harder and softer beds wherever upheaval exceeds degradation, and climatic conditions are favorable; and, further, this sapping process is carried on in regions of great declivity, where deep channels of corrasion are formed, whatever may be the petrologic conditions, the alternation of softer and harder beds not being an absolute, but only an accessory condition. In those mountain regions where the rocks are granites, schists, or extravasated masses, every little stream engaged in deepening its channel furnishes conditions favorable to sapping; and so these walls are ever yielding, in small fragments that tumble down from time to time, in large fragments when cliffs or crags topple over, and in great masses by land slides. So wherever cliffs are formed, whether by deep corrasion or unequal erosion, the cliffs themselves are degraded, disintegration beginning with the breaking of the rocks above through atmospheric causes, aided by gravity. Then the rocks are transported by gravity from the higher to lower levels when the disintegration is increased by the fall, and the rocks are left in a condition to be readily transported by the wash of rains or the flow of streams.

The extent to which degradation is carried on by this sapping though much less than either of the others, is so great that it must not be neglected in any consideration of this subject.

In a mountain region every stream forms cliffs by deep corrasion, and every cliff has a talus in evidence of the efficiency of this method, and we see its effects exhibited in the most remarkable manner in the long lines of cliffs or towering escarpments which stand athwart the Plateau Province.

In this method of degradation petrologic conditions may be more or less favorable, but within these conditions the principal factor in determining rate of degradation is declivity. The declivity must be very great for the initiation of the process. With rocks already disintegrated by atmospheric agencies, the declivity must be greater than what is usually denominated natural slope; that is, it must be so great that rock power can overcome friction so as to transport the material to a lower level; and again, that gravity may be used as a force of disintegration, the declivity must be still further increased, and with this increase of declivity the rate of disintegration and transportation by falling is increased at a great ratio until the rocks are undermined, when the conditions again multiply the power. But rapid corrasion, which depends on declivity, increases sapping; and sapping, which depends on declivity, increases corrasion by adding to the instrument of corrasion, and again declivity is multiplied as a factor in degradation.

To this rule that sapping promotes corrasion by adding to the instrument of corrasion, there are three curious exceptions, one of which is of great importance. The first is where the cliff produced by deep corrasion, before it has retreated from the bank of the stream, tumbles down so as to choke the stream. In this case the material falling from the cliffs serves to protect the underlying stream bed, and, so far as it ponds the water up stream, it causes it to precipitate its load, and thus deprives it of the instrument of corrasion. But this fallen matter is rapidly attacked by the stream, is soon taken up as load, and used as an instrument of corrasion.

The second exception is where a lateral stream enters a main one, the lateral stream having so great a declivity as to be able to transport great quantities of coarse material during local flood time, or that flood time which pertains to the secondary stream, but not to the primary. In this case it may sweep along its greatly-inclined bed into the main channel, load derived from sapping, or even from erosion, which cannot be farther transported by the main stream, and this new matter for the time being serves as a protection to the bed of the main stream. In the Colorado River, with very few exceptions, all the falls and rapids which beset its course through the great cañons are caused by dams made by side streams having great declivity. A few of the falls are made by dams formed by the sapping of the immediate cliffs of the main river.

The third exception is found where streams having great declivity run through beds of incoherent sands. Here load is rapidly added to the stream by gravity, and the stream not being confined by water tight rocks, its waters penetrate the interstitial spaces of the sands and serve to overcome the friction of slope, and thus assist rock power in transporting the sand into the stream. Here the stream cannot have high banks, and the channel is greatly widened and is engaged in transporting load furnished it from the sides, and can make but little progress in corrasion, for every particle carried from the bottom of the stream is rapidly replaced by one from the sides. This condition is finely illustrated in many places along the course of the Virgin River, a tributary of the Colorado. In one place where its course is through indurated and homogeneous rocks, its channel is from 20 to 50 feet in width, and from 1,500 to 3,000 feet in depth; it runs through a narrow but profound gorge. But when it passes a well defined geological horizon from these coherent into extremely incoherent beds, its channel abruptly widens, and the stream is a broad sheet of water many hundreds of yards in width and but a few inches in depth. Again this condition is well illustrated in the Platte River where it crosses the Plains. Here the beds through which the river runs are incoherent, and although the river has as great a fall as the Colorado through the plateaus, and although the climatic conditions are essentially the same, yet the former runs in a broad sheet scarcely below the level of the plain, while the latter runs in a narrow groove at profound depths below the general surface. Thus it is that the streams, though they may have great fall, and though the stream beds may be of material that can be rapidly transported, yet they do not succeed in excavating deep channels, for every particle taken from the bottom is replaced. Nevertheless general degradation is carried on by such streams at a rapid rate, but not at a maximum rate, for the water permeating the sands on either side is steadily and rapidly evaporated, and is thus lost as an agent of degradation. There are many streams in the arid region of America, running alternately through harder and softer beds, which are continuously degrading the coherent rocks and intermittently degrading the incoherent rocks; that is, the streams are ever living where the beds are coherent, but when they reach the sands the waters sink and re-appear where the beds below are harder. Through these harder beds the streams cañon, and through the softer beds low plains stretch either way from the course of the stream; and it is only during flood time that the channels are cut across these plains from cañon to cañon.

But dropping these exceptions, all of them interesting cases, let us return to the main argument. We have seen that ever are the effects of declivity in degradation multiplied directly and indirectly. Wherever the rate of degradation by any one method is increased it is due chiefly to increased declivity, and wherever the rate of one method of degradation is increased, the rate of all other methods is increased.

We may not be able to give mathematic expression to rate of degradation in terms of declivity, but Hopkins and Babbage have shown that the power to transport load of a given size of particles increases with the sixth power of the velocity of water, and it is probable that the rate of degradation increases with the velocity of water in very nearly the same ratio, but modified slightly by a multiplicity of climatic and petrologic conditions.

It will be seen that in the above discussion I have neglected one term of climate, that is temperature. My field of study has been limited to the frigid and temperate climates, and for the effect of a torrid climate I have no facts to guide me to valid conclusions, but within my field of study the temperature term, though modifying the methods and topographic results of degradation, does not invalidate the result I have reached as to the overshadowing importance of declivity. Increased cold diminishes the protection derived from vegetation and permits greater rainfall to produce greater degradation. But in a given latitude increased cold is due to increased elevation. (This increased elevation is also increased declivity.) But this is again modified by the fact that moisture descends as snow, and to that extent the beating power of rains is lost. Where these snows accumulate as ice, forming glaciers, another modification of degradation is introduced, diminishing the effects of the water in degradation and changing the topographic features; that is, any given amount of precipitation of water will produce more degradation acting as rains and rivers than as snows and glaciers. By the former condition atmospheric disintegration is more rapid, and corrasion is confined to narrower channels, and thus sapping is promoted. Transportation in ice and water are governed by the same conditions of flotation, and the greater heterogeneity of river chamel promotes greater flotation, so that degradation in each of its elements of disintegration and transportation is faster by rains and rivers than by snows and glaciers. Hence, as cold increases, degradation is promoted by the decrease of protection derived from vegetation until that degree of cold is reached where the moisture is precipitated as snow, when low temperature serves to decrease degradation.

Having considered all the modifying conditions of climate and petrology, it yet remains that degradation increases with declivity through the combined forces of water power and rock power in a rapidly-multiplying rate from that low degree of declivity which permits the transportation of finely-comminuted load to that high degree of declivity which permits the load to be moved by its own gravity, when the effect of declivity is again multiplied at a still higher rate until verticality is reached and undermining begins and another multiplication of the effect of declivity ensues.

There are conditions of degradation in the extremes of declivity worthy of mention. In high degrees of declivity transportation in a horizontal direction is limited, the cliffs soon tumble down, and degradation by this process ceases. In a very low degree of declivity approaching horizontality the power of transporting material is also very small. The degradation of the last few inches of a broad area of land above the level of the sea would require a longer time than all the thousands of feet which might have been above it, so far as this degradation depends on mechanical processes—that is, driving or flotation; but here the disintegration by solution and the transportation of the material by the agency of fluidity come in to assist the slow processes of mechanical degradation, and finally perform the chief part of the task.

We may now conclude that the higher the mountain, the more rapid its degradation; that high mountains cannot live much longer than low mountains, and that mountains cannot remain long as mountains; they are ephemeral topographic forms. Geologically all existing mountains are recent; the ancient mountains are gone. But existing mountains may be old or young as compared with other existing mountains. We may speak of the age of mountains, referring to the age of the rocks of which they are composed, but this will have no reference to the age of the mountain form. We may speak of the age of a mountain with respect to the inception of the upheaval which exposed the rocks to that degradation which has produced the mountain form; and this epoch will not be very long ago, geologically, for the rate of upheaval must be greater than the rate of degradation, else mountain forms will not be produced. We may speak of the age of mountains, referring to the completion of the upheaval by which the mountain forms were produced through degradation; the time which has elapsed since the epoch to which we then refer must be short indeed; but if, in speaking of the age of mountains, we refer to the time when those topographic forms were produced, they are all newly born.

Having found that degradation is accelerated by increased declivity at a high rate, let us apply this law to the degradation of the Uinta uplift and see what topographic features would have been produced if the uplift had been abrupt or greatly faster than degradation. As the area was uplifted in large part as an integer, its steep flanks would then have been regions of great declivity, while its axial region would have comparatively gentle slopes, and as the first streams heading along the axis ran toward the flanks, these streams would not only have had channels suddenly increasing in declivity at the flanks, but the amount of water carried by the streams would have steadily increased from axis to flanks, and hence corrasion on the flanks would have proceeded at a rate determined by these multiplied causes. As the main channels were thus corraded all the lateral channels would in like manner have been rapidly corraded; this would have induced rapid sapping and rapid erosion, and the degradation along the flanks would have far exceeded degradation along the axis, and this would have resulted in the production of an ever narrowing axial ridge. An examination of the map reveals the fact that these are not the topographic characteristics of the Uinta Mountains. The axial region is higher in the western portion of that part of the range under consideration, but the difference in elevation between the flanks and axis is inconsiderable when compared with the whole amount of degradation; while in the eastern portion of the part of the range under consideration the axial region is much lower than the flanking region on either side. Here the excess of degradation in the axial region is accounted for by remembering that the degradation of consequent drainage has been assisted by the degradation resulting from extra limital or through drainage. But in the former case, *i. e.*, the western portion of the region under consideration, the drainage is all consequent on the upheaval, and to account for the plateau like character of the region, we have to suppose either that the elevation being constant has been but little faster than degradation, or else that elevation has been intermittent.

Let us further consider these two hypotheses, one of which must be true. If elevation was constant but slow, the axial region was first attacked by degradation, and as it was slowly uplifted, degradation kept this axial region down so that an axial ridge was not produced. If elevation was intermittent it might have been fast for a time, and then ceased until the region was planed down to a general level now represented only by the summits of the highest peaks, and then a new upheaval carried it to its present elevation. But the rate of this last uplift must have been slow or the axial ridge would have been more pronounced, and hence we may infer that the elevation was either slow by continuous motion, or what would be its equivalent, slow through intermission of movement, with the last epoch of elevation slow. Further light will be thrown on this subject when we consider sedimentation. It is manifest that if elevation was slow so that degradation progressed nearly as fast as displacement, then degradation was slow. Again consider the amount of degradation. From this portion of the Uinta range a block three and one-half miles in thickness has been carried away, all since the close of Mesozoic Age; and for this degradation the declivity was small so that its progress was slow, and we have some conception of the amount of time which has elapsed since the beginning of the Uinta upheaval.

SCHOLIUM.

Let us now turn aside for a moment from the main argument to consider a statement which I have elsewhere made concerning the Basin Ranges. These are monoclinal ridges of displacement, of narrow base and steep declivities where conditions for rapid degradation obtain, but the amount of degradation of any Basin Range is exceedingly small as compared with the Uinta Range, and we are forced to conclude that the epoch of its upheaval is much later than that of the inception of the Uinta uplift, but may be of about the same date as the last throw of the Uinta displacement.

SEDIMENTATION.

Soon after the inception of this upheaval, sedimentation began on either flank and continued during the progress of the uplift until on the north side more than 6,000 feet of sandstones and shales had been deposited, and where the Brown's Park beds overlap Bridger beds about 8,000 feet. On the south side also there was a great accumulation, the extent and characteristics of which are not yet fully known. Geologists will understand that the thicknesses given refer only to the beds which remain to be studied. There may have been much greater sedimentation; beds may have been formed during periods of sedimentation which were carried away during periods of dry land conditions, and especially during the last great period of degradation not yet ended, and of which sediments there are no residuary fragments attesting to their former existence.

On both sides of the range, but especially to the north, we know that the progress of sedimentation was interrupted by periods of dry land conditions. These dry land conditions prevailed over a large area during the epoch separating the Lower Green River from the Bridger period, but a part of this interval of time at least was occupied in sedimentation over a portion of the great lacustrine area. Again, a period of dry land conditions prevailed between the deposition of the Bridger and the Brown's Park Groups. The latter was deposited over areas in the region of uplift beyond the reaches of the antecedent lakes represented by the four lower Cenozoic groups. How far the Brown's Park Lake extended over the region which had previously been occupied by the waters in which the earlier Tertiary sediments were deposited we do not know. Wherever the overlap of the Brown's Park beds on the Lower Cenozoic groups has been studied the former terminate in escarpments, and no evidence of shore line has been seen. The Bishop Mountain Conglomerate which has been found to lie unconformably on all the other geological formations of this region, except the Brown's Park, and possibly on this latter also, is neither a marine nor lacustrine deposit, but is believed to be a subaerial gravel. It is possible many geologists would ascribe it to the action of ice, but in any case it need not be considered in our account of sedimentation.

Such were the general changes from emergence to submergence throughout the region of downthrow, but there was a narrow belt of country between the general region of uplift and the general region of downthrow which was subject to more frequent changes than the greater ones described above.

We find, first, that there are many overlaps, *i. e.*, that later beds extend beyond the limits of earlier beds. To accomplish this result it is manifest that the waters of the lakes must have risen or the land subsided. Again, we find that certain beds thin out shoreward. It is manifest in this case that the waters of the lakes must have fallen or the land have risen. Again, we find upper lake beds unconformable on lower lake beds. Here it is manifest that a dry land period separated their deposition, and that displacement occurred. These outthinnings, overlappings, and unconformities appear from time to time from the base to the summit of all the fresh water beds older than the Brown's Park.

There are some other interesting facts relating to the belt under consideration, viz, the appearance of many conglomerates which are rapidly changed into sandstones in a direction farther from shore. These conglomerates are found to be made up of the more or less water-worn fragments of limestones, sandstones, and quartzites similar to those outcroppings in the mountain region or area of uplift, and often contain the same fossils, leading us to conclude that they are derived from that region.

It should be remarked here that the appearance of these conglomerates, together with the overlappings, outthinnings, and unconformities before mentioned, furnish the evidence on which we decide that this was the old shore-line, and that the lake beds were never continuous over the great Uinta area. On the other hand, the fact that no such phenomena have been observed in the outcroppings of the Mesozoic and Paleozoic beds leads us to conclude that they were at one time continuous over the Uinta area, and this is strengthened by the fact that in all these lower groups any bed found on the one flank re-appears on the other with all its lithologic characteristics; and it is thus that we fix the epoch of the inception of the Uinta upheaval after the close of the deposition of the Upper Hogback Sandstone of the Point of Rocks Group, and before the deposition of the lowest bed of the Bitter Creek formation.

Returning again to the consideration of sedimentation in the region of downthrow in its relation to displacement and degradation in the region of uplift, we have first to consider the amount of sedimentation or building up of the sediments on the flanks of the uplifts to the extent of many thousand of feet; next, the general unconformities which separate some of the formations; and, lastly, the minor unconformities, overlappings, and outthinnings observed in the zone of ancient shore-lines. From all these facts it appears that displacement, degradation, and sedimentation were in a general way simultaneous and continuous up to the close of the Bridger period, but interrupted by many minor cessations in the progress of displacement and some cessations in the progress of deposition, and that between the Bridger and Brown's Park periods there was a long time when no sediments were accumulated.

The Uinta uplift in the region of Brown's Park was at one time several thousand feet greater than we have represented it to be; but after the deposition of the Brown's Park beds it fell down that much; the evidence of this will more fully appear when we have discussed the Yampa plateau, Diamond Peak, the Dry Mountains, and Brown's Park.

RECAPITULATION.

We will now recapitulate some of the important conclusions reached in the study of the geology of the Uinta Mountains. First, the upheaval began at the close of the Mesozoic Age, and continued with slight intermissions until after the Bridger period, and the total amount of upheaval in the axial region was more than 30,000 feet. The region was upheaved partly as an integer and partly as a body of minute parts. Second, *pari passu* with upheaval degradation progressed, and in some places along the axial portions of the region this degradation amounts to more than 25,000 feet, and the mean degradation is three and one-half miles, and from the entire area there has been a total degradation of 7,095 cubic miles. While we have no means of determining any absolute rate of degradation, we are led to conclude that a maximum rate was not established; that, as upheaval was slow, degradation was slow. Third, *pari passu* with displacement and degradation in the region of uplift, there was sedimentation in the region of downthrow. This sedimentation was sometimes intermittent over large areas, frequently intermittent along the shore-line zones. These sediments were derived in part at least from the region of uplift, but probably mingled with materials brought from districts not embraced in the region under discussion. On the north side of the mountains the amount of sedimentation was more than 6,000 feet, and where the Brown's Park beds overlap Bridger beds the amount of sedimentation was about 8,000 feet.

THE YAMPA PLATEAU.

DISPLACEMENT.

The structural sections of Plate I embrace not only the Uinta Mountain region, but also extend over the region which I have designated as the Yampa Plateau. The facts relating to the present position of the formations are there fully set forth. On Plate V we have separated the stereogram of the Yampa region from the general stereogram, Plate III. Referring to Plate V, attention is called to the Island Park sag *d*, *d*, to the Echo Park sag *e*, to the Split Mountain cusp *c*, to the monoclinal flexure of Cliff Creek *m*, *m*, *m*, to the Fox Creek flexure *f*, and to the Yampa fault *g*, *g*, which branches midway in its course.

A comparison of this stereogram with the geological map will be instructive.

The Yampa Plateau is on the south side of the Uinta Mountains, and all the lines of displacement in the stereogram, except the Yampa fault, show the upheaval to be northward corresponding to the general upheaval of the Uinta Mountains, but the exception mentioned exhibits a northward throw. This great displacement is a flexure at its eastern end; but it finally changes into a dragged fault, where the thrown beds are flexed upward at the end, and then into a clean fault; midway in its course it branches; the northern branch is a fault as far as it has been traced; the southern branch changes from a fault to a monoclinal flexure, and finally these branches of the great displacement fade out, but in a manner not clearly understood, as the region is marked by an accumulation of late subaerial gravels, by soil and by vegetation, and on the stereogram this uncertain area has been represented by broken lines. By referring to the map it will be seen that the main fault with its branches is represented in the topography of the country by bold cliffs. These lines of cliffs are broken by many deep gorges of corrasion descending from the plateau to the lowlands where the stratigraphy is plainly revealed, and the lower beds of Triassic sandstone are seen on the same geographic level as the upper beds of Uinta Sandstone, so that the total displacement is about 5,000 feet. These cliffs are due immediately to displacement; where this displacement is by faulting the cliffs are escarpments, but where it is by flexure the flexed beds remain, and the slope of the cliffs conforms in a general way with the dip of the strata. Hence these lines of cliffs have not receded from the locus of displacement, although they are so precipitous as so furnish conditions favorable to rapid degradation by direct sapping, corrasion, and general erosion. From these facts we inevitably conclude that the displacement is of late date. But the Triassic beds on the upheaved side are gone, and in many places a great thickness of Carboniferous beds also, while on the thrown side a notable thickness of Trias yet remains. The non-recession of the cliffs proves that the displacement was not ended long ago, if indeed the movement has yet ceased, while the occurrence of the beds on the thrown side, which have been degraded from the upheaved side, lead us to refer the inception of the upheaval to an epoch of much earlier date, and to infer that the displacement was slow, yet not so slow that degradation was able to keep apace.

When we come hereafter to discuss the relation of this displacement to other facts of displacement, degradation, and sedimentation, it will appear that this displacement was not upheaval in relation to the general region under discussion in this chapter, but was in fact downthrow, whatever it might have been in relation to the level of the sea or in that other relation, which yet may be a very different thing, *i. e.*, to the center of the earth.

SCHOLIUM.

Early in this volume I distinctly defined my use of the terms "upheaval" "subsidence," "uplift," and "downthrow," and restricted the meaning of these words in such a manner that they should relate only to adjacent and compared beds of rock, but I recognize three categories of relations that may be expressed by these terms, viz, the relation of parts of a geological horizon to each other, the relation of parts of a geological horizon to the level of the sea, and the relation of parts of a geological horizon to the center of the earth. For these several categories it would be a great advantage to geological science, by leading to greater simplicity and precision of description and to clearer conceptions, if different verbal representatives could be used for the different ideas.

DEGRADATION.

The amount of degradation in the region of the Yampa Plateau though less than in the Uinta region as defined above, is still great. The maximum degradation is found at the few points where deep cañons cut the cliffs of the Yampa fault, and Uinta Sandstone is found in the floor. In these places there has been more than 15,000 feet carried away since the close of Mesozoic time; the mean degradation over the entire area has been 8,000 feet, or a little more than one and a half miles, and the total more than 1,200 cubic miles.

SEDIMENTATION.

A part of the rock material taken from this region was doubtless deposited in the Tertiary lake region to the south, another portion probably into the Brown's Park Lake, and still another and very considerable portion has been carried away by the Colorado River to the distant sea.

JUNCTION MOUNTAIN.

This district was studied in the earlier years of the exploration of the region, and since that time it has not been carefully reviewed. In my notes I make mention of a fault running in a north and south direction to the east of the axis of upheaval, with a throw to the westward, but the magnitude and general characteristics of the fault are not given. The sections given in Chapter I of this volume, figures 1 and 2, represent the idea of its structure obtained at the time it was studied, but subsequent years of observation in other regions lead me to place no great value on the observations made and conclusions reached at that time.

DIAMOND PEAK.

To the north of O-wi-yu-kuts Plateau is Diamond Peak. The principal mass of the mountain is on the north side of the great Uinta fault, but the foot of the mountain stretches across from the thrown to the upheaved side of the fault.

For a long time this mountain was an enigma. From its position it ought to be a monoclinal ridge, but it is not. Again, its base rises chiefly from the thrown side of the fault, but its summit rises many hundreds of feet higher than the plateau on the upheaved side of the fault, and it seems to stand as a contradiction to all known laws of the progress of degradation. On a first visit to the mountain no clew to this enigma was obtained; on a second visit a better understanding of its lithologic constitution was obtained; and on a third and final visit, which was somewhat protracted, it is believed that the problem was solved.

All that portion of the base of the peak north of the fault is composed of beds of the Bitter Creek period lying horizontally. On the horizontal beds sandstones and limestones are piled in confusion. In the sandstones no fossils were found, but they resemble lithologically the sandstones of Carboniferous Age. The limestones contain Carboniferous fossils. We have in fact a huge pile of Carboniferous rocks resting on a base of horizontal Tertiary sandstones. Now to explain how rocks of an older horizon were piled on a later, we have a fact which was discovered after the second visit, but before the third, viz, that there had been two movements along the line of this fault in opposite directions. By the first movement the Uinta or upheaved side was carried about 3,000 feet higher in relation to the beds on the north side than now appears. Subsequently by a reverse movement it fell back the 3,000 feet. After the former displacement and before the latter, we may reasonably suppose that here a great cliff faced northward, for the total displacement by faulting was about 23,000 feet, and the only hypothesis necessary to the explanation of such a line of cliffs is that displacement was in its later development faster than degradation. Such cliffs would rapidly tumble down, and beds of Carboniferous Age might thus be placed on beds of Tertiary Age. But further, immediately to the west and immediately to the east along this zone of displacement, the line of faulting in its meanders back and forth through the zone of flexure, which has heretofore been described, passes some distance from the upheaved side of the zone toward the thrown side, and hence the beds on the upheaved side dip at a great angle to the northward, and are in a position to more readily tumble down, and doubtless this condition obtained where the

O-wi-yu-kuts cliff overhung the Tertiary sandstones that form the base of Diamond Peak.

This double movement along the plane of the Uinta fault is seen farther west beyond Red Creek, where it was first discovered, and where the sandstones of the Point of Rocks period are found to have been dragged down by the later and southward throw. Similar evidences are seen farther eastward, between Diamond Peak and Red Creek, and the topographic features of the region in like manner give evidence of the later movement, for some of the peaks composed of Bitter Creek sandstones are higher than the mountains and plateaus of quartzite and Uinta Sandstone. To the east of Diamond Peak this second displacement did not follow the old plane of faulting, but trended irregularly northward and bent downward the edges of the beds which originally abutted against the southern wall of the fault, which was composed of Uinta Sandstone and underlying rocks. Subsequent degradation has carried away the upper part of these beds that were turned down, and we now see fragments standing on edge and the younger beds are on the south side, the older beds on the north side, a fact which I have stated in a former chapter, and which is thus explained. But we have still further evidence of this later throw on the south side. The beds of the Brown's Park Lake were deposited against the foot of Diamond Peak, and this later displacement was subsequent to the deposition of these beds, and the plane of faulting cuts them in twain. Those fragments on the north side of the fault lie high upon the side of Diamond Peak, while the beds on the south side of the fault are low down in the valley at the foot of the peak. The latter are nearly horizontal; the former have a general dip southward, but are broken and greatly contorted.

This mountain, of origin so strange, was curiously enough the scene of the great diamond bubble, so skillfully burst by my brother geologist, Clarence King.

THE DRY MOUNTAINS.

This low range of mountains extends in a southeasterly direction from Vermilion Creek to the Snake River, and, topographically, appears to be a continuation of the great monoclinal ridge of Carboniferous sandstone northeast of Po Cañon, but, in fact, these mountains are made up of beds of Tertiary Age, though there are outcrops of Mesozoic beds in the depths of the deeper gulches.

This range marks the continuation of the displacement that I have called the great Uinta fault, and the evidences of the reverse movement are complete. The first movement, which was upheaval on the Uinta side and throw on the northeast side, seems to have been by monoclinal flexure, while the last movement, which was throw on the Uinta side and upheaval on the northeast side, was in part by flexure and in part by fracture. But in the period of time separating the two movements the Brown's Park beds were deposited across the zone of original flexure which had been greatly degraded; still farther to the northwest there is another line of displacement approximately parallel to the first, with its throw also on the southwest side, corresponding in this respect with the throw of the last displacement in the Dry Mountain district. This northeast displacement fades out in a northwest direction, and entirely disappears at the divide between the water-shed of the Vermilion and the water-shed of the Snake River. When it is first seen near this divide it is a gentle monoclinal flexure, and steadily increases in abruptness along its line in a northeasterly direction until the bluffs of the Snake River are reached, where it is seen as a dragged fault. There seems to be no doubt that these displacements having throws to the southwest were synchronous, while the evidence that the monoclinal flexure with throw to the northeast was of earlier date is complete, for between the two periods the Brown's Park beds were deposited—that is, the Brown's Park beds are seen to have been involved in the displacement having a southwest throw, but took no part in the displacement with a northeast throw, as this last displacement was made and the beds involved in it were truncated prior to the deposition of the Brown's Park beds, and these beds were placed over their upturned edges.

In the Dry Mountains some interesting facts have been observed. Along or near to the line of double or reverse displacements we sometimes find an escarpment facing the southwest, composed of beds of the Bridger period, or of still lower Cenozoic rocks, and dipping back toward the northeast, but as often we find escarpments facing the northeast composed of beds of the Brown's Park period, horizontal or gently dipping to the southwest, *i. e.*, the escarpments of this range are sometimes reversed, because of the reverse movement along the planes of fracture or the zone of flexure.

BROWN'S PARK.

In this discussion I shall not only include Brown's Park proper, but a district of country stretching to the southwest, between the Dry Mountains and Escalante Peaks to the Snake River. Here we have a geological basin with a floor of Uinta Sandstone and Carboniferous and Mesozoic rocks. Its longest diameter is in the same direction as the axis of the Uinta uplift, and while the basin extends somewhat southward across the axis, yet the larger part of the basin is on the north side of the axis. But the old lake basin extended eastward and northward far beyond the area included in the Uinta uplift and beyond the present channel of the Snake River, and here the floor is unknown; but this latter region is not within the limits of present discussion.

Within the region under discussion on the floor of the old lake basin beds of the Brown's Park period were deposited; these beds lie chiefly in a horizontal position, but on the north side of Brown's Park the beds are abruptly turned up against the Uinta Sandstone of the O-wi-yu-kuts Plateau, with a dip of about twenty-five degrees. Farther to the east, near the divide between the waters of the Green and the Snake, south of the monoclinal flexure and fault of the Dry Mountains, a deep synclinal flexure is observed; parallel with it and still farther south another of less magnitude, and still beyond a third but slightly developed.

Let us now consider the effect which the reverse throw along the great Uinta fault and the throw along the Yampa fault has had on this valley. In the former the downthrow at Red Creek is perhaps less than 1,000 feet; at Diamond Peak, about 3,000 feet; and the total throw of the two displacements in the Dry Mountains and vicinity is probably more than 4,000 feet. The throw of the Yampa fault, from its inception on the west, soon attains a magnitude of 5,000 feet, and where it is lost by transverse structure, near Junction Mountain, it is about 3,000 feet. Thus it is seen that the great block between these two faults has fallen down from 1,000 to 5,000 feet in its different portions. Prior to this downthrow there was a great elevated valley drained into the Green River. When the downthrow commenced it is probable that the Brown's Park beds were not yet deposited, but after it had continued for some time the region was so depressed that the waters of the stream were ponded and a lake formed. In this lake, then, the Brown's Park beds were accumulated.

We know that the Brown's Park beds were involved in a part at least of this downthrow, and hence were deposited before the downthrow was accomplished, because the beds themselves were involved in the displacement; they are severed by faults and bent by fractures where they are seen to overlap or extend beyond the area of downthrow.

Hence it is seen that Brown's Park is not a valley of displacement or of subsidence, but was originally formed as a valley of degradation—an elevated valley in a mountain region. It subsided or fell down as a part of a greater block. But the whole of it did not thus subside, for the Dry Mountains stand across the site of this ancient depression.

ASPEN MOUNTAIN DISTRICT.

In this district we have a great upheaval with its axis in a north and south direction, at right angles to the Uinta upheaval. On either side of the upheaval there are zones of maximum flexure.

The beds brought to view in the degradation of this upheaval are all the Cretaceous formations above the Henry's Fork Group and all the Cenozoic groups below the Brown's Park; hence the inception of this upheaval dates from some epoch in Post-Bridger time. The whole of the uplift is not within the area embraced in the map. The section, together with the geological map, presents all the important characteristics of this uplift, but there are some minor features of interest. In the northwest, northeast, and southeast angles or corners of the uplift there are many minor faults normal to the strike of the beds. Quien Hornet Mountain stands on the southwest corner. No faults have been discovered here.

There is a gentle synclinal between the end of the Aspen Mountain uplift and the side of the Uinta uplift. At the south end of the uplift the axis passes through the eastern end of Aspen Mountain. Farther northward the axial region, topographically, is a valley, for Bitter Creek divides the uplift, a stream having an extra limital source—a stream whose course was determined antecedent to the uplift.

In the heart of the uplift Cretaceous beds of extreme friability are found, and the secondary drainage or lateral wet-weather tributaries to Bitter Creek have excavated these valleys to the very heart of the uplift.

Here 10,000 feet of beds have been carried away by the waters since the inception of the uplift.

INDEX.

www.ingramcontent.com/pod-product-compliance
Lightning Source LLC
LaVergne TN
LVHW050527100826
845148LV00002B/460

* 9 7 8 1 4 2 5 5 2 0 1 3 7 *